The Command of Grace

The Command of Grace

A New Theological Apologetics

by
Paul D. Janz

t&t clark

Published by T & T Clark

A Continuum imprint

The Tower Building   80 Maiden Lane
11 York Road   Suite 704
London SE1 7NX   New York NY 10038

www.continuumbooks.com

British Library Cataloguing-in-Publication Data
A catalogue record for this book is available from the British Library.

ISBN-10: HB: 0–567–03358–9
        PB: 0–567–03359–7

ISBN-13: HB: 978–0–567–03358–1
        PB: 978–0–567–03359–8

Typeset by RefineCatch Limited, Bungay, Suffolk
Printed on acid-free paper in Great Britain by CPI Antony Rowe, Chippenham, Wiltshire

To my mother and father, Lydia Janz and Leo Janz

CONTENTS

Preface

This book sets forth a new critical initiative in theological apologetics that calls for a fundamental reassessment of theological self-understanding and method today, especially in its attentiveness to the present reality of God in revelation. It can be seen in a way a companion to the 2007 publication of a co-authored monograph entitled *Transformation Theology* (by Oliver Davies, Clemens Sedmak and myself), in that it seeks to lay out in more critically structured and formally defined ways some of the basic positions that were initially put forward there. In other words, in its designation as a 'new theological apologetics' the present volume can be seen also secondarily as an apologetics for 'transformation theology'.

The primary motivation for writing the co-authored book was a perceived disconnect between the life of faith itself in the church on the one hand – where God is witnessed, confessed and experienced as a present and living reality, active with dynamic transforming power at the center of embodied human life today – and what has frequently become a standard procedure in contemporary theology on the other, which often confines its endeavors fundamentally to the conceptually self-sustaining safety of textual and doctrinal theory, grammar and interpretation. Because of the basic format of the book, however – three authors writing toward a shared vision, but from within quite different and only loosely connected registers – and because it purposively avoided any strongly polemical edge by which it might have positioned itself more explicitly on the current theological landscape, a recurring theme in initial responses to it has been a certain puzzlement as to what 'transformation theology' most essentially stands for, or what it is exactly that sets it apart distinctively as a 'new' theological outlook, and most importantly, what it expects from the theological reader; what it wants theology to do differently. It is hoped that the present volume can bring some greater clarity to answering these kinds of questions.

There are many, past and present, to whom this book owes much, but I limit acknowledgments of gratitude to those who have most integrally informed its development. I am especially indebted to my colleagues Oliver Davies and Clemens Sedmak for providing the critically energetic and stimulating intellectual space which has allowed the germinal ideas from which this book began to flourish and develop. The intense conversations with Oliver Davies, which began early in 2005 following my arrival at King's College London, and which grew in both frequency and intensity over the next year as we discovered what for us seemed to be exciting and overlapping areas of concern for fundamental theological questioning, have profoundly shaped both the content and structure of this book. I am equally grateful to Clemens Sedmak, who arrived at King's in 2006 and who brought a whole new dynamic and this-worldly ethical urgency to bear on those initial conversations. I am likewise grateful to Susannah Ticciati for the probing clarity of her mind and critical questioning over the past eighteen months as she followed the progress of the book, and for her invaluable critical commentary and suggestions for improvement in reading the book as it neared completion. A special word of thanks also belongs to Thomas Kraft and Dominic Mattos at T&T Clark, who have been tremendously helpful, patient and constantly available both with regard to the publication of this book and in the launch of the transformation theology book series, and to Ian Howe for his critically careful work in the process of copy-editing. Finally, I owe the deepest gratitude to my wife, Beth, not only for her constant support and encouragement throughout the writing process, but also for the countless ways in which she has selflessly taken such care to contribute to the kind of home environment in which academic creativity can thrive.

Chapter 1

Theological Apologetics and the Reality of God

I

1. For Christian theology, everything depends on the present and living reality of God, as does everything in the Christian hope and everything in the Christian life. The affirmation which according to the scriptural witness itself[1] stands indispensably at the center of the Christian message, is that the incarnate and crucified Jesus, through the power of God's Spirit exerted in his resurrection from the dead and at Pentecost, is really alive today – not at some infinite distance, as if resurrection and ascension meant a departure again from the world into which God really entered bodily in Jesus of Nazareth – but presently and dynamically alive for human beings today at the center of their own embodied life. The origin and generating source of Christian hope are therefore not only the linguistic assurance of a written promise, indispensable as this is. It is much more the *presently living* hope of the Spirit of God himself – the one who through Jesus Christ is alive and active at the center of our own corruptible life – who has been given as a 'deposit guaranteeing' the promise of an incorruptible life to come (2 Cor. 1.22; 5.5). If God in his revelation is not truly present and presently real in the causally transforming power of divine righteousness and lovingkindness at the center of our own lives in the world – even and especially at points of greatest human despair and loss (Job 23.8–12): then the living hope of an eternal life in God beyond human death reduces to the psychology of a mere wish projection; then what Christians call 'faith' is a merely illusory and subjectively emotive human assurance that atheistic critiques would be right in labeling a false comfort for the 'weak-minded'; and then theology at best inevitably collapses into either a study of what is most sublime and noble in human beings themselves, or into cultural studies, or into esthetic exercises in literary theory or storytelling. Everything in Christian theology therefore depends on the present reality God, as does everything in the Christian life.

The 'apologetical' task pursued in this book is called 'theological' in that it begins with and seeks to 'defend' the accountability of Christian truth from the very center of what most indispensably and distinctively constitutes and defines it, as expressed in these opening statements. Or in other words, any apologetical endeavor that begins from the terminology of revelation, transcendence, incarnation, resurrection, redemption and so on, is inherently a theological one. One of the most immediate challenges it faces as such, however, comes in the full recognition that precisely this terminology from which it must begin has today often become remote, anachronistic and meaningless with regard to its truth or reality in life. And a primary concern therefore must be to allow this terminology itself to speak with a new and accessible relevance again at the center of life.

A 'theological apologetics' is thus somewhat different from what we are more familiar with today as 'Christian apologetics'. For this latter, as we shall see, seeks in most contemporary cases to defend Christian truth predominantly by beginning from more general arguments about theistic 'plausibility' in order to work 'inward' to greater Christian specificity from that. Whereas the former begins from what seems to be most intractably difficult about the Christian truth affirmed in faith – and thus, at least prima facie, most 'implausible' – and seeks first simply to *understand* this, albeit not in theory but in reality, and in the full rigor of reason. For similar reasons, the defining concerns of a theological apologetics can be distinguished also from those of 'Christian doctrine', and we will address that difference in a moment.

But before coming to that, there is one seemingly innocuous and unassuming term that I want to single out in the otherwise rather declamatory opening paragraph as carrying a particularly vital import for any form of apologetics or doctrine – important especially today where it is often forgotten – and this is the term 'dependence'. For to say that theology (whether doctrinal or apologetical) itself *depends* on the revealed reality of God which grounds and precedes it implies that theology is both a fundamentally *contingent* discipline with respect to this ground (because it is dependent on it) and a fundamentally *limited* one with respect to this ground (because it cannot contain it).

This immediately means two things, one negative and one positive. Negatively, it means that theology may never – as it can often tend to do – simply 'presuppose' within itself, as a set of concepts or as any phenomenological 'given', the living truth of the reality on which it depends. This is disallowed firstly for the obvious reason that a presupposition or any theoretical 'given' is by definition never anything other than a concept, whereas the truth of the self-revealing God is not merely the truth of a concept but the truth of a reality in life. But it is disallowed also for theology's own methodological integrity. For in converting the truth of the reality of God in life into the truth of something merely conceptually presupposed or cognitively 'given', theology would essentially subsume its own ground to within itself, thereby becoming something conceptually or doctrinally self-guaranteeing. And it would thus cease to be the dependent and limited discipline that it indispensably is.

But this disallowed negative now also has a positive corollary in the other direction, which is as follows. If we want to take with full seriousness (i.e. not in any 'demythologized' or 'ideal' sense) the scriptural declaration that God has really revealed himself in temporal history in a mortal body in Jesus Christ; and if the resurrection-reality of God is indeed a reality which is through Pentecost disclosed in dynamic livingness even today to the same world of embodied life into which God became incarnate in Jesus: then this means something vital and indispensable for theology. It means that in searching out or attending to the truth of the grounding reality of God on which it depends, theology must even today always look nowhere else but *to* the world of sensible-rational human embodiment, in and for which the reality of God is disclosed, and never away from this world.

It is true of course that Christian theology always looks first to the Bible, and therefore first to the narratives of an inspired written text. Yet precisely as it does so, it finds that the Bible itself, by its own inspired testimony, is not a self-referentially enclosed text, but that in all of its most central declarations it always points beyond itself to the present revealed reality of God in the real created world in which humans actually live. By the Bible's own witness, therefore, theology's dependence is not only on the scriptural texts, indispensable and inviolable as this is, but also, through the text, always back to the dynamically creative and causally transforming reality of God at the center of embodied life now. The apologetical enterprise as pursued in this book will thus implicitly agree with Bonhoeffer's important statement, echoing Luther (and paraphrasing): that because in the reality of Jesus Christ the reality of God has entered into the reality of the world fully, therefore theology may not look away from the world but nowhere else than to the world of real embodied life to engage with the revealed reality of God.[2] The present book will develop the basic disposition voiced in such a statement in quite different ways than Bonhoeffer did, and with an apologetical rigor that he himself did not, or became unable to do. But its basic orienting disposition is the same.

Or again, the present enterprise seeks to develop, in a new and quite different apologetical way than Rahner did, what he calls an 'axiom' for understanding 'every relationship between God and creatures'. This axiom, as he puts it, is that creaturely relational closeness and distance, respectively, to God and to the world, 'do not vary for creatures in inverse [proportion] but in direct proportion'.[3] In plain language this means that it is only as I draw closer to the real world of my own creaturehood, or to the real world of sensible-rational human embodiment in space and time, that I may also draw closer to God. And with every retreat from this world into conceptual abstraction, God also must inevitably become more distant. Or likewise, in the other direction, the closer God draws us to himself, the more deeply we will find ourselves drawn into the real world of embodied sensible-rational life in space and time. Or yet again, it seeks to pursue along new lines and with full apologetical rigor a basic disposition voiced by Rowan Williams, who suggests that the 'foundational events' of Christianity themselves – the life, death and resurrection of Jesus Christ – receive their true and definitive 'authentication' and theologically accountable 'defense' in the way that, *as* real historical foundational events, they are still *generative today* as presently real.[4]

2. Before beginning to pursue all of this constructively, however, it will be helpful to amplify further what was mentioned only cursorily above in distinguishing a 'theological apologetics', first from the defining concerns of

'Christian doctrine' on the one hand; and then secondly from what we are familiar with today as 'Christian apologetics' on the other.

Christian doctrine is by broad agreement today characterized as that exercise of theology which is concerned essentially with the faithful *interpretation* or *description* of the proclamations of scripture with regard to the theoretical analysis, clarification and coherence of its *meanings* internally.[5] If this is so, then we might say that a theological apologetics is concerned more basically with a reasoned *explanation* of these interpreted meanings with regard to questions of their *truth* in embodied life, or more exactly with regard to the truth of their ground in the revealed reality of God as a presently living reality. Or to phrase the relation between the two slightly differently, one could say that a theological apologetics is, at least in one of its primary concerns, interested in the accountability of doctrine per se to the truth of its ground in the revealed reality of God at the center of life, a reality that doctrine itself cannot contain but on which it depends. In short, whereas doctrine is concerned essentially with description and faithful interpretation with regard to questions of internal meaning, a theological apologetics is concerned with explanation with a view to the question of the truth of these meanings in life.

Now it is well known that Christian doctrine over the past century has not infrequently come to take a rather dismissive or even hostile view of the value of apologetical questioning for theological endeavor. This is especially pronounced for example in Karl Barth, who famously asserted that 'the best apologetics is good doctrine'. Indeed, Barth himself goes so far as to set his own 'defense' of Christian truth in direct opposition to any sort of apologetical endeavor that might seek to find 'common ground' with other disciplines, by claiming that his own account is not an apologetic but rather a 'polemic' against any such possible common ground.[6] However, Barth's main objection to apologetics as such (at least to his portrayal of it) is in a way understandable and legitimate. For what he rejects in this understanding of apologetics is what he sees as its implicit claim to be able to provide a 'prolegomenon' for theology per se, which is to say the provision of a preparatory structural framework within which the basic parameters of theology are first rationally or epistemologically set out, on which basis it can then go about its business of doctrinal interpretation as something 'well defined'.[7]

Barth's objection here, however, is not so much to the ability of reason per se to provide its own guidelines for right thinking apart from theology, guidelines that theology itself will duly follow as it engages in its own rational activity.[8] The objection is much more to the assumption implied in a prolegomenon that an activity of human reason could by itself contribute something 'preparatory' for the revelation of God. For divine revelation is entirely a work and act of God, given in unmerited grace. And the point is that any such rationally worked out 'preparation' for revelation, even in theological study, would by definition be a preparation by human achievement or merit. But while there is undoubtedly an important and basic theological soundness to Barth's concern here, it is also accompanied by a certain basic flaw or insufficiency. We will be engaging with Barth in some depth in due course, but let us

set aside those concerns for the moment and turn now to consider more exactly
the other distinction: i.e. how the 'theological apologetics' pursued here is
different from what we are more familiar with today as 'Christian apologetics'.

With a few exceptions,[9] Christian apologetics today is mostly undertaken
from non-theological terrain. And as such, it does indeed quite frequently see
its function essentially in the way that Barth rejected, i.e. as providing a prolegomenon or an intellectual preparation for the truth of the Christian gospel,
or as setting out a 'common ground' on the basis of which more specifically
Christian and theological themes can then be brought to bear subsequently.
The essential concern here, in other words, is often with establishing accounts
of 'plausibility' in more general ways – e.g. the plausibility of 'theistic' belief
per se, or of 'religious experience' per se – as a basis for the more specific
plausibility of Christian content, which is why some evangelical apologetical
endeavors call these approaches 'pre-evangelistic'.

For example, the general plausibility of theistic belief can be undertaken
by demonstrating the reasonableness of affirming the existence of God
(although again not yet specifically the God of the Bible, but the theistic
idea of God as supreme being) through cosmological, teleological or empirically evidentialist argumentation. Or it can be done by demonstrating the
credibility of religious or mystical experience as the experience of something
genuinely 'noumenal', and not merely something psychologically aberrational
or paranormal. Or again it can be done by arguing for the plausibility of the
existence of a good God even in the face of horrendous evil in the world, and
so on. Still others seek to demonstrate the plausibility or warrantability, not
generally of theistic belief, but specifically of 'Christian belief'. This is in some
instances done on the epistemological argumentation that certain beliefs can
be shown to be 'self-evidently basic' to the Christian community; whereupon
this community is then found to be as much within its properly warranted
'epistemic rights' for holding to its own self-evident basic beliefs as other
communities are theirs. At any rate, since all such approaches are concerned
in one way or another fundamentally with questions of plausibility, it would
not be improper to term them collectively as 'plausibility apologetics'.

Now Barth's critique notwithstanding, such non-theological apologetical
endeavors can clearly have a great value and importance, not only in
providing rigorously reasoned theistic and Christian perspectives in academic debate itself from minds that can match the sharpest non-theistic
arguments, but also in providing supportive 'reasons to believe' for concerned
Christians more broadly. However, for the really central and therefore
unavoidably *theologically* apologetical task, which must begin from where
God himself begins as he meets us in his own revelation in history, their
value and importance as such must always be something secondary or
supplemental. For no amount of theistic argumentation, religious experiential
argumentation, empirically evidentialist argumentation, or Christian epistemological argumentation can ever, on the basis of its own purely cognitive
trajectories of plausibility, penetrate to the center of where the God of the
Bible really meets us himself in Jesus Christ, in his bodily life, in his bodily
death, and in his resurrection into an incorruptible life.

It is indeed possible to show, with critically historical reliability that virtually no qualified historian today would question, that Jesus of Nazareth really lived in and died in history. And such apologetical ventures have great and extremely important merit as such, in being able to demonstrate that Jesus Christ is not just a mythological figure but a real man who lived as we do and who died as we do. But even these enterprises can always only be secondarily apologetical. For no amount of the most dedicated historical scrutiny can show us that the Father of Jesus Christ is God; or that he was conceived of the Holy Spirit in Mary; or that it was really the immortal God who tasted death on the cross in Jesus Christ; or that the resurrection was a resurrection into a radically new and incorruptible life and not merely a resuscitation back into corruptible life, as we see, for example, in the biblical account of the raising of Lazarus.

No non-theological apologetics working from the outside in can penetrate to the reasonable 'plausibility' of the truth that in Jesus Christ the eternal, invisible and immortal God becomes finite, visible and perishable in a human body. The only prospect of engaging in a 'defense' of the accountability of what we affirm with the not-merely-subjective 'certainty' of faith to be the truth of such statements, is to begin from the center. But we must as such immediately reiterate the vital and indispensable point made above. To say that the present enterprise in a theological apologetics *begins* from the truth of the reality of God does not mean that it begins from this merely as something conceptually 'presupposed'. Far from presupposing the truth of this reality as a set of analytically self-securing theological concepts – and thus in effect setting the question of its truth aside or ignoring it as an earnest theological concern – it rather *seeks out* the truth of this reality with the full attentiveness and integrity of all human faculties of awareness. And it does so at the only place where, on the affirmation of faith and under the inspired direction of the scriptures, this reality demands to be sought out: at the center of life in the world.

II

3. It is under impetus of these basic motivations that the present volume seeks to set forth a new critical initiative in theological apologetics, one that advocates a fundamental reassessment of theological self-understanding and method today, especially in its attentiveness to the present reality of the transcendent God in revelation. It will therefore proceed apologetically in a quite different way than the discussions in 'Christian apologetics' with which we are more familiar today, as mentioned briefly above. And it will accordingly from here on no longer take these as primary points of comparative reference. It will rather proceed through what might be called a kind of critique of theology itself, one which for important reasons will need also to become strongly philosophically engaged. The 'critique' of theology is not meant of course in the sense of a 'criticism' of it or an attack against it but precisely in the opposite sense. It will in fact be a support of it by seeking to ascertain in specific ways

the defining limits of its own integrity with respect to its ground in the reality of God in life, a ground that it cannot contain but on which it depends.

The enterprise as such might thus also be called an exercise in 'fundamental theology', although it would quickly have to be added that it does not as such pretend to act as a 'prolegomenon' or preparatory exercise for doctrinal theology, still less as something 'foundational'. For doctrine knows full well that it begins properly and rightly in the Bible, and as such already always 'in the middle of things',[10] without needing to wait for an introductory or foundational exercise which seeks to demonstrate its 'possibility' as an intellectual discipline. If the present enterprise can be called 'fundamental' therefore, it is so only in the sense of its concern with the relation of theology per se to the grounding reality of God on which it depends. It is, in other words, a grounding kind of questioning to which all doctrinal endeavor itself will eventually have to lead whenever it seeks, as it must, to ask about the living truth and reality of its meanings.

The project as such, however, will need to express itself throughout not only along its own affirmative lines, but also, as a contextual backdrop to that, through several sustained critiques of recent trends under the impact of which theology's ability to be properly attentive to the revealed reality of God as present and living has become diminished. In this more negatively critical mode, the book will identify especially an array of powerful idealistic, analytical, phenomenological, foundationally textual and cultural-linguistic developments over the past two centuries, under the influence of which theology has in many of its most predominant and influential trends today effectively ceased to be a discipline which is genuinely *dependent* on the reality that grounds it, and has instead become essentially something self-sustaining within itself. Or in other words, it has under these influences come to exercise itself predominantly within what we might call a 'conceptually cognitive mono-vision', whereby it has not only become self-guaranteeing within itself ('tauto-theological'), thus forfeiting its rationally rigorous edge, but has also inadvertently violated its indispensable incarnational (embodied) ground.

Against this, the book seeks to refocus fundamental theological questioning also through other basic modes of human awareness, beyond the conceptually cognitive, which under the aforementioned influences have become largely lost to theology over the past two centuries, even though they continue to thrive in the life of faith in the church itself, and even though they can be shown to have informed much of our theological and philosophical history fundamentally. If God in his very 'Godness' meets us in revelation at the very center of created life, and reveals himself only *here* as the hope of the life to come, then theology must again seek to be attentive to God in the full contingency of embodied-rational life in a multi-faceted way, which is to say in the engagement of all of its constitutive faculties of awareness (which we will address briefly in a moment) and not just the conceptually cognitive.

We will begin to engage with the specifics of this task itself in Chapter Two. But for introductory purposes of orientation, let me just explain briefly what this 'multi-faceted attentiveness' is supposed to mean, before then going on through a brief historical survey to consider introductorily different ways in which the relation of God to the world has been viewed in the past. This will be done with a view to crystallizing what can only be described as a broadly-cast current 'predicament' of theology in this regard.

4. Normally, or at least very widely today, theology understands itself and accounts for its activity most essentially as a kind of 'grammar'. Indeed, theology is understood almost axiomatically today most basically as 'talk about God';[11] as 'discourse about God';[12] as concerned essentially with the question of 'how to speak rightly of God';[13] or again, as most essentially a kind of 'depth grammar' that builds on 'faithfulness in intratextuality' and so on.[14] This occurs even where one might not expect it. The recent self-described 'revisionist' or 'revolutionary' 'theologies of the cross', as espoused by Eberhard Jüngel or Jürgen Moltmann for example, quite explicitly define the essential difference of what they are presenting as most essentially a 'revolution' *within* the semantics of thought. We will discuss this somewhat further in Chapter Three, but consider here the explicitness with which Jüngel himself expresses this. In his words, what is required of theology today in light of the cross is most basically 'to query again the *linguistic meaning* and function of the word "God" '[15] or to 'learn to *think* God in a new way'.[16]

Now the point here of course is not in any way to question the indispensable and utterly central place of grammar, discourse and cognition for theology. For indeed theology is predominantly just this, given that in all of its written, spoken and thinking exercises, it is intrinsically a form of talk, speech, narrative, reading, thinking, language, grammar, discourse, description and interpretation. It is only to say that in the full and complete sense of what the term 'theo-logy' denotes, theology cannot be solely or *exclusively* a noetic (mentally discursive) exercise in grammar and linguistics. For this would make theology essentially into a kind of philology, which is to say a science of language and literature, which finds its defining and authoritative points of reference entirely within the confines of discursive, lexicological or textually grammatical domains.[17]

But if the God of the Bible with whom theology is concerned is indeed, in his resurrection-reality and Pentecost-reality, present today as a *living* actuality at the center of life and not only as an 'ideal actuality'[18] in grammatical or linguistic domains, then this means that theology in its fullness cannot be something fundamentally or exclusively philological, indeed not even something fundamentally doctrinal. To the contrary, it means further, and now positively, that in its very elemental nature theology must also be constituted by another, quite different kind of activity. And this other elemental activity, in addition to 'talk about God', can in the most basic of terms be identified simply as 'attentiveness' to God in embodied life. And by 'attentiveness' I do not mean only a kind of 'hearing' as this is more frequently meant in theology, for example when we speak of what it means to be 'hearers of the Word'. I do of course, and very importantly, also mean attentiveness in this sense, only not exclusively so. For there are quite different modes of attentiveness that are also constitutive of human life, modes of attentiveness which do not reduce to conceptually-cognitive and grammatically discursive domains, and which are in fact both temporally and logically antecedent to them. Let me take this opportunity to introduce preliminarily a brief overview of what these other modes of attentiveness are, especially insofar as certain discernible delineations between them will serve as a basis for the essential structuring of this book into a loose bipartite focus.

5. There is a long history of agreement in both theological and philosophical anthropology[19] that the multifactedness of human life-consciousness manifests itself from within two most basic orientational faculties. Or one might also speak of two most fundamental ways that human beings *relate* to the reality in which they find themselves alive. The one basic relational orientation or consciousness-faculty has been called the *cognitive* faculty, or the *faculty of cognition*. This refers to that faculty of consciousness by which humans relate to themselves and the world through perceiving and thinking, or through percepts and concepts. (Sensible perceptions are no less 'cognitions' than rational concepts are.) The other has been called the *appetitive* faculty, or the *faculty of appetition* ('appetition' stemming from 'appetites'). And this is meant to refer to that faculty of consciousness by which humans relate to themselves and the world not through percepts and concepts but through desires and motivations. (We shall speak to the more exact derivations of these terms later, but for convenience sake, I use here the English derivatives of the Latin distinctions between *cognitiva* and *appetitiva* as they appear thematically in Aquinas.)

Now both the 'cognitive' and 'appetitive' modes of awareness are comprised in turn of both sensible and rational components. We are sensibly aware in our cognitive consciousness most obviously and straightforwardly through our five external senses. As intrinsically receptive capacities, these 'external' senses are perceptively responsive to the causally dynamic physical realities that we encounter as bodies in space and time. By the rational component of our cognitive consciousness we mean of course that consciousness in which we are conceptually or thinkingly aware. This is an awareness or capacity which, beginning from Aristotle's first explicit characterization of it as such, has been called the 'judging power' (or also the 'discriminating' or calculating' power) of human beings. And as a judging or discriminating power, it is not intrinsically 'receptive' as the senses are, but rather something intrinsically spontaneous and active in its discriminating and calculating functions. Moreover, because the use of reason for the cognitive faculty is a reasoning in and for thinking and language – which is to say for 'discourse' – it is often called the *discursive* use of reason. And we should add to this also that when this cognitive use of reason seeks to remain entirely within thinking per se – i.e. when it seeks to engage entirely with concepts and language, and not with sensible percepts at all – it is called the *speculative* use of reason.

But now the faculty of appetition or desire will be shown likewise to have both rational and sensible components. The sensible aspects of this faculty are located in the bodily passions, and the rational component is located in the will, or in what Aquinas calls the 'intellectual appetite'. Moreover, what vitally distinguishes appetites or desires from concepts or percepts (cognitions) is that they provide the fundamental *motivating* influences for reasoned action in life, with the bodily or sensible passions motivating from physical desire or need, and the will being able to motivate to embodied action apart from sensible sources.

Nothing in this brief introductory taxonomy is to suggest of course that these faculties and capacities operate entirely separately or dissociatively from each other in real life. It is only to say that even though I find them often to be inextricably interwoven and intermingled in what I experience and know to be the singleness of my embodied-rational constitution, nevertheless they will be found at bottom to be irreducible to each other. And what 'irreducible' means most essentially is simply that when we observe them critically and reflectively, each of these different modes of awareness will be recognized as being in certain basic ways originary to itself, such that it is not possible to understand it as a product or function of the others.

But we can now bring this to bear in an introductory way also on the basic rationale underlying the more negatively critical aspects of the book. For as we shall begin to see in Chapter Two, under the impact of the aforementioned idealistic, analytical, phenomenological and linguistic influences, the sensible and appetitive modes of awareness have in both theology and philosophy today often come to be subsumed under what is predominantly seen as the higher authority of conceptually cognitive consciousness or discursive intellection (i.e. thinking consciousness). Or they have come to be subsumed under what Hegel called the 'lordship' of the discursive or thinking intellect over the other modes of awareness. And what will be shown to have occurred as a result is that both theology and the human sciences have come to exercise themselves very broadly today within a kind of 'conceptually cognitive monovision'. This is not to say of course that sensibility and desire are not indeed popular themes in many current discussions. It is only to say that it is precisely in their treatment *as* 'themes' – or in their treatment as always subservient to the conceptually 'determining' and thus 'meaning-giving' structures of conceptual cognition – that genuine attentiveness to their originary authority as sensible and appetitive modes of awareness at the center of life has been lost.

An important double aspect of what this book will be seeking to do in this light is to explore the uniqueness of each of these modes of attentiveness as they together constitute the unity of human life-awareness, in order from there also to say something vital about what this means for theological attentiveness to the reality of God at the center of life. More specifically, it will seek to show that just as human awareness of the reality within which they find themselves alive is constituted by all of these modes of awareness together: so also the living and present reality of God in God's self-revelation to the world is disclosed to *whole* embodied-rational human beings and not only to the discursively cognitive aspects of human life. And this means that theology must also be attentive to the present revealed reality of God in the wholeness of human life and not just in the conceptual-linguistic aspect.

III

6. We have until this point spoken only cursorily of certain 'powerful intellectual developments' over the past two centuries, under the impact of which theology has found it possible to shift its attentiveness away from the real world of sensible human embodiment as the indispensable site of the revealed reality of God even today, and to isolate itself rather within the self-sustaining securities of linguistic and conceptually cognitive domains. In defending and qualifying this observation, in order to set out the book's own constructive alternatives, we will at several points throughout the course of the volume need to engage in a sustained critique of those aspects of the theological and philosophical tradition and history by which this shift has occurred. But it will be helpful for introductory purposes of orientation and backdrop to present briefly a very basic overview of how this question of the reality of God has been addressed and attended to in the past, and how the current widespread confinement or isolation of theology within a conceptually cognitive mono-vision has occurred.

Let me caution before proceeding, however, that the introductory overview offered here will at this juncture have to be stated in quite inadequately over-general terms, although many aspects will be supported more rigorously in subsequent chapters. It also unavoidably reflects a particular perspective on this history. But I would only want to assure the reader that even if there are aspects of this introductory overview that are met with disagreement or found wanting, this will not mean that there will have to be disagreement with the more constructive positions put forward later. In other words, the affirmative positions developed in this book do not themselves depend on any particular reading of intellectual history.

Prior to what is often called the 'enlightenment'[20] period of the sixteenth to the eighteenth centuries, questions about the reality of God in relation to the reality of the world were usually addressed in philosophy and theology via various kinds of appeals to what has come to be referred to as 'metaphysics'. (It will be clear from the way that this sentence is formulated that we are speaking here of a somewhat different question than the more strictly epistemological one of how it is possible to speak of a transcendent God, e.g. through analogy, symbolism, etc.) While the origins and meaning of this term are disputed – especially as it was editorially attributed originally to Aristotle (who himself does not actually use the term) – what has come to be understood by it roughly in the 'pre-modern' and early modern (pre-Kantian) usage, is the postulation of a supposed objectively real 'supra-sensible realm' surpassing or lying beyond the physical (hence 'meta-physical') or material world of space and time we live in. This was understood as a realm or sphere 'out there', a 'realm' of unchanging and constant realities that are not susceptible to the transience and passingness of embodied existence. The scholarly postulation of objective metaphysical realities in pre-modern times was thus in a sense a mirroring, in more critically reflected and less superstitious ways, of what in the popular understanding was broadly seen as an 'enchanted' world.

Now while the appeal to a real metaphysical realm in this 'pre-modern' sense was engaged philosophically in an array of different ways, it is nonetheless roughly accurate to say that this was generally pursued either along broadly Platonic lines or somewhat differently along broadly Aristotelian lines, even in theology. Augustine, for example, followed neo-Platonic thought in approaching the question of transcendent reality by appealing to what were seen to be the eternal and thus meta-physically real Platonic 'Forms' or 'Ideas', Forms that have an ultimate reality in themselves and in supra-sensible purity and perfection. (This, however, is not to say that Augustine by any means saw God as a Platonic Form, and we will address this further in a moment.) The Ideas of 'the good', 'the true', 'the beautiful', of justice and love,[21] and also other, more subordinate Ideas: all of these were seen as eternal Forms, in the 'participation' of which the particular empirical things constituting or encountered in sensibly embodied life were deemed to have their character and identity, or to be what they are and the way they are. Or more exactly, it is in virtue of these supra-sensible Forms that sensible phenomena and bodies are deemed to possess the qualities or 'perfections' that they do, to the greater or lesser degree that they 'participate' in these Forms or 'instantiate' them.

The appeal to metaphysical realities was undertaken somewhat differently by Aquinas, who followed more strongly Aristotelian influences. Put simplistically, the direction in Aristotle did not proceed from the reality and perfection of the Forms down to their imperfect instantiations in empirical particulars. It proceeded rather from empirical particulars to underlying 'substance' or 'essences' (and hence also in a way to supra-sensible 'forms', albeit now in a somewhat more moderated way than in Plato). And because of their empirical orientation these Aristotelian outlooks came thereby to assume also a more metaphysically cosmological character than Plato. In all cases, however, what was sought in the *meta*-physically real – as opposed to the *physically* real, or more broadly the empirically or spatio-temporally real – was something essentially unchanging, reliable and constant, something which is not susceptible to the contingencies, vicissitudes and transience of passing and corruptible spatio-temporal existence.

It must importantly be acknowledged, however, that for any of the Christian figures who used these Greek outlooks for theological purposes, the reality or 'being' of God was not simply numbered as another 'Form' among what were seen as the ideally perfecting higher Platonic 'realities', or as a 'substance' among what were seen as the cosmologically underlying and grounding 'realities'. Thomas's thought, for example, is much too rigorous in its 'negative' directions to allow for any such obvious error. But they served nonetheless in certain ways as fundamental courts of appeal or as points of leverage that enabled theology to bring the uncreated reality of God to bear on the created reality of the world, or to account for the reality of God in relation to the reality of the world.[22]

However, when we come especially to the later stages of what is today broadly called the 'modern' or 'enlightenment' period, this view of an objectively substantialist metaphysics, or of a real metaphysical 'realm' populated by supra-sensible 'essences', changes decisively. The subject of 'metaphysics' did indeed even in these later stages continue to be pursued as a philosophical discipline, but now in a fundamentally different kind of way, one that showed the older views of objective metaphysical substances, essences and substrates to be rationally unsustainable and thus effectively irrational. We will discuss this in more detail in subsequent chapters, but it is important even at this point to understand that the stances taken toward the question of a meta-physical or supra-sensible reality were quite fundamentally different at the beginning of this period – i.e. in what we today refer to as the 'early modern' views in sixteenth- and seventeenth-century 'rationalism' – than they were nearer the end of this period in Hume and Kant. In fact, the views on substantialist or essentialist metaphysics at the earlier and later ends of this period were quite radically opposed to each other. For in the earlier 'continental rationalism' of the sixteenth and seventeenth centuries, the 'pre-modern' commitment to the primacy of substantialist metaphysics in accounting for the 'fundamentals' of human, cosmic and divine reality, was in fact reinforced with a new and sharpened intensity, whereas in Hume and Kant, the new rationalist intensification of metaphysics was entirely dismantled.

But let us look just briefly at the intensification of substantialist metaphysics in rationalism. Descartes, for example, located the elementary and foundational basis of human reality not physically in sensible embodiment, but rather meta-physically in the *'thinking* substance'.[23] Leibniz likewise, although now with greater cosmological import, located (at least in one vital aspect of his philosophy) the elementary and underlying components of nature in windowless 'monads'. Monads are described by Leibniz as 'simple substances', which is to say foundationally real or ultimately real metaphysical 'things in themselves' which, as both simple (indivisible) and meta-physical, have neither parts nor spatial extension.[24] Accordingly, they lack any spatial dynamism, which is to say they are dynamically inert. As 'supra-sensible' realities they are seen as entirely inaccessible to the sensible faculties, and are apprehensible instead solely through the light and activity of 'pure reason'. And pure reason itself is only able to operate with full clarity and distinctness in these regions when it is purged of any sensible input, by which it becomes 'confused'. Spinoza too, under similar rationalistically metaphysical orientations, spoke of the elementary authority and reality of 'thoughts which themselves think'.

Others, such as Christian Wolff or Nicolas Malebranche, could be added to this group, but there are in sum two characteristics above all by which we today set this in many other ways disparate set of thinkers together under the designation of 'seventeenth-century rationalism'. The first is the shared supposition that 'pure reason' by itself, unaided by any sensible input or experience, which always introduces misapprehension, confusion and error, is able to give us the clearest and most certain insight into the true 'nature of things', or into the fundamental and ultimate reality of the world or the nature of this reality. The second is a new reinforcement, in more speculatively intricate ways, of the earlier 'pre-modern' metaphysics which postulated the real existence or real 'subsistence' of another 'realm', beyond the one in which we are sensibly aware and embodied. This is an 'ultimately real' meta-physical realm, constituted by 'things in themselves' that are changeless, constant, simple and incorruptible. And it was deemed further that the 'metaphysical reality' arrived at on this supra-sensible level then also permitted us to address questions about the reality of God, since divinity likewise transcends the corruption and decay of sensible or empirical reality in the extensive magnitudes of space and time.

7. At this juncture, however, we must pause to acknowledge that in the midst of all of this, and even prior to the rejection of the old substantialist metaphysics through Hume, Newton and Kant, there was one immensely powerful theological voice – that of Martin Luther – who even in the 'pre-modern' period, prior to the seventeenth century, had been rejecting not only the Platonic, but also even any of the more moderated Aristotelian appeals to substantialist metaphysics, for a proper attentiveness either to the reality of the world or to the reality of God in the world. Luther's own primary motivation here of course was not a philosophical one but a thoroughly theological and indeed an incarnational one. His pre-eminent concern was that of preserving the unquestioned primacy of the scriptural declaration that God is truly and fully present in the embodied history of Jesus Christ, and not more truly and fully in some 'meta-physical' reality underlying this, which would lead to Christological error.

Luther himself read the then dominatingly influential Aristotelian texts avidly. But in light of what he saw to be theology's indispensable incarnational commitments to real embodiment, he rejected the residual substantialist and essentialist elements in them. And indeed it was arguably largely on this basis that he was able to find a compatriot of sorts in William of Ockham. Ockham had a century or so earlier, and from what are today seen as unsustainable 'nominalist' philosophical perspectives, held that only individually existing things and their individual sensible properties are real. And he had therefore also rejected the metaphysically essentialist or substantialist elements remaining in Aristotle. However, Ockham's position as such, because of what came to be regarded as other quite basic epistemological failures, proved unable to sustain itself philosophically with any longevity. And it is perhaps partly because of his perceived association with Ockham that Luther's own important 'incarnational' insights and contributions in this particular area against the old substantialist metaphysics were also forgotten by the subsequent theological tradition (especially in the nineteenth and twentieth centuries), an oversight that Bonhoeffer, for example, strongly laments. But the Lutheran exception notwithstanding, the subsequent theological tradition after him continued by and large to trace its orientations in its questions about the reality of God in relation to the world through the more predominating meta-physicalist theological trends.

8. It was in Immanuel Kant, however – under the strong influence, it must be added, of Hume and Newton – that the definitive, and what for subsequent thought proved to be the insurmountable defeat of the old substantialist

and cosmological metaphysics, for which Luther was seeking assistance in Ockham, finally occurred. And it is primarily in light of this particular philosophical achievement by Kant that Bonhoeffer, who was always more basically attentive to Luther even on these epistemological issues than he was to Kant, pondered whether Kant should not be given the title of 'epistemologist of Protestantism [i.e. of the *original* Lutheran positions] par excellence'.[25]

But of course it was hardly only in 'Protestantism' that the defeat of the old substantialist or essentialist metaphysics was felt. Virtually all of continental philosophy changed dramatically in these respects within a matter of three decades following the publication of Kant's *Critique of Pure Reason* (1781). This remained true even when his own insights were used subsequently in ways fundamentally opposed to what he himself intended, as for example in the resurgence in new ways of the primacy of the supra-sensible in the idealisms of Fichte and Hegel.[26] And Roman Catholic theology too, while for its own specific reasons[27] somewhat slower to respond to the Kantian challenge than nineteenth-century Protestant theology, has in many of its most influential directions in the twentieth century – e.g. Karl Rahner, Hans Küng, Bernard Lonergan or Joseph Maréchal – come to orient itself methodologically away from the old substantialist metaphysics. It is true that there remain in Roman Catholic theology powerful vestiges – even at the very highest levels as we shall see – of either the Platonist metaphysics of effusion and emanation, or also of the more moderate Aristotelian metaphysics of substance through neo-scholasticism. But again, in its most widely influential expressions (e.g. Rahner or Küng), Roman Catholic theology too has found that it has had no choice, in the wake of modern science and the Kantian critique of metaphysics, but to abandon the old metaphysics of supra-sensible essences, substances or substrates in asking the question of the reality of God in relation to the world.

Whatever the subsequent disagreements with Kant and departures from him – and there were many such disagreements and departures – what is unquestioned today is that continental philosophy changed fundamentally after him. And the basic summary point here then is that Kant's critique of traditional metaphysics proved so forceful that theology, just as much as subsequent philosophy, found itself unable any longer to sustain its questioning about God and the world through substantialist and often cosmological appeals to an 'objectively real' supra-sensible meta-physical 'realm' underlying physical reality.

IV

9. But it is here that we reach finally what was to become the really decisive crossroads for present-day theology, especially in regard to what I have suggested has become its current conspicuous silence with respect to its fundamental ground and source in the present reality of God. For as a consequence of the loss of externalist and objectivist metaphysical appeals, theology in the

nineteenth century now began to turn its attention in the opposite direction: to mental domains of 'inwardness', or to the 'non-objective' domain of human 'subjectivity', in order to account for the intelligibility of its foundational claims about the relation of God to the world. In doing so it followed in the footsteps of the powerful 'idealisms', which is to say the foundational philosophies of mind or phenomenologies of mind, which arose after Kant.[28] (Kierkegaard's 'inwardness' was quite fundamentally different as we shall see in a later chapter.) The impact of this 'spirit of idealism' has proved so far-reaching – especially as it came to be reinforced in new and more subtle ways in twentieth-century Husserlian phenomenology – that even the great Karl Barth could not escape its gravitational pull, and he remained quite fundamentally in its orbit as we shall see more fully below.

This turn away from the objectively substantialist supra-sensible metaphysics and toward a new kind of supra-sensibility in the 'inwardness' of subjectivity, was then subsequently fortified even further with the advent of what is sometimes called the 'linguistic turn' in the twentieth century. What made the 'linguistic turn' to the primacy of language, grammar and interpretive structures all the more powerful was that it occurred almost simultaneously on several fronts and therefore with massive impact. It occurred in structuralism and post-structuralism in the human sciences; in the emergence of literary theory as a growing force in philosophical discussions; in the linguistic implications of the mental 'internalisms' exemplified in both post-Husserlian phenomenology, and in similarly oriented 'antirealist' discussions in America and Britain; and finally, as well, in the centrality of the philosophy of language for Anglo-American analytical philosophy. It is under the overwhelming impact of these influences together in the human and literary sciences, that theology also has been unable to resist the increasingly intensified movement in orientation away from the real world of sensible human embodiment, and into cognitively abstract regions, as it looks now to fundamental forms of phenomenology, textualism, narrative and grammar in accounting for the intelligibility of its claims. One of the most definitive theological expressions of this is consummately articulated in George Lindbeck's often quoted and influential view that in 'a Christ-centered world' it is 'the text . . . which absorbs the world rather than the world the text'.[29]

The point in sum is that under the influence of both of these 'turns' – the 'turn to the subject' after Kant and the 'linguistic turn' in the early twentieth century – theology has come to account for its own intelligibility and validity vis-à-vis divine revelation entirely internally to itself, i.e. in self-guaranteeing ways, or in what I will call 'tauto-theological' ways. But while theology has thereby indeed been able to assure a kind of 'analytical' success within itself theoretically and linguistically, it has also lost touch not only with what the Christian scriptures themselves indispensably affirm, but with what practicing Christian communities across the world also affirm indispensably: namely, that the reality and power of God are through the resurrection and Pentecost dynamically present and alive in the real world of space and time at the center of embodied human life today.

10. It is against these trends that this book seeks, in the spirit of Luther and others like him, to return to a genuinely 'incarnational' account of the resurrection-reality of God through Pentecost even today, a reality on which everything in theology depends. Or stated differently, it seeks in new ways to return theological attention to the real world of sensible-rational human life in space and time as the indispensable 'site' of the present revealed reality of God, no less than it was exactly this same real created world which was the 'site' of the revelation of Jesus Christ in the days of his mortal flesh.

In the second half of the book we will begin to put forward a new way of addressing the problem of 'revelation and reason', in which both the question of what revelation *is* will be reassessed, and a mode of reasoning which has in the past been prominent but which has now lain dormant for the better part of two centuries will be reinvigorated. This will then require also a further exploration of the nature of faith. In its philosophical orientations, the general structural framework of certain aspects of the book will borrow strongly from the Aristotelian, Thomist and Kantian traditions, all of which share in many ways remarkably similar dispositions in their philosophical (or for Thomas, theological) anthropologies.

We can say no more as yet about the basic destinations that will be reached in the concluding chapters, destinations which I hope will be able to open up important new vistas for theological self-understanding and attentiveness to revelation, especially by means of a particular theological breakthrough into a new focus on the righteousness of God through what we will be calling 'the command of grace'. But that can only speak properly for itself once various basic difficulties and questions have been worked through, and a new basis for forward movement has been set. I would only add that because some of the approaches pursued here will be unfamiliar, or I dare even say 'new' in a qualified way, at least by many current standards, and in order therefore to facilitate ease of access from an array of perspectives, the book has as much as possible been constructed in such a way that the chapters can be read individually as thematic essays, even though they are meant to fuse together into a tightly knitted overall argument.

Notes

1 E.g. Matt. 18.20; 2 Cor. 13.4; Gal. 2.20; Col. 3.6; Heb. 12.8; 1 Cor. 3.16; 2 Cor. 4.20; Rom. 6.13; 12.1.

2 Dietrich Bonhoeffer, *Ethics* (Minneapolis: Fortress, 2005) DBW (Dietrich Bonhoeffer Werke), vol. 6, pp. 55, 59.

3 Karl Rahner, *Foundations of Christian Faith* (New York: Crossroad, 1978), p. 226.

4 See especially 'Trinity and Revelation' and 'The Finality of Christ' in *On Christian Theology* (Oxford: Blackwell, 2000), pp. 131–47 and pp. 93–106.

5 See e.g., George Lindbeck, *The Nature of Doctrine* (London: SPCK, 1984), pp. 112–14.

6 *Church Dogmatics* I.1 (Edinburgh: T&T Clark, 1975), 2nd edition, p. 341 (hereafter CD).

7 More generally, a 'prolegomenon' is seen as a preparatory exercise for engaging in any particular field of study, an exercise that sets in place or clarifies certain structural parameters and frameworks on which that discipline rests and within which it operates, and therefore on the basis of which it is 'possible' as a discipline at all.

8 Although Barth himself, as we shall see, on certain basic levels takes theology as permitted to 'exempt' itself from the rigors of reason which it otherwise accepts, in order to accomplish particular theological purposes.

9 So-called 'presuppositionalist' apologetics is indeed theological in character. But without wanting to deny the important value of such approaches in other ways, they can never be *genuinely* apologetical, but rather something else. For any such summary reconfiguration of Christian truth into conceptually presupposed truth would essentially be apologetically self-defeating, in that it would thereby precisely cease to be an explanatory 'account' or reasoned 'defense' of theological truth but merely a conceptual presumption of it.

10 Rowan Williams, *On Christian Theology* (Oxford: Blackwell, 2000), p. xii.

11 Eberhard Jüngel, *God as the Mystery of the World* (Grand Rapids: Eerdmans, 1983), p. vii; Barth, *CD* I.1 p. 4.

12 Wolfhart Pannenberg, *Systematic Theology*, vol. 1 (Grand Rapids: Eerdmans, 1991), p. 7.

13 Elizabeth Johnson, *She Who Is* (New York: Crossroad. 1997), pp 1–16. Johnson herself, however, by no means limits theological activity and attentiveness to linguistic discourse but is also concerned with many of the directions we will be pursuing in this book.

14 George Lindbeck, *The Nature of Doctrine* (London: SPCK, 1984), pp. 113–24, 130.

15 *God as the Mystery of the World*, p. 9.

16 *God as the Mystery of the World*, p. 9, original emphasis.

17 Several voices are willing to admit outright that philology is exactly what they are seeking most essentially to do as theologians. See e.g. John Milbank, 'The Theological Critique of Philosophy' in *Radical Orthodoxy* (London: Routledge, 1999), pp. 21–37, 29.

18 Donald MacKinnon, *Explorations in Theology 5* (London: SCM, 1979), p. 68.

19 The history of agreement I refer to will come to fuller expression as the book proceeds. Speaking generally, however, it is one that begins already in some of the pre-Socratics, but which comes to its first fully structural formulation in Aristotle, follows through in Aquinas and other scholastics, and is repeated in new ways in Kant under the additional influence of Locke, Hutcheson and Hume, and is carried through also in the nineteenth century by writers such as Schleiermacher and Kierkegaard. It is acknowledged at the same time, however, that there have also been extended periods in our intellectual history – most notably in early neo-Platonism, in seventeenth-century rationalism, and in nineteenth-century German idealism (e.g. Hegel, Fichte) and its aftermath – in which the human relation to the reality in which they find themselves alive has been viewed differently, and we will be addressing the differences in detail in due course.

20 By enlightenment is meant roughly that period from Copernicus, Galileo and Descartes through to Newton and Kant during which, both scientifically (cosmologically) and epistemologically, human understanding of themselves and the world they inhabit became dislodged from what had hitherto been virtually unquestioningly held as theological underpinnings. As modern science advanced, and as philosophy changed along with it, basic aspects of the cosmic order and the human constitution were found to be explainable by

natural means, or by the natural 'light' of reason and empirical discovery, and hence 'autonomously' from God. This met with stern reaction from the then regnant authorities. Galileo, as is well known, was imprisoned for espousing views of the cosmos that we today find unproblematic and take for granted, but which at that time were deemed to be dangerous and heretical, because they began to explain by natural means aspects of physical reality which up until that time had been understood as inherently mysterious, and explainable only through theology.

21 See e.g., *On the Trinity*, Bk 8 (Cambridge: Cambridge University Press, 2002), pp. 5–22.
22 See e.g. *On the Trinity*, Bk 8, preface and ch 3, pp. 4, 7.
23 See e.g. *Meditations on First Philosophy* in *The Philosophical Works of Descartes* (Cambridge: Cambridge University Press, 1981), pp. 152–3.
24 See e.g. G. W. Leibniz, *Philosophical Essays* (Indianapolis: Hackett, 1989), pp. 213–14, 333–4.
25 Bonhoeffer, *Act and Being*, DBW 2 (Minneapolis: Fortress, 1989), p. 34.
26 The details of the difference between Kantian philosophy and subsequent 'German idealism' will be discussed more fully below in Chapter Two.
27 ... largely because of its stronger rootedness especially in Aristotelian but also in Platonic metaphysical presuppositions through Thomism and scholasticism.
28 Johann Gottlieb Fichte, *Fichte: Science of Knowledge (Wissenschaftslehre)*, ed. Peter Heath and John Lachs (New York: Appleton-Century-Crofts, 1970; 2nd ed., Cambridge: Cambridge University Press, 1982); Georg Wilhelm Friedrich Hegel, *The Phenomenology of Mind* (London: Allen & Unwin, 1931).
29 George A. Lindbeck, *The Nature of Doctrine* (Philadelphia: Westminster, 1984), p. 118.

CHAPTER 2

CAUSALITY AND CONCEPTUAL MONO-VISION

I

1. Any request for an 'explanation' of something is a request for a reasoned account of it; and a reasoned account, in turn, involves most essentially a tracing of connections between events or ideas. Explanations or reasoned accounts therefore are always given in accordance with an expectation to be able to demonstrate a connected sequentiality of one form or another. When we stop to reflect on it, we will see that all of our explanations or accounts as such take place inevitably in one of two ways, and *only* in these two ways. One kind of explanation or accountability is concerned with the connections involved in causal sequences in space and time, and the connections made here are based on what is perceived through sensible observation. The other kind of explanation or accountability is concerned with the connections involved in conceptual sequences in thinking; and the connections made here are not directly based on sensible observation but on what is calculated through the operations of logic or ratiocination.

Now in everyday life this distinction between causal accounts or explanations and conceptual accounts can seem like an obvious and really quite unproblematic one. For example, no one will disagree that the causal-sensible way I am expected to be able to explain or account for the fact of this irregular scar on my left forearm (an effect caused by a fall from a ladder while pruning a row of holly bushes in my back yard five years ago) is fundamentally different than the conceptual-logical way I am expected to be able to explain or account for the geometrical 'fact' that the square of the hypotenuse of a right triangle is equal to the sum of the squares of the other two sides, or for a reasoned proof of a theorem in the propositional calculus. Or again, no one will disagree that the causal-empirical reasons I am expected to give in explaining my late arrival at an airline gate for a flight departing to San Diego – my incoming flight from London to Chicago was late due to unexpected headwinds in the Atlantic crossing – is completely different than the reasons I am expected to give for my arrival at a conclusion deduced via the formal logic of a syllogism.[1]

The two kinds of explanation or accounting here are entirely different. The former explanation in each of the above pairings of examples has to do with observations of sensibly perceptual connectedness in the relation of physically causal processes and events between bodies in space and time; whereas the latter kind of explanation in each pairing has to do with observations of logical connectedness in the relation of mentally inferential processes and computations between concepts in discursive intellection. And our recognition of the requirement and ability both to ask questions and to give reasons in these two different ways corresponds most directly to the human organism itself, which precisely *in its unity* recognizes itself as *both* sensible (susceptible and responsive to bodily or causal influences) *and* rational (susceptible and responsive to conceptual or logical influences). So again, not only are these the only two ways in which we are able to give explanatory accounts, but they will also be found to operate on essentially different criteria, such that the one kind of accounting or explanation can never act as a substitute for the other.

Now this distinction, which is clear to common sense, has also been quite carefully observed and respected throughout most of our theological and philosophical history, and continues to be observed fully today in the natural or physical sciences, just as it is in everyday life. But when we come to developments within the philosophy and theology over the past two centuries, we find that for an array of reasons this twofold kind of attentiveness has with a few exceptions almost entirely disappeared from view. Or more exactly, we find that the question of causal explanation based on the dynamic interactions between bodies in space and time has in one way or another become entirely subsumed under the mental authority of conceptual explanation or conceptual 'determination', in a way that effectively makes the cause–effect processes in the world a function of the subject–predicate relation in sentences, or of the 'intentional–referential' processes in human consciousness. As a reflection of this, dictums such as: 'Where the word breaks off no thing may be',[2] or 'The phenomenon of understanding pervades all human relations to the world',[3] are now often taken as providing the standard or default orientations for proper enquiry. The result, to borrow a like-minded turn of phrase from Emmanuel Levinas, is that the most prominent strains of philosophy and the human sciences more broadly mainly operate today from within the confines of a kind of 'consciousness obsession',[4] or what I will be calling a conceptually cognitive mono-vision.

Now as we shall see, this has had a powerful impact on theology today as well, especially in the understanding of the basic character of divine revelation, and from there also to theological self-understanding per se as an intellectual discipline. And in order to make clear the deep extent to which the current mindsets depart from past views – not to mention also the growing gulf between the 'humanities' and the natural sciences today – it will be necessary in this chapter to look at the history of the distinction in both theology and philosophy. We will be concerned in so doing with showing both the exact reasons for the considerable magnitude of this shift and certain unsustainable errors which occur in it, in order in the next chapter to demonstrate the extent of its effects on theology. It should be added importantly, however, that the objective here will of course not be to suggest that God becomes 'visible' in his revelation 'causally' as a sensible percept, but only that theological attentiveness to the reality of God in revelation may not exclude the sensible aspects of human life-awareness, or may not confine itself to the mental.

2. We can see the distinction between causal and conceptual explanations clearly sustained and structurally developed, for example, already in Aristotle. In fact, a vitally important aspect of what distinguishes Aristotle's more empirically oriented philosophy from Plato's is precisely the sharp separation he draws between '*aitia*' (that is, reasons which explain in a genuinely causal or 'etiological' way or 'in the explanation of a change'[5] in the real world); and '*dioti*' (that is, reasons which 'explain' in a merely logical way, i.e. by showing merely deductively the analytical 'consequences' that follow from given pre-mises or presuppositions).[6] It is true that Aristotle found a way of expressing this difference between causal and logical explanations entirely on the syllo-gistic level: i.e. by distinguishing between syllogisms that provide genuinely 'scientific' understanding and those that do not; or between syllogisms which, in his own words, provide causal 'demonstration' in a way 'productive of scientific knowledge' and those that do not.[7] But the sharpness and consistency with which Aristotle more generally holds these two kinds of authorities for questioning as at bottom separate, are made fully clear in his own unmistakable insistence that one kind of explanation or reasoning can never at bottom act as a substitute for the other.[8]

It is not for nothing that Aristotle, for all his great depth and sophistication, is sometimes referred to as the quintessential 'philosopher of common sense'. And indeed, these particular philosophical clarifications about the two differ-ent ways in which we reason through explanation were so resonant with the actual human experience of the world that they remained very broadly adhered to in the centuries following Aristotle and throughout the medieval period, even by those who departed strongly from him in more basic ways. For example, while Augustine's main philosophical influences are neoplatonic rather than Aristotelian, he nevertheless fully recognizes the critical importance – even and especially for theology – of distinguishing between explanations from causal sequence and explanations from logical sequence. This can be demonstrated on several levels and from several sources but it is shown with particular clarity in book five of *The Literal Meaning of Genesis*, entitled 'The Two Narratives and the Causal Reasons', where Augustine deals extensively with 'causal reasons' (and also for him the related 'seminal reasons'). As reasons which are integrally connected to *material* processes and sequences, these are seen as fundamentally distinct from reasons derived purely from *mental* or discursive processes and sequences.[9]

But for theology it is in Thomas Aquinas that these basic Aristotelian orientations and distinctions are carried forward with particular force and illumination, and now especially so in Thomas's employment precisely of *causal* explanation as an authority for *theological* reflection. It is well known, for instance, that all of the 'proofs' in Thomas's celebrated 'five ways' precisely do *not* proceed from a consideration of the activity of discursive reason per se. Thomas does indeed acknowledge a fundamental and thoroughly logical form of discursive reasoning which proceeds on a consideration of '*ratio*' as this 'advances from one concept to another' inferentially on the basis of certain 'first principles': i.e. principles that he sees as immediately present in the intellect.[10] But the arguments for the 'five ways' do not proceed in this way. All of them proceed rather from what is encountered causally in *sensible* observation and then move inductively to the 'proofs' from there.

I have discussed this more fully elsewhere,[11] but Thomas's attention to causality for theological purposes can also be shown in another way. The term 'revelation', which has today become a common shorthand for speaking of God's 'self-communication' to the world, contains within it a certain ambiguity which as we shall see has contributed to a basic confusion as to how it is to be paid attention to theologically. In Aquinas, however, no such potentially ambivalent term as revelation ever becomes operative with any prominence. Thomas rather speaks less ambiguously of the divine disclosure to the world essentially and originally in terms of a 'divine causality', or a divinely causal disclosure.[12] To be sure, this divine causality is not for Aquinas encounterable or made visible in its full power and efficacy in the world except as human awareness is enlivened by an 'illumination of faith'.[13] But the fact remains that *what* the illumination of faith first makes 'visible' for human beings is the God who deals 'causally' with and in the world, and who is known 'through his effects' in the world and not first through the inferences of pure ratiocination.

Aquinas's understanding of 'divine causality' should not be misunderstood, however. It is true that the common medieval mind at the time of Thomas's writing still inhabited what we would see today as a kind of enchanted or superstitious world, one which was structured within a 'three-tiered' cosmology (heaven above, earth here, hell below). And it can be freely admitted accordingly that such a mindset might have tended to see the divine causality at work in everything, reflecting a God who, as one commentator has put it, was actively supervising the affairs of the world from moment to moment. But this is hardly the understanding of divine causality as it is theologically developed by Aquinas, whose treatment is anything but 'naïve' in this sense and in fact mainly 'negative' in approach, even though it reflects the cosmology of his day in a properly sophisticated way.

This philosophical and theological attention to causal relations as distinct from conceptual relations then came to be not only preserved but even further amplified in certain ways through the major intellectual transitions that immediately followed Thomas and scholasticism. This can be seen both in the movement from the so-called *via antiqua* (roughly, Aristotelian scholasticism culminating in Aquinas and Scotus) to the *via moderna* (roughly, the emerging anti-Aristotelian nominalism exemplified most prominently by William of Ockham); and then also as these influences were carried further into some of the reformers (most notably, Luther). In fact, there occurs in this period what is today broadly perceived to have been an unhealthy and in some ways theologically impoverishing movement in the other direction, in an overemphasis or even a radicalization of the sensibly particular and therefore of empirically causal awareness in nominalism. In the subsequent reformational discussions the focus on causal authority as distinct from conceptually cognitive authority also remained predominant, although here in more essentially doctrinal ways, especially in the treatment of grace, covenant, predestination and election.[14]

3. With the emergence of continental rationalism in the seventeenth century, however, something begins to change fundamentally, not only for the philosophical understanding of 'reality' per se, but also for the status of causal authority itself. Let me try to make this clearer. Because of the obvious susceptibility of sensible perception to error and misjudgment, rationalism began to view the senses as inherently unreliable guides for questions about what is 'real' and 'true'. The most that can be expected of the senses, it was claimed, is the delivery of a truth which, as Leibniz put it, is inherently 'confused', clouded and inconstant. What begins to be re-affirmed instead (not entirely unlike Platonism) is a more truly real, unchanging and constant *supra*-sensible or *meta*-physical 'realm', of which the embodied empirical world is only a changing and imperfect expression, or a subservient manifestation. And what rationalism saw here, specifically with regard to the question of empirical causality, was that *if* such a metaphysical 'realm' really exists or subsists, then the cause–effect relations, which dynamically pervade every aspect of physically embodied life, must also have their explanation in a deeper meta-physical and thus purely 'rational' reality.

And here we come then to the really fundamental shift over earlier treatments of causality. Causal authority now begins to be understood philosophically as no longer something fundamentally empirical or sensible – that is, no longer even essentially *about* the relations and physical dynamics of extended bodies – but rather now as more correctly something *about* this meta-physical 'realm' itself. And because this realm is defined as supra-sensible, therefore it can be accessed philosophically only through pure reason. Or to use the language that was common at the time, the empirically dynamic authority of *causa* becomes completely absorbed into the discursive authority of *ratio*.[15] It is directly as a reflection of this subsumption that many of the most distinctively characteristic doctrines of seventeenth-century rationalism come to development: the doctrines of supra-sensible monads, pre-established harmony, sufficient reason in Leibniz; supra-sensible substance, and 'thoughts which themselves think' in Spinoza; causal 'occasionalism' in Malebranche; 'substrata' and 'real essences' in Locke (Locke remained a unique hybrid of empiricist and rationalist on these matters); not to mention the definition of the human causal agent itself as most fundamentally a 'thinking substance' in Descartes.

In sum, then, the really decisive point for our purposes is that in seventeenth-century rationalism causal reasons or explanations, which had hitherto been seen as pertaining fundamentally to dynamic relations between bodies in space and time as these are sensibly observed, were now fully subsumed into ratiocinative reasons or explanations, pertaining to a putatively more genuinely objective reality at work on deeper or higher supra-sensible levels. And the vital corollary here is that all of these relations between essences, substrates, substances or monads on the metaphysical level are seen as fundamentally closed to sensible awareness and open only to the sensibly abstracted, or *purified activity of reason itself*. It is specifically this purified activity of cognitive or discursive reason, having purged itself of all potentially misleading sensible orientation, which is denoted by the term 'speculative reason'. The 'reality' that rationalism thus aspires to in its purest forms is no longer the spatial and temporal, sensibly dynamic reality in which we live and die, but rather a purely speculative 'realm' which is absent of all spatio-temporal dynamism and therefore inert.

Now it will be easy to see in this light that in any of its different manifestations continental rationalism at its heart was most essentially a philosophical *project* of 'pure reason'. And it is important to recognize that it was precisely this *'project* of pure reason' that became the primary polemical target of what Kant, in his <u>*Critique* of *Pure Reason*</u>, would specifically bring under such sustained attack as a form of what he polemically called 'dogmatism'. In Kant, this term 'dogmatism' designates most essentially an over-reaching activity of the purely speculative (i.e. supra-sensible) exercise of reason in which it makes claims or asserts its jurisdiction in ways that cannot themselves be rationally justified. This is by no means to say, however, that for Kant there is anything 'wrong' with the speculative use of reason per se; indeed, he shows it to be entirely indispensable for philosophy within its proper limits. It is only when speculative reason ceases to recognize the limits of that over which it may legitimately claim jurisdiction and ownership that it becomes 'dogmatical'. Kant was able to support this critique by exposing what came subsequently to be recognized broadly as a fatal error in such rationally dogmatic approaches.

The basic error here has two sides to it. On the one side Kant demonstrates that rationalism's reification[16] of its metaphysical 'substances', 'essences', 'substrates', 'monads' and so on, is itself an *ir*rational move. Or in other words, the only way the objective reality of such entities can be affirmed is through a kind of 'despotic' decree of the understanding, a decree which cannot itself be rationally justified and which thus must enforce itself with an authority that is simply 'dogmatically' posited. What the Kantian critique shows to the contrary is that the most that reason itself can rationally demonstrate about any such supposed metaphysical entities, is that they are 'mere ideas of the understanding', ideas which reason must itself produce as it strives intrinsically for unity as a faculty of coherence. Somewhat more exactly, rationalism's affirmation of a real objective metaphysical realm is under the Kantian critique shown to be the product of certain rational illusions, such that what is claimed to be metaphysically real (objectively) is in truth only a domain of the mind's own speculative ideas.

But this error also has an inverse side to it. For the Achilles heel of rationalism according to the Kantian critique was also its failure to realize that just as reason has a limit on the margins of thinking (i.e. the inability of reason to demonstrate the objective reality of its own sensibly purified ideas, as rationalism claimed this), so also reason has a limit at the center of embodied life. The point is that in empirical reality discursive reason also encounters a basic limit for the legitimacy of its rational claims of jurisdiction or ownership. For it is quite obvious that reason does not itself *engender* or produce the empirical reality of the world from within which it finds itself active in a human body. It rather discovers this reality as something that is 'given' to it nowhere else than through sensible awareness.

And this brings us back inevitably to the question of the causal dynamism of the embodied world. For the basic authority with which the empirically real world announces itself on its *own* terms through sensibility to discursive reason, and thus as a limit to reason, is again the authority of an empirically *causal* dynamism. The Kantian enterprise thus showed that discursive reason must always, *for its own very integrity*, hold itself to account before the tribunal of the real empirical world in space and time. Or more fully, it showed that whenever reason seeks to make fundamental pronouncements about the 'nature' of the reality of the world it inhabits, or about any 'structure' the world reflects, it must always, even in its most abstract and theoretically speculative reaches, be directed 'critically' and thus self-limitingly back to its 'empirical use'.[17]

II

4. The impact of the Kantian critique was of such magnitude that it quite fundamentally changed the course of epistemological procedure in subsequent continental thought, no less among those who rejected its conclusions than among those who supported them. Nevertheless, it was precisely this critical or self-limiting character of Kantian philosophy that the subsequent idealisms (e.g. of Fichte and Hegel), who otherwise built fundamentally on his insights, perceived as a kind of betrayal or humiliation for true philosophy, whose goal as they saw it must be to establish the 'absolute freedom' and spontaneity of reason in its speculative use. And so they undertook once again to free the discursive intellect from what they saw as its embarrassing confinement to sensible reality in space and time. And one of the primary ways in which they undertook to achieve this – here as in rationalism, although now even more definitively – was once again through a renewed and sustained attack on the causal authority of empirical reality.

We can only document this in the sketchiest of terms here in Hegel. In his *Science of Logic*, for example, Hegel undertakes to achieve an intellective conquest of causal authority by claiming that the cause–effect relation in the world can be reduced to what he explicitly calls a 'tautology' in conceptuality or grammar.[18] And he seeks to achieve this in what can be seen roughly as a basic two-stage strategy. First the cause–effect relation itself is removed from the context of the sensible world and reconfigured as a subject–predicate relation in language – i.e. where the empirically dynamic 'cause' is transported onto the linguistic level and made into a grammatical 'subject', and where the empirical 'effect' then becomes a 'predicate' of that subject.[19] But then secondly, in this subject–predicate relation itself, what the grammatical predicate (i.e. the reconfigured 'effect') is seen to bring to the subject (i.e. the reconfigured 'cause') is not something that amplifies or brings any new or contingent information to the grammatical subject in any way. Rather, the predicate (the 'effect') merely restates what is already contained and can be found 'analytically' in the very definition of the subject (the 'cause') itself. This then is what Hegel means when he speaks of 'the relation of causality' as fundamentally the relation of a linguistic 'tautology'.[20] Dynamically causal relations as experienced in the embodied world are thus entirely absorbed into the logical relations of the discursive intellect, as self-consciousness 'rises to the universal' through the 'power of abstraction'.[21]

This basic subsumption of the sensible authority of causality into the analytical authority of logic is just as pronounced in Fichte's *Wissenschaftslehre*, although demonstrated in different ways. We cannot go into that any further here except to say that what transpires in German idealism can be summed up for present purposes as something importantly twofold. First, and more basically, the *sensible receptivity* that we naturally encounter dependently as that which governs our embodied awareness in the dynamic empirical nexus of cause and effect, is reconfigured in Hegel and Fichte to mean something that is more originarily a feature of the *speculative activity* of the discursive intellect. Or to restate this more fully: the basic sensible susceptibility and awareness that we experience obviously in everyday life to be both dynamically *causal* and therefore dependently *receptive* (the icy February wind in my face; the steep incline of a particularly brutal hill on my jogging route; the unusually excessive noise, due to a construction detour, of the city traffic this morning as I walk to work): this sensibly receptive and thus dependently causal character of embodied life has been transformed into a spontaneous activity of cognitive consciousness.

This subsumption of the authority of natural physical causality under the 'determining' ownership or 'lordship' of the mind's own ideas, is what stands behind Hegel's well-known belief, following Schelling, that 'nature' is most essentially *versteinerte Intelligenz*, i.e. ossified (or petrified) intelligence. Indeed, Hegel famously was willing to push these positions to the point of contending that nature per se does not have a causally sequential past at all apart from what consciousness gives to it, going even as far here as to maintain that fossil remains were never living organisms. It also explains the jarring causticity of Hegel's polemic against Newtonian physics. Newton is characterized by Hegel as a 'complete barbarian as regards his conceptions', who made 'bad observations and drew worse conclusions', and whose scientific findings 'are so untrue and devoid of sense or understanding . . . that they may also serve as an example of how we should neither experiment nor draw conclusions, of how nothing at all can be learned'.[22]

Despite these eccentricities, however, there is undeniably a great beauty and intellectually brilliant power to Hegel's work, a power that continues to exert its influence often in subliminal ways even today after the less palatable 'totalizing' aspects of his work have been rejected. The particular subliminal influence with which I am concerned relates to a point made with especial eloquence in Gadamer's *Truth and Method*, specifically in its brilliant opening assessment of early nineteenth-century European intellectual development in the wake of German idealism.[23] I speak particularly of Gadamer's tracing – under what he shows to be the direct impact of idealism – of a newfound confidence and even supremacy within the

Geisteswissenschaften or the human sciences (e.g. philosophy, anthropology, sociology, history, literary studies, etc.) over the *Naturwissenschaften* or the natural sciences. As Gadamer explains, the *Geisteswissenschaften* had hitherto often labored under something of an inferiority complex vis-à-vis the *Naturwissenschaften*, especially as these latter had been able to provide a 'scientific objectivity' that had until that time eluded the former. The emergence of idealism, however, created the groundwork for a fundamental change in that inferior self-assessment, and Gadamer's essential point now, as to the lasting impact of idealism in this regard, is the following vital and truly far-reaching one.

If, as idealism had claimed, the most fundamental and originary constituents of human 'reality and truth' are features of the creative or spontaneous speculative intellect in abstraction from what is sensible: then it follows as a matter of course that the purest and most genuine apprehension of reality and truth will always be undertaken first and foremost as a *Geisteswissenschaft*, which is to say fundamentally as *a science of human mental or phenomenal consciousness per se.*[24] Or we can state this also in the following way. One of idealism's most defining claims had been that the causally dynamic, spatio-temporally extended sentient 'world' may not be spoken of as properly 'real' or as yielding any 'truth' in any case, except as it has come to an appropriately sophisticated 'determination' *as* a 'world' by the mind. Now if this is true, as it indeed came to be accepted, then the *Geisteswissenschaften* are capable of asking the authentic questions of truth and reality not only in a more genuine and originary way than the *Naturwissenschaften*, but indeed without reference to them or their empirical interests at all. For these latter are still tied to asking the question of truth in its merely naïve definition as the 'agreement of cognition with its object'.[25] We can summarize Gadamer's observations then as follows. Under the continuing influence of these lingering aspects of idealism, even after other onerous totalizing aspects of it were rejected, it did not take long in the human sciences more broadly for the speculative intellect to assert a kind of absolute supremacy over sensible embodiment, such that the influence of idealism today remains tacitly but still pervasively embedded within many contemporary versions of phenomenology, philology, textualism, structuralism and so on.

5. Before making some concluding remarks in preparation in the next chapter, where we will look at the impact of all of this on theology, let us look more specifically at just one such continuing influence in the example of present-day phenomenology following Edmund Husserl. Without any question, one of the major factors for the re-emerging influence of idealistic orientations in current thought has been the continuing impact of Husserl's phenomenological project, along with the host of other phenomenological (and 'post-phenomenological') responses it has spawned. Outside of certain developments in French philosophy early in the twentieth century (e.g. Kojève, Koyré, early Merleau-Ponty), it is Husserl who most influentially brings a modified spirit of Hegel (and Fichte) back to the center of intellectual exchange, thereby strongly influencing a wide array of disciplines in the

process, including theology.[26] There is of course an important departure from Hegelian idealism in Husserl, in that what we are speaking of as a 'conceptually cognitive mono-vision' or 'consciousness-obsession' no longer appears on the grand metaphysically idealist scale of Hegelian 'absolute knowing' or 'absolute idea'.[27] Phenomenology describes itself rather as a 'science of consciousness' or a 'science of essences' in consciousness.[28] And it therefore restricts itself purposively, and with all the rigors of an exact science, solely to the descriptions or logical analysis of whatever 'appears' in consciousness as well as the manner of such appearing in consciousness.

Now in order for phenomenology to achieve the full rigor that it seeks as an exact science of consciousness alone, it must 'bracket out' any and all questions that do not concern phenomenal consciousness – e.g. any questions about things or events in the world that might be spoken of as existing independently of human consciousness. And the mechanism by which it undertakes this bracketing-out activity it calls the *epoché*. It should be noted, however, in phenomenology's defense, that certain 'realist' critiques of phenomenology can often misunderstand the basic character of the *epoché*, which is not an outright denial of non-phenomenal physical reality. It rather denotes a complete withholding of judgment – either of assent or dissent – over the 'external' common-sense world, for the simple reason that this can have no bearing on a science which has confined itself by definition exclusively to what appears within consciousness. But even though the *epoché* is thus invoked legitimately for its own stated purposes – i.e. in order to retain the clarity of phenomenology as a 'pure' science of 'notions in the [mental] horizon of their appearing', or as a pure science of 'intentional analysis' (Levinas) – nevertheless the commitment that remains constant and in harmony with idealism is that the whole of nature or reality is always to be treated as 'nothing but a correlate of consciousness',[29] and as always hermetically enclosed within this. The basic consonance of phenomenology on this level with the conceptually mono-visional spirit of idealism can be encapsulated in terms of three basic kinds of 'suspensions' or rejections in the *epoché*.

First, there is in phenomenology, as in idealism, a 'suspension' of *the authority of sensibility* as something actually originating in embodiment. I do not mean of course that sensibility is not a concern in phenomenology. Indeed it is a very important and even defining feature of many phenomenological projects (e.g. Levinas or also for Deleuze, Merleau-Ponty and others). I mean only that sensibility in phenomenology is by definition never treated in a way that allows for its origination in the body through empirically causal forces, but rather treats it first as something already subsumed under 'intentional' (mental) consciousness.

Secondly, *the reality of material nature* is 'suspended' in phenomenology; or in other words, the real externality to the questioning mind of any such material or physical nature is suspended. Consider how radically and quite explicitly Husserl is willing to remove even the empirical reality of his own extended body from reflective consideration. Or more exactly, consider how willing he is to remove or suspend any authority that this sensible embodiment might be able to exert on human enquiry. In his own words, within phenomenology 'the actuality of all of material Nature is therefore kept out of action and that of all corporeality along with it, including the actuality of my body, the body of the cognizing subject'.[30] Husserl goes on to admit freely that 'this radical suspension of Nature stands in conflict, to be sure with our most deeply rooted habits of experience and thinking'. But then he adds that 'it is precisely for this reason that a fully self-conscious phenomenological reduction is needed' if the systematic investigation of consciousness as a project of 'pure immanence' in cognitive conception is going to be successful at all.[31]

It is in the third area of suspension, however, that we come back to our main theme in this chapter. And indeed, this is the one that is necessary for the sustainability of the other two. The third suspension in the *epoché* is once again the suspension or denial of *the reality of causal connections*. More exactly, here as in Hegel, it is a denial that the authority of causal sequences in space and time can be understood as anything really different than the authority of logical or semantic (meaning-oriented) connections or sequences in the activity of consciousness. To use Husserl's own language, in our perception of causal relations, we are in no case ever *really* 'dealing with an external causal relation', that is, never with an authority different than what can be provided by mental 'intentionality'.[32] Rather 'such apparent causation' is always 'itself through and through intentional' (i.e. mental), such that any consideration of causal realities or authorities apart from the authorization of cognition is deemed by Husserl to be 'absurd in principle'.[33]

6. Let me emphasize, however, that our own objection to phenomenology in all of this is not to the phenomenological discipline per se, as a kind of philosophy of mind. Indeed, it has contributed much of great value, perhaps especially (for theological concerns) in that it provides what Paul Ricoeur calls the 'indispensable presupposition' for hermeneutics.[34] But as Ricoeur himself will then go on to add, there is nevertheless a strong objection that must be raised against phenomenology, even from a hermeneutical perspective, insofar as it projects itself as something foundational for *all* enquiry, that is, as the 'science of sciences' or as the 'ideal of scientificity'.[35] Yet, critiques like Ricoeur's notwithstanding, such a foundational consciousness obsession has indeed become virtually the default view in many sectors of study today as these mono-visional perspectives in philosophy have in turn permeated current intellectual views of 'reality' more widely and deeply throughout the human sciences and theology. Indeed, it can seem astonishing to witness the lengths to which such outlooks are often willing to go to preserve the supremacy of conceptual or 'determining' consciousness over causal dynamism, or to make the latter fundamentally subservient to the former. This, even to the point of being willing to insist, for example, that the reality or 'authenticity' of the actual, unrelenting empirical advance of an affliction such as cancer or Alzheimer's disease, *depends* on the thematizing activity of a conceptually 'determining' consciousness which gives it its 'significance' and therefore its 'reality'.

But this is not only 'counter-intuitive', as Husserl freely admits, but also surely absurd. For the fact remains that these afflictions continue to run their own real course, inflict their real pain, and do their own real damage in the body – even prior to the conscious detection of them and even when the afflicted one might in the later stages of illness have become unconscious or comatose. Indeed, they do so with a causal dynamism and harshness of authority that precisely *defies* capturability in the 'signifying' abstractions of *any* cognitive classification or linguistic expression, and in a way that remains causally constant across all cultural interpretations or ethnographies. The fact that we name them and identify them under these 'intentional' designations does not make their reality 'through and through intentional' or mental. We need to continue with some further examples which to many readers may seem unnecessarily extreme, given the apparent obviousness of the observations. But the view that all reality must (at least for humans) be understood foundationally as 'mind-dependent' reality has become so prevalent today in broad sectors of philosophy and theology that we need to push the matter further.

We can look, for example, to the destructive causal power of a spate of recent near-cataclysmic natural disasters to witness with especial grimness the failures of these prevailing consciousness-centered views that deny the real non-conceptual authority of causal forces. Among these are the tsunami in Southeast Asia, the hurricane devastation of New Orleans and the massive landslides in the Philippines in which a mountainside of mud swallowed an entire town with its 1,800 inhabitants. To say that the deaths of these people, many of whom would have perished instantaneously and entirely without warning (and thus without the possibility of assimilating what was occurring into any 'signifying' framework or linguistic structure of 'meaning'): to say that the *reality* of the death and suffering of these victims actually *depends* on this coming to expression in a language game or conceptual scheme and not vice versa, is not only to miss something important about human life. It is also to make a fundamental misjudgment whose basic character verges into the moral and not merely epistemological.

These events are not 'up to us'; nor are they 'up to language' or 'up to culture'. Their *reality*, their authenticity, their authority, especially for the embodied human organisms affected, do not *depend* on their receiving 'authentication' from a different non-causal source, or on achieving a 'proper significance' within a conceptual scheme. They are not 'through and through intentional' or mental. The morally troubling implications of such a view become even more accentuated in real instances of unspeakable evil. The evil of Auschwitz or Rwanda does not depend for its reality or 'authenticity' on being brought to a 'determining' expression in a conceptual scheme or language game. Indeed, it is precisely in the face of the mind-stopping brutality of their evil in their actual causally embodied enactment that language itself must often simply learn to 'shut up'. We can for emphasis invoke a well-known Wittgensteinian dictum here and apply it in a quite different way than it is normally understood. For it is exactly in relation to these manifestations of bodily and causally enacted reality, and not in relation to some noumenally abstract esthetic sublimity, that Wittgenstein's dictum comes to its truest and most soberingly intractable expression: '*Wovon man nicht sprechen kann, darüber muss man schweigen*' ('Whereof one cannot speak, thereof one must remain silent').[36]

But we need not look only to tragedy and unspeakable evil to illustrate this point. We can look to the causal generation of our human life to make it as well. The point is that the reality of my own physical birth, of which I have no consciousness or memory, does not *depend* on my now being able to place that event into a meaning-giving conceptual scheme or language game. More than this, the causal, empirical reality of the early-stage human embryo or zygote that was secretly formed, grew and found nourishment in a mother's womb several weeks before being 'discovered', and thus before receiving a certain 'significance' by the bearing mother, does not *depend* for its reality on the placement within that 'signifying' conceptual scheme or language game. The reason for this is that its reality – its biotic *life* – is first *engendered*, according to a causal, embodied dynamism and authority, and not first cognitively *determined*, according to a 'signifying' authority or a logical or cultural-linguistic authority. Indeed, the very possibility of the conceptual 'determination' depends *on* the causal reality of the 'generation', and not vice versa.[37] In any such considerations, the simple question 'which came first?' will assure the right directionality in the relation of dependence. To deny this crucial distinction in the authority between 'causal generation' and 'conceptual determination' is equivalent to denying with Hegel that fossil remains were ever really living organisms, or more broadly to deny that nature can have a causally sequential dynamism and past apart from or prior to human conceptual determinacy of it.

None of this is of course to deny that everything we can *say* about the world occurs necessarily within conceptual schemes and language games, that is, in the relation of signifiers and signifieds. Just as little is it to suggest that, for human awareness, things and events in the world do not acquire their essential 'meaning' and signification through concepts and language. It is only to reject the idea that things and events cannot have their own genuine authenticity and reality, or that they cannot speak with their own originary causally dynamic authority in ways that do not reduce to language games. Or it is simply to point out the fundamental mistake involved in moving from the obvious fact that all our accounts and explanations and interpretations must inescapably *take place* in language and concepts, to the much stronger and very different kind of suggestion that intentionality and language are somehow the real *origin* or the fundamental generation of these realities.

7. One must grant again that to many readers these distinctions may perhaps seem too obvious to warrant this kind of elaboration. And in fact it is impossible for any of us actually to live our real lives without a tacit full acknowledgement of them. What then are the reasons for the undiminished hold that the above orientations continue to exert on much intellectual endeavor today? Let me suggest just two.

The first can trace its roots back to Hegel's charge against Newton and Hume (and Kant): i.e. that their willingness to grant to sensible reality a causal authority on its own terms (an authority not deriving from conceptual determination) amounts to a kind of 'barbarism'. The same kinds of suspicion still prevail strongly today, where approaches that seek to be attentive to the empirical and causally dynamic aspects of life are often judged to be too 'naïve' or too 'simplistic' or insufficiently conceptually problematized to warrant serious consideration. Or they are seen as capable of yielding only 'the poorest kind of truth', as Hegel put it, and as such are unable to contribute adequately to the deeper questions of reality and truth, which must be always rooted *first* in 'the significance of a complex process of mediation'.[38]

It must be admitted, however, that such criticisms are not entirely without warrant. For there can indeed be a tendency to move in the opposite direction and to be too readily reliant on agreement with 'common-sense' explanations, in a way that can reduce to a flat materialism or a naïve empiricist 'positivism' (which we shall discuss in a later chapter), and which thereby ignore the depth and importance of what thinkers like Hegel or Husserl are seeing in other ways. Nor do statements like Bertrand Russell's 'Better an hour with Newton than a year with Plato' contribute to any softening of this antagonistic perception today. Nevertheless, anyone who has considered seriously Aristotle's *Posterior Analytics*, for example, or Aquinas's *Commentary* on this among his own other writings, or Kant's *Critique of Pure Reason*, or, in the twentieth century Donald Mackinnon's *The Problem of Metaphysics*, or Bernard Lonergan's *Insight: a Study of Human Understanding*, will very quickly realize that the best and most rigorously critical empirically attentive kinds of thinking are very far from 'naïve' or 'barbaric'.

The second reason is directly related to the first, and is the more powerfully motivating one for staying the course in the idealistic retreat from the causal authority of the real world of space and time, even in the face of what Husserl admits can be its deeply 'counter-intuitive' character. The point is that to allow that the world of embodied human life might indeed be able to exert itself causally with an authority 'on its own terms'[39] would amount effectively to a forfeiture of the hard-won intellectual supremacy that the *Geisteswissenschaften* had gained for themselves over the *Naturwissenschaften* in German idealism. For such an admission would by definition be a forfeiture of their foundationalist status, in that it would imply a certain dependence on and therefore a certain subservience of the *Geisteswissenschaften* to the causal dynamism of the reality in which we find ourselves alive. Such a superiority, once gained, is hard to relinquish. And so, while the totalizing aspects of German idealism are today indeed willingly rejected, nevertheless the more fundamental spirit of idealism lives on undiminished in more tempered forms of a conceptual or phenomenological mono-vision, yet where the discursive intellect retains its full 'lordship' over the real world of causal dynamism in space and time.

It thus remains the case that in a broad spectrum of intellectual endeavor today the fallback to the mono-visional spirit of idealism remains powerfully influential. The consciousness obsession of the spirit of idealism, in part through its revival in phenomenology, has also had significant continuing impact within twentieth-century structuralism and post-structuralism. It is true that structuralism and post-structuralism almost invariably have their origins more specifically in linguistic developments, for example, those following from Ferdinand de Saussure's theory of language. But the fact remains that the newfound boldness and confidence that phenomenology was able to claim, as an exact analytical science of pure consciousness through the *epoché*, provided for these also the impetus and boldness to transport what had hitherto been seen as essentially linguistic principles directly onto human domains for use in the human sciences.[40]

In sum, what all of this has been seeking to make clear is the ongoing pervasive influence today of a conceptual or phenomenological mono-vision, which in many ways originates in idealism, and which has been able to reinvent itself in a multitude of ways in various forms of discursively analytical endeavors. And when one adds to this the differently focused but still similarly dispositioned underlying orientations in Anglo-American analytical philosophy, not to mention the emergence of 'antirealism', which has become virtually the default view in Anglo-American epistemology: it is then hardly surprising that theology too should have come to express and orient itself fundamentally in such conceptually or phenomenologically mono-visional and linguistically analytical ways. It is to a study of that influence that we will turn in the next chapter.

Before commencing with that, however, let me emphasize again the earlier point, that our objective in seeking to rejuvenate causal and sensible attentiveness for theology will not of course be to suggest that God becomes 'visible' in his revelation 'causally' as a sensible percept, any more than he does as a rational concept. It is only to say that if God is truly alive in his revelation at the center of life today through the resurrection and Pentecost, and if he reveals himself in the fullness of this life, then theology must be attentive through all human faculties and may not confine itself to the discursively mental.

Notes

1 A syllogism is an argument in which a conclusion follows necessarily from given premises.
2 Both Gadamer and Heidegger make thematic use of this line from the poem 'Das Wort' by Stefan George. Gadamer cites it at the very conclusion of *Truth and Method* in its culmination. Martin Heidegger, *On the Way to Language* (New York: Harper & Row, 1971), p. 139. Hans-Georg Gadamer, *Truth and Method* (New York: Continuum, 2004), p. 483.
3 Gadamer, *Truth and Method* (New York: Continuum, 2004), p. xx.
4 See Emmanuel Levinas, *Totality and Infinity* (Pittsburgh: Duquesne, 1969), p. 122. See also Levinas, *Otherwise Than Being* (Pittsburgh: Duquesne University Press, 1998), p. 101, where this expression appears directly, albeit as two nouns, and in a somewhat inverted sense, but still in keeping with my usage here.
5 Stephen Everson, *Aristotle on Perception* (Oxford: Clarendon Press, 1997), p. 289 and pp. 36–55.
6 See e.g. Aristotle, *Analytica Posteriora*, Book I.13 (78a 25–35) in W. D. Ross, ed., *Aristotle's Prior and Posterior Analytics: a revised text with introduction*

and commentary (Oxford: Clarendon Press, 1949). See also *Physics*, Book II.3 (194b 16–23) in *Aristotle's Physics: Books 1&2*, tr. W. Charlton (Oxford: Clarendon Press, 1970).

7 Aristotle, *Analytica Posteriora*, Book I.2 (71.b 18–24) in W. D. Ross, ed., *Aristotle's Prior and Posterior Analytics: a revised text with introduction and commentary* (Oxford: Clarendon Press, 1949). See also especially Book I.13 (78a 25–35), where Aristotle gives three examples of the distinction between reasons that explain in a genuinely causal way (*aitia*) and reasons that explain by merely deducing logically from given premises (*dioti*). See also *Physics*, Book II.3 (194b 16–23) in *Aristotle's Physics: Books 1&2*, tr. W. Charlton (Oxford: Clarendon Press, 1970).

8 *Analytica Posteriora*, Book I.2 (71.b 18–24). See also Wesley Salmon, *Scientific Explanation and the Causal Structure of the World* (New York, Oxford: Oxford University Press, 1984), p. 18 n. 7. It will be evident at this point that I am not wanting to appeal in any deeper sense at all to Aristotle's own fuller theory in terms of his four kinds of causality, or four factors of causal explanation. (Aristotle worked with what he saw as four kinds of causality: material, formal, efficient and final. What we understand today in the straightforward empirical cause–effect relation is most clearly captured under efficient causality.) I am simply emphasizing the conspicuous distinction that runs throughout his philosophy that causal accounts which explain on the basis of sensibly encountered processes in the dynamics of real proximity in space and time, are at bottom explanatory in fundamentally different ways than purely conceptual accounts which are based on logical rules of inference in the relations of ideas.

9 Augustine, *The Literal Meaning of Genesis (De Genesi ad litteram libri duodecim)* Vol. 1, tr. John Hammond Taylor Howard (New York: Paulist Press, 1982). See also especially 146–55, 18191, 1959. See also Vernon J. Bourke, *Augustine's View of Reality*, (Villanova, PA: Villanova Press (1964)), which brings this out clearly, especially p. 127; and also Howard J. Van Till, 'Basil, Augustine, and the Doctrine of Creation's Functional Integrity,' *Science and Christian Belief*, Vol. 8, No. 1 (1996), pp. 21–38.

10 *Summa Theologiae* Ia 79.8c (New York: Benzinger Brothers, 1948; hereafter *ST*). See also Robert Pasnau's commentary in Thomas Aquinas, *The Treatise on Human Nature (Summa Theologiae* 1a 75–89) (Indianapolis/Cambridge: Hackett, 2002), pp. 294–5.

11 Paul D. Janz, 'Divine Causality and the Nature of Theological Questioning', in *Modern Theology* 23:3 (Oxford: Blackwell, 2007), pp. 317–48.

12 See e.g. *ST* Ia Q8 A1; and *Commentary on the De Trinitate of Boethiu*s in *Faith Reason and Theology*, tr. Armand Maurer (Toronto: Pontifical Institute of Medieval Studies, 1987), pp. 22–3.

13 *Commentary on the De Trinitate of Boethius*, p. 24.

14 The association of Ockham's nominalism with Martin Luther is well known and well documented, with its strong empirical emphasis on spatio-temporal particulars and its rejection of universals. Luther's own distinction as such, in his doctrine of justification, between the 'ontological causality' of justification as found in the scholastics and his own anti-scholastic 'covenantal causality', can be seen as a direct reflection of the nominalist unwillingness to recognize anything 'universal' or 'ontological' in human nature per se that could be causally 'efficacious' as a recipient of grace. What this means more fully is that for Luther the causal efficacy of grace is never received *ex natura rei* (according to some receptive capacity latent in the nature of human beings 'in general') but only *ex pacto divino* (according to the divine covenant to the individual). This is not to suggest that there are not significant differences to be found here

among the reformers themselves, especially with regard to the question of divine causality. Luther, as we have just seen, ties this directly to the doctrine of justification by faith, whereas both Zwingli and Calvin see the divine causality at work most comprehensively in predestination and election. See e.g. Otto Scheel, *Martin Luther, Vom Katholizismus zur Reformation*, 2 vols (Tübingen: Mohr 1923), 2:161–203; W.J Courtenay,'Nominalism and Late Medieval Thought: A Bibliographical Essay', *Theological Studies* 33 (1972) 716–34; Frederick Coppleston, *A History of Philosophy*, Volume III, *Ockham to Suarez* (London: Burns Oates and Washbourne, 1953) pp. 16, 72–4. See also G. W. Bromiley, 'General Introduction', in *Zwingli and Bullinger* (Philadelphia: Westminster, 1953), p. 33.

15 So, for example, Leibniz: a 'cause in the realm of things corresponds to a reason in the realm of truths, which is why causes themselves – and especially final ones – are often called reasons'. And again, 'A reason is a known truth whose connection with some less well-known truth leads us to give our assent to the latter. But it is called reason, especially and par excellence, if it is the cause not only of our judgment but also of the truth itself – which makes it known as an a priori reason' (*New Essays on Human Understanding* (Cambridge: Cambridge University Press, 1981) 6.6.475). See also e.g. Samuel Shirley, 'Translator's Preface' in Seymour Feldman, ed., *Baruch Spinoza The Ethics; Treatise on the Emendation of the Intellect; Selected Letters* (Indianapolis: Hackett, 1992), p. 25: 'Spinoza's "cause" is not quite what [we are] used to. It need not imply temporal succession: indeed, for Spinoza a cause is more the logical ground from which a consequent follows . . . For example, it "follows" from the nature of a triangle that its three angles are equal to two right angles. Hence, Spinoza occasionally couples the word "cause" with the term "reason" ("ratio")'.

16 To 'reify' in this case means to claim an objectively real status for something not demonstrably real.

17 See e.g. *Critique of Pure Reason*, Paul Guyer and Allen W. Wood (tr. & eds.) (Cambridge: Cambridge University Press, 1998), A671/B699–A681/B709 passim.

18 G. W. F. Hegel, *Hegel's Science of Logic*, tr. A. V. Miller (London: George Allen & Unwin, 1969), pp. 560–1.

19 *Hegel's Science of Logic*, pp. 558–69.

20 *Hegel's Science of Logic*, pp. 560–1.

21 Hans-Georg Gadamer, *Truth and Method* (London and New York: Continuum, 1975), p. 11.

22 *Lectures on the History of Philosophy*, Vol. III (Lincoln: University of Nebraska Press, 1995), pp. 323–4.

23 See especially Chapter 1, 'Transcending the Aesthetic Dimension', in *Truth and Method*, pp. 3–86.

24 In Gadamer's words, 'in the [new] "understanding" practiced by the *Geisteswissenschaften*, the question of truth is raised in a new way.' *Truth and Method*, p. 87.

25 This is what Kant refers to as the 'nominal definition of truth' *CPR* A58/B83.

26 See e.g. Gadamer, *Truth and Method*, p. xxxiii, Levinas, *Totality and Infinity*, pp. 44–5; Vincent Descombes, *Modern French Philosophy* (Cambridge: Cambridge University Press 1980), pp. 9–16, 67.

27 See Hegel, *Phenomenology of Mind*, pp. 479–93; *Hegel's Science of Logic*, pp. 824–44.

28 . . . although it must quickly be added that 'essences' here are no longer the metaphysical reality essences supposedly existing externally to the mind as

'substances', but rather essences now understood as essential meanings within consciousness.

29 Levinas, *Otherwise than Being* (Pittsburgh: Duquesne University Press, 1981), p. 183; Dermott Moran, Timothy Mooney eds, *The Phenomenology Reader* (London: Routledge, 2002), p. 11.

30 Husserl, *Pure Phenomenology, its Method, and its Field of Investigation* in McCormick and Elliston (eds) *Husserl, Shorter Works* (Notre Dame: University of Notre Dame Press, 1981), pp. 15–16.

31 Husserl, *Pure Phenomenology, its Method, and its Field of Investigation*, pp. 10–17, 130–1.

32 Husserl, *Logical Investigations* (London and New York: Routledge & Kegan Paul/Humanities Press, 1970), p. 576.

33 *Logical Investigations*, p. 576.

34 Paul Ricoeur, *Hermeneutics and the Human Sciences* (Cambridge: Cambridge University Press, 1981), p. 101.

35 *Hermeneutics and the Human Sciences*, p. 102.

36 Ludwig Wittgenstein, *Tractatus, Logico-Philosophicus* (London: Routledge, 1961), p. 150.

37 Even Jacques Derrida, when asked in an interview about the status of his physical birth versus his 'true birth', finds himself forced to admit that 'if there is anything that cannot be "up to me", then this is it'; although he then quickly goes on to draw even this admission into a broader 'circumfessing' linguistic narrative. 'A "Madness" Must Watch Over Thinking', reprinted in *Points . . . Interviews*, Palo Alto: Stanford University Press (1995), pp. 339–43.

38 G. W. F. Hegel, *Phenomenology of Mind* (Oxford: Clarendon Press, 1977), p. 55.

39 i.e. an authority that does not depend on conceptual determination or conceptual identification but rather one on which conceptual determination itself depends.

40 See my treatment of this in Chapter Two of *God, the Mind's Desire* (Cambridge: Cambridge University Press, 2004).

Chapter 3

Tauto-theology

I

1. We have in the last chapter been tracing what throughout the predominance of our intellectual history have been carefully observed as two separate
modes of attentiveness and accountability that we naturally employ as we
relate to and seek to understand the reality within which we find ourselves
alive. These are: (a) conceptual accountability, based on attentiveness through
logic and language to the connections between ideas in the grammatical
relations of subject and predicate in intellection; and (b) causal accountability, based on attentiveness through sensible observation to the connections
between physical events in the dynamic relations of cause and effect in space
and time. The separateness and non-reducibility of each to the other, moreover, are clearly recognized as reflective of the very constitution of the human
being in the world. For in its embodied-rational unity the human organism
recognizes itself as *both* sensible (susceptible and responsive to bodily or
causal influences and constraints) *and* intellective (susceptible to and operat-
ing under conceptual or logical influences and constraints).

We have also seen, however, that in philosophy and the human sciences
especially, and under an array of recent influences (idealistic, phenomenological, literary theoretical, structuralist, post-structuralist and so on), causal-
sensible authority and accountability has come broadly to be subsumed under
conceptual authority and accountability. Or to put this somewhat differently,
questions of causal dynamism in embodied life have in these discussions come
to be made subservient to and dependent on questions of their conceptual
meaning. In this chapter we look more closely at the actual outworkings
and effects of this within theology itself. And what we will find here is that
while these effects are initially primarily methodological, their impact has
also run deeply enough to have an effect in the area of doctrinal content as
well, especially with regard to a basic shift that has occurred over the past
two centuries in the understanding of divine revelation itself.

The underlying and unifying focus of this chapter will be to demonstrate
that in both its doctrinal and apologetical or 'fundamental' modes, theology
has in many of the most dominant recent exchanges come to exercise itself and

to justify itself as a discipline in internally self-guaranteeing ways. Or to introduce now a term that will become thematic in this chapter, it has in its fundamental methodological orientations become committed to resolving its most defining questions and problems 'analytically' within itself. And wherever this has occurred it has ceased to be able to be properly attentive to its incarnational ground.

This 'analytical' orientation to problem-solving, moreover, will be found to be just as predominant in current philosophical discussions as it is in theological ones; and so let us begin by contextualizing the term itself more broadly. Restricting ourselves first to its philosophical expressions, when we speak of the 'analytical' disciplines we mean broadly those disciplines that are concerned solely with what reason can come to by itself, or can establish by itself, i.e. purely by a conceptual *analysis* of a certain hypothetically 'given' or presuppositionally specified subject matter. Or more exactly, it means what reason is able to derive simply by drawing out the 'predicates' which can be found to be contained within the linguistic definition of an allocated 'subject', through a conceptual analysis of the subject itself, which is again to say, purely by *analytical* means.

So, for example, that a square has four sides, that a bachelor is unmarried, or that a 'supreme being' cannot be subordinate to anything, are all 'analytically true' statements, because in each case what is predicated of the subject is already contained within the linguistic definition of that subject, and can be yielded through a conceptual analysis of this alone. Of course analytical procedures can be much more complex and sophisticated than this, as we shall see. But the common underlying feature is that analytical disciplines are concerned with authority or 'accountability' entirely as this reflects itself in the *logical* and linguistic development of a 'subject matter' which is presumed or presupposed as a conceptual or textual 'given', and descriptively analyzed as such.

Analytical procedure can manifest itself as such on different kinds of levels and from within a wide variety of traditions and orientations. But the context within which many of us today would be perhaps most readily familiar with the term 'analytical' is in its association with what has become known as 'analytical philosophy', in the particular twentieth-century Anglo-American mode as reflected in the thought of A. J. Ayer, Rudolph Carnap, early Wittgenstein, Bertrand Russell, and others. Ayer's book *Language, Truth and Logic*, although it is now seen as in many ways outdated, set a certain kind of standard for analyticity whose effects are still felt strongly today, not only within contemporary analytical philosophies of language, mind and science, but even among the newer so-called 'post-analytical' orbits of Quine, Davidson, Goodman or Putnam and their followers. We will later in the chapter return to this particular manifestation of analytical procedure, especially with respect to its expression in what came to be known as 'logical positivism', in order to understand what is meant exactly by a similar charge of 'positivism' that Bonhoeffer levelled against Barth.

But for the present it is important to note that this particular captivation with analyticity, language and logic is by no means an anomaly limited to

Anglo-American thinking. It can also be found in nineteenth-century German idealism, for example – and indeed, here in a much more ambitious form – as the fundamental motivating orientation of both the Hegelian and Fichtean projects. Both of these are at bottom concerned with giving an account of reality entirely, or at least fundamentally, in terms of mind and logic. And within these outlooks, as we have seen, nowhere is the commitment to the primal authority of conceptual abstraction over sensible embodiment more evident than in the full subsumption of the *sensible* authority of the *cause–effect* relation in space and time into the *analytical* (mental/linguistic) authority of the *subject–predicate* relation in language and logic.[1] It is on this line of reasoning that Hegel finds it possible to speak explicitly of the cause–effect relation itself as a linguistic 'tautology'.

But we have also seen the commitment to the essentially analytical character of human enquiry about reality just as strongly in contemporary phenomenology. To be sure, what appears here is no longer analytical in exactly the same linguistic sense of an analysis of grammar and syntax; and indeed, Husserl himself was especially concerned to distinguish what he was doing from analytical philosophy of language. Phenomenology calls itself rather a discipline of *Bedeutungsanalyse* ('meaning analysis') and is it thus 'analytical' in the sense of an analysis of what 'appears' in phenomenal consciousness per se, including the modes of the appearance of images in consciousness. Its analytical and mentally enclosed character no longer comes to expression in the relation of 'subject' and 'predicate' in language, but rather now in the relation of 'intentionality' and 'reference' in consciousness, or in more exact Husserlian language, in the relation of 'noesis' (i.e. the mental act of perceiving and knowing) and 'noema' (i.e. the mental 'object' *within consciousness*, which is 'perceived as perceived').

We will return in a later chapter to amplify these phenomenological discussions somewhat further for different purposes. But the point at present is simply to summarize under a different terminology what the previous chapter has already shown to be the deep extent to which these trends toward cognitive self-enclosedness pervade current endeavors within the human sciences, in order now in the present chapter to go on to look further at the impact this has had on theology. Let me reemphasize before commencing with that, however, that there is of course nothing 'wrong' with analytical or linguistically confined procedure per se, even within theological contexts. In fact, the rigors of analytical method are indispensable for conceptual integrity within itself. It is only when theology seeks to make statements concerning its indispensable ground and source in the revealed reality of God that it must ensure that it remains a genuinely dependent and secondary discipline and not an analytically self-guaranteeing one within conceptuality or grammar. Indeed, it is quite proper to some theological disciplines such as the historical-critical and textual-critical ones, that questions about the truth of what the biblical texts proclaim in their 'content' are provisionally set aside, so that the technical correctness and precision that must guide these disciplines can be pursued with the kind of integrity and purity that is expected of them and in which they have their particular value and importance.

2. At any rate, with these caveats in mind, one need not look far to see the influences of the analytical mindset at work in theology more generally. Indeed, they are present not only where one might expect to see them – for example, in the many cross-disciplinary endeavors today which operate in dialog with phenomenological, deconstructionist, literary or semiotic discussions – but they appear also right at the heart of doctrinal and apologetical engagements themselves. One could point to a whole array of examples here but let us look a just a few.

Among major recent theological figures, these basic analytical dispositions can be seen most prominently and influentially perhaps in the work of Karl Barth, the essentially analytical character of whose work is explicitly admitted, even stipulated, by Barth himself, and is quite clearly evident on many fronts. Let me add before proceeding, however, that my treatment of Barth here and in later chapters will focus primarily on aspects of the first two volumes of the *Church Dogmatics*; and it is to be granted that later in the *Dogmatics* Barth expresses himself somewhat differently on related matters, specifically also with respect to the kinds of moral or ethical issues that will concern us in subsequent chapters. (John Webster, for example, offers a trenchant and much more broadly engaged argument for why the Barthian dogmatical project overall should be viewed at heart as a 'moral ontology'.)[2] Nevertheless, it is in the first two volumes that Barth's own fundamental or theologically grounding orientations to revelation are voiced, and these orientations are again and again developed under the stipulation of an analytical validation. The full force of the analytical security of the Barthian enterprise within itself on these fronts will not become entirely clear until later in the chapter, where we will discover a crucial reconfiguration that has occurred in the understanding of divine revelation itself in these directions. But its basic analytical character can be made clear enough in a more rudimentary way with regard to his development of the doctrine of the Trinity, which he puts at the 'head' all dogmatics, and which therefore provides the indispensable perspective for all his subsequent doctrinal endeavors. The doctrine of the Trinity thus serves for Barth as the equivalent of a 'fundamental theology' or a 'theological epistemology'.

In the first volume of the *Church Dogmatics* Barth begins his treatment of the doctrine of the Trinity by describing the essential character of revelation as demanding to be developed entirely 'analytically'. In keeping with our own foregoing definitions of analyticity, Barth likewise describes this further as meaning that revelation must be understood solely and entirely 'in terms of its subject',[3] that is, God, or more specifically around a conceptual 'analysis' of the primary statement 'God reveals himself'.[4] When this statement is then analyzed with due diligence in light of the scriptural texts, it will be found of itself to yield two further corollary statements or predicates which, now in content as much as in form, complete the basic analyticity that is already contained in the original statement, so as to yield the following three: '*God reveals himself. He reveals himself through himself. He reveals himself*'.[5] These three statements which, as Barth goes on to say, are really analytically 'identical' and thus 'inseparable', then become the basis of Barth's doctrine of the Trinity. And this doctrine in turn, on still further analysis of the original statement, is found to have its source in a single unifying statement which Barth calls the 'root' of the doctrine of the Trinity: 'God reveals himself as *the Lord*', that is, as 'the only One who is [absolutely] free'.[6] Having thus in its primary stage completed what he repeatedly stipulates must be an analytical task, Barth then seals its character as such, finally, by declaring explicitly that all of this, as it comes to be summarized in the foregoing root-statement, 'is to be regarded as an *analytical* judgment'.[7]

Before going further with this, however, let me again insert a caveat that even though this book will itself at points appear to be quite heavily critical of Barth, this should quite emphatically not be understood as an attempted vilification or disparagement of the Barthian enterprise per se. Strongly to the contrary, the Barthian theology is unquestionably one of massive intellectual power and integrity, with a depth of rigor and passion of Christian commitment hardly surpassed in recent times, a work of immense value and importance. Any critiques offered here therefore are to be understood in the spirit of Eberhard Bethge's description of Dietrich Bonhoeffer's often intense criticisms of Barth – i.e. that despite the severity of his own objections, Bonhoeffer always 'criticized as an ally'.[8] In fact, as a theological apologetics, the book affirms and follows many of Barth's starting points but develops them differently.

For example, there is full agreement with Barth that theology's primary and inviolable concern must be with the 'Godness of God' and that based on the scriptural witness it must therefore start with the statement that 'God reveals himself'. But rather than taking this as a statement that can guarantee its own truth and solutions within itself or within doctrine through a conceptual analysis of it, a theological apologetics sees the statement instead as confronting theology with an entirely different kind of challenge. It sees 'God reveals himself' as a statement that points us indispensably back to the real world of embodied life, since it is at the center of *this* life in the fullness of its embodied contingency – and not merely in concepts (not even 'concrete concepts' as Barth will call them later) – that God really reveals himself even today through the resurrection and Pentecost. The basic orientation for the apologetical 'defense' of this statement is therefore not toward linguistic or conceptual resolutions within analyticity or grammar. It is rather toward the dynamism of real life in the world, which never offers up the cognitive comforts of conceptual guarantees, and which must therefore seek an authenticity for the statement on different grounds.

3. It is well known in any case that Barth has not been immune from criticism for what can be seen as a certain self-guaranteeing and self-enclosed character of his theology. Wolfhart Pannenberg, for example, is especially critical of this feature of Barthian thought for the part it has played in leading much contemporary theology into what Pannenberg calls 'the dead end of faith subjectivism'.[9] Even Eberhard Jüngel, one of Barth's most distinguished followers, acknowledges this analytical and theoretically self-enclosed character as a weakness in Barth and seeks to correct it. And he does so by making not Lordship and absolute freedom the root of the Christian understanding of

God, but rather the cross. Yet Jüngel too will be unable – at least as he seeks to account for theology's orientation to its fundamentals – to escape the self-securing lures of analyticity, and we can find in Jüngel a striking example of how even a 'theology of the cross' can guarantee its own success in essentially linguistic and conceptual ways. Let me explain this.

It is well known that both Jüngel, and Jürgen Moltmann with him, maintain that there is something essentially misconceived and misleading about what they call the 'classical' understanding of God: that is, God understood in Anselm's terms as 'that than which nothing greater can be conceived'; or in John of Damascus as 'ineffable and incomprehensible'; or in Aquinas as 'known in his unknowability'.[10] Against such views, both writers advocate what they call a fundamental 'revisioning' or even a 'revolution'[11] that is needed in the modern understanding of God. A revolution is needed in which God's truest essence is expressed no longer in the language of the freedom, incomprehensibility and inapproachability of God, but rather most fundamentally as the 'perishability of God'. Now there can be little argument but that both Jüngel and Moltmann have indeed contributed to an important refocusing and rejuvenation of theological attentiveness in these directions. But it is specifically the way that they see fit to accomplish and support this renewed focus which is testimony once again to the extent to which the prevailing analytical and linguistically self-guaranteeing spirit of the times pervades theological self-understanding. Indeed, in his determination to remain within these securities, the impact of what Jüngel calls a 'significant correction' over the traditional theological understanding of God becomes significantly diminished.

To explain this, let us remain with Jüngel who, as the more critically rigorous of the two figures, is also the more explicit in this regard. The point specifically is that Jüngel at bottom achieves his significant correction over the classical doctrine of God essentially through a fundamental redefinition of the analytical *meanings* of central theological terms themselves – in this case, the meaning of the term 'God'. And on the basis of this linguistic redefinition of theology's 'subject', certain crucial new 'predicates' will be found to follow from it automatically, predicates by which theology will be able again to guarantee its desired results within itself simply by a linguistic analysis of the redefined term.

But to illustrate this more fully, consider the directness and explicitness with which Jüngel himself expresses the essentially analytical and linguistic character of the correction he advocates. In his own words, the cross of Christ demands that we must come back 'to query again the *linguistic* meaning and function of the word "God" ';[12] or again, that in light of the cross we must 'learn to *think* God in a new way'.[13] And this altered 'linguistic meaning' of God is then expressed more exactly as follows: 'the *Crucified One* must be the criterion for any possible concept of God'. Indeed, as Jüngel summarizes, 'for responsible Christian usage of the word "God", the Crucified One is *virtually the real definition* of what is meant with the word "God" '.[14] Moltmann likewise speaks of a 'revolution' that is needed 'in the *concept* of God'[15] in light of the cross.

Now despite all of the other ways that Jüngel's theology can be powerfully reasoned and of great value, there is nevertheless no getting around a certain hollowness in the entirely analytical or grammatical 'success' achieved, at least with regard to these sorts of fundamental questions. And Jüngel along with Barth can act as a good example for a much broader trend I am seeking to identify here. For by redefining God's nature ahead of time *linguistically* as in its most basic essence radically 'self-emptying', Jüngel makes the cross a logic-ally necessary analytical corollary *within doctrine* of the very meaning of the term 'God'.[16] And because the 'truth' of the statement of the self-emptying God has thereby been able to be established with the full certainty of a logical necessity (based in the meanings of terms), we find even in Jüngel the tendency to suppose that theology has therefore with force been able to complete its task of the 'defense' of the truth of the cross through doctrinal theory alone. What has been forfeited thereby, however, is an opportunity to draw theo-logical attention to the reality and power of the cross at the center of life even today in the resurrection-reality of Christ, a reality that theology does not contain self-guaranteeingly, but on which it depends contingently. The sum-mary point then, is that the cross here, in its *theological* force, becomes again essentially a logically necessary predicate which a conceptual analysis alone of the re-defined meaning of the 'subject' – i.e. 'God', redefined as the Crucified One – can be shown already to contain logically or analytically within itself.

But there are two quite basic errors or oversights that have occurred in this process, both of which reflect what Jüngel himself admits are the strong alignments of his own thinking to the philosophy of Hegel. And indeed, the ease with which Jüngel is able to bring Hegel and Barth into alignment is testimony again to the presence of those idealistic orientations in Barth him-self. But let us get to the errors themselves, the first of which concerns the theological status given to God's kenotic self-emptying. Now as Jüngel will of course fully agree, God's kenotic self-emptying does not itself occur in theo-logical grammar by linguistic definition but in embodied history and in real suffering on the cross, and thus in the dynamism of the causal nexus in space and time. Nevertheless, by allowing the divinely causal and embodied self-emptying to be transported easily and summarily into the subject–predicate relation through a *linguistic* redefinition of God – and by making this lin-guistic domain the sole or primary focus of theological attention – Jüngel's position has followed exactly and with precision the Hegelian error of suppo-sing that the cause–effect relation in embodied history can be subsumed within the subject–predicate relation in language.[17] Whereupon then in its theological articulation God's kenotic self-emptying can be expressed and 'verified' with all the conceptual guarantees and securities of a mere tautology.

But there is also a related and more specifically theological error which occurs here. For to declare that because God has met us in his fullness in Jesus Christ on the cross: that therefore we can effectively *dispense* altogether with the 'classical' doctrine of God's aseity, incomprehensibility and inscrutability is surely to miss something essential. Or to presume that in his 'perishability' *alone* we have 'the virtual real definition of the word "God" ', is surely to miss something vital. Indeed, in order for Jüngel's theology to speak with the real 'revisionary' power it intends, what demands to be affirmed in the reality of the Crucified God is not simply that the 'Crucified One' has become perishable (which is the heart of the tautology). What must be affirmed rather is that it is truly the incomprehensible, inscrutable, eternal and immortal God, who lives in unapproachable light and whom no one has ever seen or can see (1 Tim. 6.16), who has become finite, visible, perishable on the cross in a real human body in Jesus Christ.

Some version of the 'classical' doctrine must therefore be upheld together with the 'crucified' doctrine, otherwise the message of 'the Crucified *God*' entirely loses its power. The point in short, therefore, is that God's self-emptying on the cross in no way *solves* the theological problem of God's relation to the world in 'kenosis'; it rather *sharpens* this problem with a kind of conceptual difficulty and sheer intractability against which all attempts at analytical resolution into concepts fall short, and indeed must fall silent. Now again, the intention here has not been to single out Jüngel for special criticism. It has only been to demonstrate in another way, beyond Barth, just how deeply the linguistically and phenomenologically analytical orientation runs, even in contemporary doctrine, where it has often become virtually the default theological self-understanding, just as we have seen it is the default method-ology in the human sciences and broad reaches of philosophy. Further theo-logical examples are even easier to find in cross-disciplinary ventures, such as John Milbank's reconfiguration of Christology itself as a *philologia crucis*, or a philology of the cross.[18] Or again, the same orientation is visible in Christian philosophical discussions, for example in Alvin Plantinga's philosophically analytical approach to Christian apologetics, which is at bottom equally self-securing through its conceptually failsafe appeals to 'proper basicality' and proper warrant.[19]

What theology effectively becomes therefore in all such analytical exercises is at bottom the equivalent of a self-guaranteeing tautology, or what might be called a 'tauto-theology'. A tauto-theology is any theological or apologetical endeavor which, by linguistic or other cognitively authenticated assurances, is able to solve its own deepest problems theoretically within itself, and thereby commits the error of putatively 'overcoming' its indispensably *dependent* status in relation to the revealed reality of God which grounds it at the center of embodied life.

II

4. But we must return now to deal more fully with something addressed cursorily above, something that goes to the heart of what has made possible the movement of theological self-understanding into analytical self-sufficiency. It concerns a fundamental shift that has occurred in the understanding of divine revelation itself under the influences of the predominating conceptually cognitive mono-vision elsewhere. As we have seen in the previous chapter, the more traditional and predominating view in the past has understood revelation as at its origin a divinely *causal* disclosure to the world, which can

be active and dynamic even where human beings do not become aware of it in the illumination of faith. This is clear enough from the scriptures themselves, for example from the declaration of the Johannine prologue, that the incarnate Logos of God 'was in the world, and though the world was made by him, the world did not recognize him' (Jn 1.10); or again that the light of the incarnate Logos of God 'shines in the darkness, but the darkness did not comprehend it' (Jn 1.5).

But now under the aforementioned influences, and in the past century especially, the understanding of God's revelational activity has shifted away from the view of it as a *causal disclosure in the world* to the view of it as a *communicative event in the mind*. Even Karl Rahner, who in other epistemological respects is quite closely aligned with the basic orientations of this book, restricts himself to speaking of revelation most fundamentally in terms of a 'communication'.[20] The difference between revelation understood as a causal 'disclosure' or 'manifestation', and revelation understood as a mental 'communication' may on the face of it seem subtle, but its effects have been profound. For it is precisely in the movement away from the former view and into the latter that theology has found it possible to become conceptually self-guaranteeing within itself. So let us look more carefully at what is involved here.

The point is that by the very definition of the term – that is, by the very denotation of what it *means* analytically in the English language – a 'communication' by strict entailment involves not only someone who communicates, but also the cognitively conscious reception in an 'addressee' of what is communicated. By the very analytical meaning of a 'communication', therefore, if there is no cognitive apprehension or acknowledgement in an addressee, then by definition no 'communication' has occurred. We will see in a moment how deeply this view has taken hold in a paradigmatic example in Barth. But let me just reiterate here that it has been under the influence of the predominating foundationally cognitivist views elsewhere, which see all 'reality' as to one degree or another essentially 'mind-dependent', that this view has also been able to take hold right at the heart of theology itself.

At any rate, we can try to illustrate on a human and empirical level the basic difference between a causal disclosure or manifestation on the one hand and a mental communication on the other. We all know what it is like, after the fact, to recognize that the real import of a series of relational events or of a personal exchange has failed to communicate itself to us even though, as we see later, it was 'staring us in the face' all the time in the empirically causal relational character of the events themselves. Or let us follow this through to a more specific example. Marriage counselors will tell us that in failed marriages it is often the case that one partner has for months or years, either indirectly through changes in behavior, body language, innuendo, or even directly in speech, been expressing or manifesting certain kinds of dissatisfaction, loneliness, isolation or other states of being which the other partner has entirely missed – perhaps through an obsessive preoccupation with vocational work or whatever – and which have therefore failed to pass over into a communication. Indeed, the other partner may after the relational breakdown come to recognize these expressions and manifestations full well for what they actually were, and wonder how he or she could have been so blind to them. But now the fact that the gestures and expressions failed to communicate cognitively or meaningfully to the intended recipient does not in the least diminish the reality of the manifestations themselves. Or it does not diminish the reality of their disclosive character as gestures and expressions of actual states of being and feeling. It does not nullify them or make them void for what they really were, and are afterwards recognized to have been.

Now these are admittedly rather manufactured and inadequate examples for the theological subject at hand. For divine causality is by no means a merely efficient or empirical causality of which we can be aware directly through sense perception as we are aware of empirical objects. But they can be used analogically nonetheless to clarify something crucial that Schleiermacher states in quite explicit terms about the inalienably causal character and authority of revelation. Writing in 1830, and in direct opposition to the idealistic philosophy of Hegel which declared that 'God is attainable in pure speculative knowledge alone',[21] Schleiermacher was still mounting a rigorous defense of the traditional, genuinely incarnational view of revelation as a divinely *causal* disclosure to whole embodied-rational human beings in the world. Much differently than Hegel, for Schleiermacher, the original character and reality of revelation as a 'divine causality' is, in his own words, so obvious 'that it requires no further discussion'.[22] But Schleiermacher does then after all go on to discuss it at length anyway, and in that discussion he is willing to push this divinely causal stipulation so far as to declare his 'unwillingness to accept' that in its '*original* element [revelation] operates on man as a *cognitive* being' at all.[23] 'For that', as he now continues with force, 'would make revelation to be originally and essentially *doctrine*'[24].

Schleiermacher's point here is of course not to say that cognition is not involved or does not play a part in the reception of revelation. It is only to say that in its original element it is not a direct communication to the cognitive intellect, but rather first a dynamically causal divine initiative in the wholeness of life, an initiative which as such precedes and indeed makes possible the human awareness of it. But the second part of his statement – i.e. that an essentially cognitivist view of revelation would have the effect of making it 'to be originally and essentially *doctrine*' – is also important. For this is precisely what for all intents and purposes has often occurred today. Let us then push further to the most prominent recent example of this reconfigured view of revelation – in Karl Barth – where revelation is no longer understood as a causal disclosure to human beings in the full multifaceted dynamism of embodied-rational life in the world, but now rather primarily as a communicative event directly to the discursive mind. Barth's views on this have together with other influences helped to shape two generations of theological thought on the matter.

5. We can begin by citing several of Barth's own statements in these directions which make the position perfectly clear: 'the encounter of God and man takes place primarily, pre-eminently and characteristically in this sphere of *ratio*'; 'it

is the divine reason communicating with human reason'; 'revelation in itself and as such . . . is talk, speech'.[25] The depth to which this orientation pervades the *Church Dogmatics*, and the lengths to which Barth is willing to go in preserving it as such, is manifested further by Barth's explicit stipulation that revelation cannot for us today be encountered as a 'present reality' at all but always only as a 'concrete concept'.[26] In Barth's own words, whether in theology or the life of faith, it is always the case that we today can have only 'to do with the *concrete concept* of revelation which the Bible attests to *have taken place* and which proclamation promises *will come*'.[27] The reality of revelation, in other words, is for Barth essentially something past and future and never present. Or as Barth explains further – and now with clear similarities to Husserl – theology today can have solely to do with 'the concrete bracket which embraces a specific past, the epiphany of Jesus Christ, and what is always a specific future'.[28]

Barth is indeed very careful, upon asserting this, to add the vital caveat that 'naturally, the reality of revelation stands beyond the concept'; but he then immediately reiterates, and now more unmistakably than ever, that in life today '*we cannot try to deal with the reality*' itself.[29] For 'neither in proclamation nor in dogmatics can we produce the attested past and promised future as a present. Nor can we think that in any present that we can produce we are producing this past or this future'. He then concludes the discussion as he began it, by repeating that in theology today it is always and solely the case that 'we are dealing with the *concept* of revelation, i.e., with the present of God's Word *between the times*'[30] of the past and future realities of revelation.[31] To be sure, this 'concept' is for Barth not a normal abstract and generalizable concept, but rather a 'concrete' one. And what he means by revelation as a 'concrete concept' is a conceptually communicative event of divine revelation to a specific human consciousness at a specific time and a specific place, occurring through the reading of the scriptures or the hearing of the proclamation of the gospel in the church. Yet having been defined as essentially a cognitive communication, it remains the case that revelation must by this definition take place entirely on the conceptual or phenomenological level of the discursive intellect, in the direct communication of 'the divine reason to human reason', as human reason is enlivened by the Holy Spirit.

This immediate discursively communicative view of revelation then also pervades the *Church Dogmatics* more broadly, where revelation invariably comes to expression in the grammatically discursive terminology of a 'report', a 'message', an 'attestation', a 'telling', a 'proclamation' and so on.[32] Indeed, the essentially discursive constitution of revelation runs even to the heart of Barth's treatment of reconciliation. In these discussions the status even of 'God with us', which is the central basis of Barth's doctrine of reconciliation, may not, for Barth, be understood, strictly speaking, as a dynamic presence acting causally at the center of embodied-rational life. It is rather to be understood once again in the more basic and truer sense of an essentially verbal 'report' to discursive cognition of something occurring in the divine essence per se. Barth's own words here again could not be clearer: ' "God with us" ', he states, 'as it occurs at the heart of the Christian message is the *attestation* and the *report* of the life and act of God as the One who is'.[33] Or even more explicitly, '*the fact* that God is with us *is a report* about the being and life and act of God'.[34] There is indeed for Barth a real 'invasion of our history' by God, an invasion which tells us 'of the real truth about our history as a history which is by Him and from Him and to Him'.[35] But even here, Barth is careful to stipulate that this very invasion of our history is for us today grounded more fundamentally 'in the *message* of the Christian community [which] applies to us by *telling* us of a history which God wills to share with us and *therefore* of an invasion of *our* history'.[36]

We must be fair to Barth here, however, especially in recognizing the character of the theological mindset that he was countering. For this particular stance he took on revelation, and the formidable internal rigor with which it is pursued, must of course be understood in light of what he saw as the fatal mistakes of many of the nineteenth-century 'liberal' theologies, which in his view had reduced theology merely to a sublimated study of humankind and the world. So let us just briefly examine this backdrop against which Barth is speaking more carefully. For in doing so we will come to a further crucial factor underlying the deep-seated self-guaranteeing or tauto-theological orientation in both doctrine and apologetics today. It is a factor that will go to the heart of what Bonhoeffer detected in Barth as a 'positivism of revelation'. We will in what follows be attempting to put Bonhoeffer's criticism of Barth's theology as positivistic into the full philosophical context that informs it in Bonhoeffer and apart from which the criticism cannot be properly understood. But in order to do that with fairness to Barth we must first allow him his own voice.

III

6. We have already discussed in Chapter One how the massive changes in the human perception of the reality of the world, brought on by the collapse of the pre-modern three-tiered cosmology through the advent of modern science, caused theology to abandon its traditional metaphysically cosmological appeals in accounting for the reality of God and to turn rather to appeals to 'inwardness', to 'subjectivity' and so on. And it is important to recognize that what Barth himself is doing here in defining revelation as something that occurs 'primarily, pre-eminently and characteristically in this sphere of *ratio*' is *not* an appeal to anything about human 'inwardness'. Indeed it is precisely the nineteenth-century theological appeals to human capacities of 'inwardness' – or what Barth also referred to, following Ernst Troeltsch, as a 'religious *a priori*' – that Barth is most energetically seeking to overturn. For Barth, the event of Jesus Christ is an utterly unique act of God which cannot in its uniqueness correspond to any universal religious principle in human nature which a 'religious *a priori*' would imply.

In light of this we can see in Barth what amounts to a pivotal 'double rejection' residing at the heart of his critique of the nineteenth-century 'liberal' schools. And it is essentially in this double rejection that we can best understand his well-known statement that a genuinely theological engagement with divine revelation 'is not a matter of apologetics but of polemics'.[37] As a polemic rather than an apologetic, one of theology's first tasks, Barth goes on to say, is to overturn any idea that through our natural human capacities of awareness and enquiry we could be able to discover or discern any 'vestigium' or trace of God in the world, a trace by which the God of the Bible could be naturally glimpsed or apprehended apart from faith. For any such 'vestige' would for Barth be the entry again of the possibility of a merely humanly philosophical or 'religious' apprehension of God rather than a genuinely *theo*logical one.

But again, Barth's rejection of the 'vestigium' through his theological polemic occurs on two basic fronts. It is a polemical rejection first of any 'externalist' cosmological appeals to metaphysics, through which theology would become dependent again on cosmology, whereby it would lose what Barth sees as its rightful and necessary focus entirely on 'the Godness of God'. And it is a polemical rejection secondly of any 'internalist' anthropological appeals to 'inwardness' or a 'religious *a priori*', through which theology would become dependent again on anthropology, whereby it would likewise lose what Barth sees as its rightful and necessary focus entirely on 'the Godness of God'.

Now it is exactly this double rejection – i.e. both of the externality of 'metaphysics' and the inwardness of a 'religious *a priori*' – and the success with which it was achieved in Barth, that Bonhoeffer cites more than once as being the 'great merit' of Barth. Indeed, Bonhoeffer credits it as marking the origin for what he himself would go on to consider in his own theology as the possibility of a 'religionless Christianity'.[38] But here we come to the decisive point. For as Bonhoeffer continues, Barth himself then went on to put in place of 'inwardness' a 'positivist doctrine of revelation which in the last analysis is essentially a restoration'[39] of the very 'religious *a priori*' Barth was seeking to overcome.

Now again, this criticism of a 'revelational positivism' in Barth has often subsequently tended to be sidelined or dismissed as a perplexing and misdirected critique, on the supposition that Bonhoeffer himself was not entirely sure of what he meant when he wrote it.[40] But Bonhoeffer not only knew exactly what he was intending to say here, but was actually also saying something that demonstrated an important insight. And the reason it has often been misunderstood, or not understood at all, is because most attempts to understand it have not been as philosophically engaged or as philosophically equipped as Bonhoeffer was in making it. For, as will become quite clear from Bonhoeffer himself (writing in 1944), his usage of the term follows a particular philosophical denotation which had risen to considerable prominence at that time in both 'continental' philosophy (through the 'analytical' approach of the 'Vienna Circle' beginning from 1923, e.g. Schlick, Carnap, Neurath and early Wittgenstein) and in 'Anglo-American' philosophy (largely through the influential popularization of these 'analytical' views in A. J. Ayer's *Language, Truth and Logic* (1936) which combined them with the Humean influences in Moore and Russell). Indeed these schools of thought in fundamental ways bore a strong resemblance to Husserlian phenomenology, as we shall see. So let us look at this criticism a bit more closely, giving careful attention to its philosophical origins. For it will identify the heart of what makes it possible for Barth to understand theology in its foundational doctrines such as the Trinity (and indeed Christology) to be something fundamentally 'analytical', and therefore self-guaranteeing.

To begin with, it is important to understand that there was something unique about these 'analytical' movements (in both mainland Europe and in Britain) – which already by 1930 were coming to advance themselves under the name of 'logical positivism' – that made them quite different from what Auguste Comte in the nineteenth century had also been advancing as a 'positivist philosophy'. What Comte had put forward was not a '*logical* positivism' but rather, in a radicalization of Humean empiricism, an '*empirical* positivism'. This empirical positivism said that knowledge-claims and meaning-claims can only qualify as fully legitimate and fully verifiable – and hence 'positive' – as they are based directly on 'positive science' through sense experience, which is to say on 'empirical science'. The non-empirical and 'speculative' claims of metaphysics and religion are therefore in Comtean scientific positivism entirely rejected as mere superstitional and 'pre-scientific' forms of thought. In his view, all of these would eventually cede or give way to the findings of positive science as humanity continues to progress. The 'positive science' from which this form of positivism receives its name therefore means a quite radical form of empirical science. And what makes this an *empirical* 'positivism' again, is the claim that only empirical science is capable of yielding forms of verification that are fully and securely certifiable or 'positive'. 'Positive' here then *means* 'fully certifiable'.

There was, however, a basic epistemological shallowness or naïveté that soon began to show itself in this form of positivism, under which the legitimacy of its claims to be able to provide a fully verifiable knowledge through empirical science was deemed to be rationally unsustainable. And what 'logical' positivism sought to do subsequently, in light of this failure of 'empirical' positivism, was essentially something twofold. It sought first to retain what it agreed must be the two most fundamental commitments of all philosophy: (i) the commitment to establishing fully secure or fully 'positive' principles of cognitive verification, and (ii) the commitment to empiricism. But it also sought secondly to do what Comte had failed to do: i.e. to bring a proper rational rigor and epistemological depth back into verification mechanisms without losing the commitments to empiricism. And to accomplish this, it turned its focus fundamentally to *language*, or to the logic of language. More specifically, its aim as such was to find a 'common language' in which all of the separate empirical sciences could be brought under a basic 'unity of verification' which could be common to all. More exactly, by analyzing logically the unique propositional languages that each of the different sciences employed separately in their verification processes, logical positivism sought to distill a single language under which all these separate verifications could be unified into a single general mechanism of 'positive' verification.

It was towards this end therefore that logical positivism understood the primary and essential task of philosophy to be that of the *clarification of meanings*, as expressed in the concepts employed propositionally in the different sciences and in mathematics. We cannot go further into the details of this here, which are intricate, except to say that in this task of the clarification of concepts logical positivism adopted what it described as a 'verifiability principle of meaning'. And this verifiability principle acknowledged at bottom only two kinds of statements as cognitively meaningful. Statements are meaningful (i.e. in a way capable of being true or false) only if they are either (a) analytically true (true by definition), or (b) if their truth or falsity can be tested and verified by sensible (or perceptual) experience.

However, the term 'positivism' in this definition also soon took on a different and more pejorative denotation. For like Comtean positivism, logical positivism too, at least in its original formulation, soon encountered what came to be perceived generally as a fatal difficulty. What was quickly recognized was that neither of its two principles – i.e. that truth claims are intelligible or meaningful only if they are either (a) analytically true or (b) empirically testable – could *themselves* be shown to be either analytically true or empirically verifiable. And this meant in turn that these two fundamental principles themselves could only be employed if their truth or validity was simply 'posited' in a way that exempted them from the very rational and empirical criteria of certifiable or 'positive' verification they espoused. The term 'positivism' here in other words began to take on a double signification: (a) 'positivist' in its original sense, meaning certifiably assured verifiability, or 'positive' verifiability; and (b) 'positivist' in its pejorative sense, meaning something which is merely 'posited' such that, on the one hand, it can claim full authority over matters of reason and sense even while, on the other, remaining at bottom fully immune from the justificatory demands of reason and sense.

7. Coming back then in this light to Bonhoeffer's detection of a 'positivism of revelation' in Barth, it can be shown to apply in both of these senses. That Bonhoeffer sees Barth's view as positivistic in the latter sense is evident already in his earlier book, *Act and Being*. Here he takes issue directly with Barth's view of revelation as a 'concrete concept' which is 'posited' directly within the discursive intellect (indeed, 'posited' here by God himself), as 'the divine reason communicates with human reason . . . pre-eminently and characteristically in th[e] sphere of *ratio*'. While Bonhoeffer himself does not speak of it in exactly these terms, it is essentially what he is referring to in rejecting the Barthian treatment of the revelatory event as a 'pure act' of God to human mental consciousness, which is to say a direct infusion (or again a direct 'positing') of the divine self-disclosure to cognitive intellection itself. Bonhoeffer's own specific objection to this is that it completely bypasses human 'creatureliness', which is to say the contingencies of embodied life, and therefore amounts, one might say, to the equivalent of a mental telepathy.

But it is even more explicitly clear that Bonhoeffer sees the Barthian understanding of divine revelation as a positivism in the other way as well, that is, as something analytically self-contained and thus certifiably secure (positive) within its own doctrinally linguistic and conceptual definitions. And it is important to be reminded here, before coming to Bonhoeffer's statements on this, that the 'positive' verifiability that logical positivism actively pursued as such, was by its own open stipulation at bottom nothing less than the fully indefeasible certifiability of an analytical 'tautology'. Now a tautology is a statement or a system of statements whose truth is entirely self-contained within its analytical definitions and concepts, such that each segment of such a truth will be found to entail all the others within itself. And this is exactly what Bonhoeffer is pointing to when he says of the Barthian enterprise that each element in it is 'an equally significant and equally necessary piece of the whole, a whole which must precisely be swallowed as a whole or not at all'.[41] Let me try to contextualize this point to bring a further amplification to it.

What we have been trying to demonstrate in this chapter, through several prominent and prototypical examples and explanations of procedures, are the different ways in which theology under the influences of the predominating cognitivist mono-vision has been able to become self-guaranteeing within itself, or tauto-theological. And there are two basic summary assessments we can make as such in conclusion. The first is that, by allowing itself to solve its own most defining problems within itself, through whatever analytical mechanisms, theology is indeed able to make its own basic tasks considerably easier. Again, I do not mean of course that the reasoning within analytical procedure per se cannot be complex and intricate and deeply erudite. I mean rather something similar to what Donald MacKinnon says in his like-minded critique of idealistic or analytical methods for theology: namely that here revelation is simply 'converted from a problem to a solution' and thereby 'into a recipe for dissolving a multitude of problems'.[42] Or as Bonhoeffer now also says explicitly of Barth: by the positing of divine revelation directly in the mind through a kind of epistemic decree of faith, Barthian theology 'makes it too easy for itself by setting up, as it does in the last analysis an [epistemic] law of faith'.[43]

But there is also for Bonhoeffer a more alarming consequence of this. The more alarming consequence, as Bonhoeffer now echoes Luther with force, is that such an approach effectively 'mutilates' (*zerreißt*) the inalienably incarnational or embodied 'this-worldly' reality of revelation – i.e. 'that Christ has come in the flesh!'.[44] The theological 'mutilation' here occurs specifically in the transportation of what for him must remain the indispensably embodied incarnational authority of revelation into the conceptually abstract confines of the discursive intellect. Indeed, we can push this view even further, and in the same spirit say the following in summation.

If we are unable or unwilling to give up the affirmation that Jesus Christ has come in the flesh, and that this same incarnate one is still through the resurrection and Pentecost really alive in divine power for us today at the center of life (2 Cor. 13.4; Gal. 2.20; Col. 3.16); if we are unable or unwilling to give up the affirmation that the living Christ is really the same today as yesterday and forever (Heb. 12.8); that the Spirit of God really dwells in the believer causally with tangible effects in human empirical history today (1 Cor. 3.16); that the kingdom of God does not consist only in talk but in real, dynamic, life-changing power in space and time today (1 Cor. 4.20); if it is really the parts of our sensible, physical bodies that are to be offered to God as instruments of God's real righteousness in the world today (Rom. 6.13; 12.1): if we are unable to relinquish the belief in the *present reality* of all of this, then we must return to what throughout the history of Christian thought has been the authoritative and prevailing understanding of God's self-disclosure. That is, we must return to the view that God works and reveals himself *causally* in the real affairs and sensible life of human beings today in space and time. To be sure, this will show itself to be not a mere efficient causality that originates from within the causal dynamic order like any natural causality. It is rather a divine causality whose origin is not temporal or finite but infinite, yet whose effects are no less dynamic, no less empirical, no less real for human embodied life today than any natural causality, however non-finite these 'effects' may also be for the eternal redemption of human beings, and God's reconciliation of the world to himself.

The vital question that now obviously presses upon us is this. What *is* this 'divine causality' exactly? – especially if by divine causality we do not mean any merely empirical or efficient causality? There will be one particularly powerful and definitive response that revelation itself will be found to give to this affirmatively. But in order to be able to make that fully clear in later chapters, we will need for the time being to remain in more 'negative' or critical territory, especially to show exactly why it is that theological engagement with the present reality of God pre-eminently by cognitive means, or in cognitively mono-visional domains, will not work. None of this will be to diminish the necessity and importance of cognition or the discursive use of reason, either in theology or in the life of faith itself. Indeed, it will seek to bring reason to its sharpest critical integrity, by ensuring that it retains a properly rigorous self-understanding and does not seek to make claims beyond what is rationally warranted.

We will in what follows approach the question of God's present reality 'negatively' then, along two basic lines of focus: (a) via the inadequacies of 'ontology' for understanding the reality of God, and (b) via the inadequacies of 'alterity' or radical otherness for understanding the reality of God. Only after this will we be able to come to what, by the demands of revelation itself, can and must be said of this reality differently in an affirmative voice.

Notes

1 See e.g. G. W. F. Hegel, *Hegel's Science of Logic*, pp. 558–69.
2 John Webster, *Barth's Ethics of Reconciliation* (Cambridge: Cambridge University Press, 1995); and *Barth's Moral Ontology* (Edinburgh: T&T Clark, 1998). In the latter volume, see, for example, pp. 41–53, 203–10, where Webster addresses the importance of human action for the Barthian picture, a theme which will become especially important for us also later in the book.

3 Karl Barth, *Church Dogmatics* I.1 (Edinburgh: T&T Clark, 1975), p. 296; (hereafter *CD*).

4 *CD* I.1 pp. 295, 296.

5 *CD* I.1 p. 296.

6 *CD* I.1 pp. 306–7.

7 *CD* I.1 p. 306, emphasis added.

8 Eberhard Bethge, *Dietrich Bonhoeffer* (London: Collins, 1970), p. 53.

9 Pannenberg, *Systematic Theology*, Vol. 1, pp. 47, 48.

10 See e.g. Eberhard Jüngel, *God as the Mystery of the World* (Grand Rapids: Eerdmans, 1983), pp. 13, 14, 184, 232–45.

11 Jürgen Moltmann, *The Crucified God* (Minneapolis: Fortress Press, 1993); see e.g. pp. 4, 201.

12 *God as the Mystery of the World*, p. 9, original emphasis.

13 *God as the Mystery of the World*, p. 9, emphasis added.

14 *God as the Mystery of the World*, p. 13, emphasis added.

15 *The Crucified God*, pp. 4, 201, emphasis added.

16 See e.g. *God as the Mystery of the World*, pp. 13, 14, 184, 232–45.

17 See the discussion of this above, pp. 28–9.

18 *Radical Orthodoxy* (London: Routledge, 1999), p. 29.

19 See p. 155 below.

20 See e.g. *The Trinity* (New York: Herder and Herder, 1970), pp. 87ff.

21 G. W. F. Hegel, *Phenomenology of Mind* (Oxford: Clarendon Press, 1977), p. 461.

22 Friedrich Schleiermacher, *The Christian Faith* (Edinburgh: T&T Clark, 1948), p. 50; see also pp. 17–23; 200–8.

23 *The Christian Faith*, p. 50, emphasis added.

24 *The Christian Faith*, p. 50, original emphasis.

25 *CD* I.1, pp. 132, 135.

26 *CD* I.1, pp. 290, 291.

27 *CD* I.1, p. 290, emphasis added.

28 *CD* I.1, p. 291, emphasis added.

29 *CD* I.1, p. 291, emphasis added.

30 *CD* I.1, p. 291, emphasis added.

31 It is in this sense of a theology 'between the times' (*zwischen den Zeiten*) of the two realities that Barth's theology receives its clearest designation as a '*dialectical*' theology. The theological journal, *Zwischen den Zeiten*, which Barth founded together with Friedrich Gogarten, Georg Merz and Eduard Thurneysen became among other things the official mouthpiece for what was by then coming to be known as 'dialectical theology' (1923–33).

32 See e.g. *CD* IV.1, pp. 3–21 *passim*.

33 *CD* IV.1, p. 7, emphasis added.

34 *CD* IV.1, p. 7.

35 *CD* IV.1, p. 7.

36 *CD* IV.1, p. 7, emphasis added.

37 *CD* I.1 p. 341.

38 See e.g. *Letters and Papers from Prison* (New York: Macmillan, 1972), pp. 280, 286; hereafter *LPP*.

39 *LPP* p. 280.

40 See e.g. Simon Fisher, *Revelatory Positivism?: Barth's Earliest Theology and the Marburg School* (Oxford: Oxford University Press, 1988), pp. 311–14.

41 Dietrich Bonhoeffer, *Widerstand und Ergebung* (Gütersloh: Christian Kaiser Verlag, 1998), p. 415.

42 *Explorations in Theology*, Vol. 5 (London: SCM, 1979), p. 150.
43 *LPP* p. 286.
44 *Widerstand und Ergebung*, p. 416.

CHAPTER 4

GOD AND THE POVERTY OF ALTERITY

I

1. From the beginning of this book we have been concerning ourselves with a single and centrally defining question: that of how the present and living reality of God at the center of life today, as accomplished through the cross, resurrection and Pentecost, and as attested to by the scriptures and affirmed by faith, can be accounted for theologically in a way that holds intact both the integrity of what is affirmed as presently real in life and the integrity of reason. But now in making this question thematic throughout the book, we must also take care to ensure that the weighting of emphasis does not begin to fall too much on the 'familiarity' side of the 'present reality' of God, without equal attention to God's genuine 'transcendence' of everything created. For we must be able to affirm that it is really the eternal and immortal God, the one who 'transcends' all of creation as its Creator, who meets us in the birth of Jesus and on the cross, and that through the resurrection and Pentecost this same God is really alive for us at the center of life today, guaranteeing the promise of the life to come. This is the heart of the Christian affirmation and it must as such be the fundamental and deciding focus of any Christian apologetics. But this very affirmation, in its specificity and narrowness as such, brings us also into the region of one of the broadest and methodologically most 'formal' of all of theology's defining concerns: i.e. what it calls the question of the relation of God's 'transcendence' of the world and yet his 'immanence' within the world.

Now as the most rigorous of the negative theologies have shown us, before we can even begin to presume to offer responses to this question, we must ensure first that *the question itself* has been properly formed. And part of what this book is seeking to show, in a critically negative mode to begin with, is the basic limitations of discursive or cognitively speculative reason even to form the question of God's transcendence properly at all, in order from there to suggest another way that God's genuine transcendence must be attended to through a different use of reason. Before going on to those constructive responses then, we must look more carefully at the essential limitations and inadequacies of foundationally discursive or conceptually cognitivist endeavors to be able to approach, or indeed even properly to understand, the question of God's transcendence.

The understanding of God's transcendence as the transcendence of 'the Wholly Other', which has long had a place in theology, has in many recent theological and other religious discussions been given a newly defined and sharpened priority and authority as the proper disposition for questioning about God. The emergence and special prominence of the language of 'alterity' in present-day theology, which echoes similar trends in phenomenological, post-structuralist and literary theoretical thought, have doubtless to do with what is quite widely recognized today as certain basic failures of 'ontological' language to accommodate adequately what Christians affirm when they speak of the reality of God. Before moving on to this chapter's primary focus in addressing certain basic inadequacies of the language of 'alterity' for theology, let us look just briefly in an introductory way at the difficulties implicit in the 'ontological' approaches to God, to which the language of alterity is a response.

2. When discursive reason seeks to come to terms with, or to investigate claims to the 'reality' of anything, it will as a matter of course and quite rightly want to ask about this in terms of the 'being' or the 'existence' of the subject matter in question. And as it pursues this question into its full depth, it will in one way or another come to face the question of an 'ontology' of the subject matter in question, which is to say the question of the essential nature or character of its being or existence. For as the term itself conveys etymologic-ally, 'ontology' is concerned most simply with the question of being or with the question of existence. As onto-logy, it denotes the 'science of being'; or it is the intellectual discipline concerned with the question of being or existence.

There is some disagreement as to where and when it was exactly that the term 'ontologia' first arose.[1] But in fact what we today call the 'ontological' question itself, when understood simply as the question concerned with existence – whether the existence of particular things or, extrapolating from that more generally, the question of existence per se which all existing things share by virtue of their existence – this question was already present in Greek philosophy, prominently so for example in what Aristotle called 'first phil-osophy'. It was in seventeenth-century rationalism, however, that the term ontology began to take a fully formal place in philosophical discussions, through its inclusion as a distinctive and thematic element in the basic sys-temic structure of various rationalistic enterprises. It was given a formal and primary place for example in the 'universal metaphysics' of Christian Wolff, which was to become a focal point for Kant's critique of seventeenth-century rationalism more broadly.

But let us before going further already insert a basic note of caution by saying that whenever we engage in any ontological endeavor, we must be careful to retain a certain rational modesty in our questioning as such. For it is always important to keep firmly in mind that ontology, as onto-*logy*, is intrinsically *a discipline of the cognitive intellect*. In other words, it is not as if the reality of the spatio-temporal world within which human beings find themselves alive were itself somehow *dependent* on a the discipline of ontology, or were 'authenticated' through an ontology. The world and its dynamic processes, including embodied human causal agency, carry on quite well by themselves without the aid of a philosophical or theological enquiry into the nature of its being. In saying this, however, I by no means wish to diminish the importance and value of a properly modest and rigorous ontology as a philosophical endeavor, but rather only to point out again that the relation of dependence may not be reversed. That is, an ontology, as an intrinsically human intellectual enterprise, depends on the existing reality of the very existence into which it enquires, because it already proceeds from that reality, and not vice versa.

At any rate, and coming on this basis to theological concerns, as anyone who is familiar with recent discussions will be aware, the prospect of an 'ontology' with respect to God, which is to say the prospect of a 'theological ontology', is fraught with all kinds of precarious difficulties and potential dangers. For while in theology as much as in the life of faith we must of course be willing and able to affirm that God really exists (Heb. 11.6) and that he is the Creator of all that is, we do not suppose ourselves thereby to be affirming that God exists in the same way that created things exist, or that God 'is' in the same way that created things 'are'. Or in other words, we cannot view God's eternal and immortal 'being' or God's real 'existence' as merely another being or another 'existent' among other 'existents'. And this means also that God's 'being' or reality cannot appear within the essentially comparative structures of any natural ontology understood as a science of being. To assume that we could place God's infinite and eternal 'being' within an intellectual endeavor concerned with the existence of finite things, would be to engage in the error of what is today spoken of, usually pejoratively, as 'onto-theology' (a term that first appears in Kant, but it is Martin Heidegger's different usage of the term to which the current pejorative understanding of the term can be traced).

But this is by no means just a 'modern' problem. In fact this error is exactly what Aquinas in his *analogia entis* (analogy of being) recognizes better than he is often given credit for by his critics, and indeed, sometimes much better than his critics. For as Aquinas will stipulate, even the very 'being' or existence of God (i.e. not only what theology also speaks of as God's attributes or perfections) must be spoken of '*ana*logically' and thus indirectly, and not (what we would today call) '*onto*logically', that is, not directly within a cognitive ordering of being.

Let me illustrate in a more modern context the basic kind of difficulty that Aquinas saw here in seeking theologically both to affirm the 'being' of God, while not including God's 'being' in the being of what is created. During my own early university training in a strongly atheistic department of philosophy, the basic question at issue here often arose in a somewhat different way, with regard to what must be meant by the term 'universe'. As the sole 'theist' in the group I was sometimes challenged on my unwillingness to include God within the universe of 'what exists'. And the analytical argument upon which the challenge to such a position was based ran something like this. The universe, by the analytical definition of the term, includes everything that exists. Now if God exists then his existence must be included in the universe of 'what exists'.

And it follows from this that his existence as such must also be able to be accounted for according to the normal ontological criteria for existence and being. For if this is not allowed then either (a) the term 'universe' is not really being used in the analytical meaning of this as including all that exists; or (b) if the analytical meaning of 'universe' is upheld consistently, and if God does not appear as an existing element of this universe, then God does not 'exist'. The theological impermissibility, as Aquinas saw it, of speaking *onto*logically of the being of God at all is thus given added emphasis, and it is in full recognition of its difficulty in this unyielding sense that his stipulation that we can only speak *ana*logically of God's 'being' must be understood.

But let us now set our sights specifically on this problem as it comes to expression in more recent contexts. And in order to appreciate fully what is seen by many today as the unsustainability of ontological language and ontological attentiveness for a proper theological understanding of the reality of God, we need to look at the work of Martin Heidegger. For it is Heidegger who sought to reinvigorate the philosophical study of 'being' in the twentieth century, especially in the wake of the phenomenology of Husserl (Heidegger's teacher), under whose considerable impact, in Heidegger's words, 'the question [of being] has today been forgotten'.[2] (As a pure science of consciousness phenomenology brackets out ontological questioning.)

Now Heidegger sees the domain of 'being' as utterly comprehensive or total, including everything that 'is' or even possibly or potentially 'is', whether material or imaginative or conceptual or whatever. (Heidegger's ontology is thus what Levinas will later criticize as a 'totalizing' kind of philosophy.) And on his way to reviving the question of 'Being', Heidegger makes one particularly important statement about what he sees as the full breadth of the terrain or domain from within which the question of being essentially emerges. The statement is important not only in its succinctness and comprehensiveness, but also especially in the formulation of one key term at which it arrives in defining the essential domain of 'being', a term that will prove to be importantly relevant also in subsequent discussions in this book. The statement is this: 'Everything we talk about, everything we have in view, everything towards which we comport ourselves in any way is being; what we are is being, and so is how we are. Being lies in the fact that something is, and in its Being as it is; in Reality; in presence-at-hand; in subsistence; in validity; in Dasein; in the "There is" (*Es gibt*)'.[3]

Now this term '*es gibt*' or 'there is' became a defining point of focus against which subsequent theological views (but also philosophical views, as we shall see below in Levinas) sought rightly to reject any inclusion of God in this domain of 'there is'. Bonhoeffer's lapidary statement in this regard is targeted specifically against the Heideggerian locution when he says succinctly (and very cleverly in the German): '*einen Gott den "es gibt", gibt es nicht*'.[4] God is not a 'constituent' in the created realm of the 'there is' but is rather, in his eternal and living reality, the Creator of *all* 'there is'. It is therefore out of the inability of such 'totalizing' ontological language to address properly what theology understands in the 'being' of God, that the language of 'alterity' or the radical 'otherness' of God has recently become especially prominent.

What I wish to show in this chapter, however, is that while the motivations and intentions in moving to such language are the right ones, nevertheless the language of alterity too, like that of ontology, remains unable to accommodate what Christians affirm when they speak of the transcendent reality of God. And so we must undertake a theologically critical assessment of this language in order to clear the way in the next chapter to begin formulating something quite different. We will approach this primarily through the work of Emmanuel Levinas who, as is well known, develops his project of alterity with especial watchfulness and force. And let me just emphasize as such that the present critique of alterity for basic theological purposes, focused here through Levinas, is not meant in any way to be a diminishment of the importance and immense value of his work in other more specific ways, especially in the uniqueness of the ethical emphasis of his work. My concerns at this point are essentially methodological and critically epistemological, having to do with establishing proper theological orientations to revelation and therefore to the transcendence of God. And on this particular front, even the unsurpassed rigor of the Levinasian project of alterity or 'exteriority' will be found unable to address what is demanded theologically in the consideration of transcendence.

II

3. In his basic project of 'exteriority' or 'alterity', Levinas is concerned to establish a whole new grounding orientation for philosophical questioning per se, or a whole new 'first philosophy' which he describes as an 'ethics'. As a backdrop to formulating this, in *Totality and Infinity* he distinguishes between what historically can be seen as two basic and different dispositions for approaching 'first philosophy': one of which he will reject outright, and the other of which he will follow and modify or radicalize. Levinas sees the historically vastly predominating exercise of first philosophy – which he will reject – as having been concerned primarily with 'the comprehension of beings',[5] and he calls this approach 'ontology'. The philosophies of Hegel and Fichte, and also Heidegger, are in different ways for Levinas the quintessential forms of ontology, but also those of Plato, Leibniz and Spinoza. Now in its concern essentially with the 'comprehension of beings', Levinas sees ontology as inherently oriented also toward the comprehensive*ness* of being, as we have already encountered briefly above in Heidegger, and therefore as something essentially 'totalizing'. And it will be quite clear as such that *this* kind of first philosophy, as something comprehensive and totalizing *within* 'being', will be unable to accommodate a project of genuine *exteriority* or 'alterity' as Levinas wants to expound this.

But Levinas now speaks also of a second basic way of engaging first philosophy, which in its primary disposition at the very least does not close off an openness to exteriority or alterity in the way that the ontological disposition does intrinsically. And this is a first philosophy that Levinas calls 'critical'. A 'critical' philosophy is one which, as Levinas describes it, orients itself to the question of 'being', not first as a comprehensive ontology, but rather first by retreating one step and calling into question (or 'critiquing') this very propensity of reason to want a 'comprehension of beings' or a comprehensive account of being in the first place. We will come in a moment to explaining what this term 'critical' means exactly in Levinas, but we need to begin in a different way.

4. A major contributing factor to both the profundity and perplexity of Levinas's philosophical work is that for his project of *exteriority* or 'alterity' he finds it necessary to operate entirely from within the tightly enclosed *interiority* of Husserlian phenomenology – that is, from within a pure philosophy of consciousness or cognition as discussed above[6] – even while constantly resisting this confinement. This may seem initially puzzling but as we shall see Levinas has his own fully logical reasons for restricting himself to the phenomenologically 'internalist' method (i.e. a method restricting itself to what appears internally within consciousness) for the radical 'exteriority' he seeks. What remains constant throughout his philosophical writings, however, is that whenever it comes to aligning or locating the fundamental orientations of his own philosophical work overall, Levinas has no hesitation in acknowledging the indispensable placement of it fully within the Husserlian phenomenological method.

For example, in the concluding summary of *Otherwise Than Being* Levinas says of the book as a whole that 'our analyses claim to be in the spirit of Husserlian philosophy, whose letter has been the recall in our epoch of the permanent phenomenology, restored to its rank of being a method for *all* philosophy'.[7] He then fortifies this basic commitment by adding that the presentation of that book overall 'remains faithful to [Husserlian] intentional analysis, insofar as it signifies the locating of notions in the horizon of their appearing . . . in the look absorbed by the notion alone'.[8] To be sure, and as already implied, Levinas is by no means a thoroughgoing Husserlian, for he struggles against Husserl even while adopting his framework. And it is vital for a proper understanding of his work as such to recognize that wherever he *is* resistant to Husserl (from within Husserl), this resistance springs inherently from what we have already spoken of as his eminently 'critical' orientation to 'first philosophy'. (Levinas uses the term 'first philosophy' to designate 'a theory of "being" '.[9])

Now the most prominent 'critical' philosophy as such is of course that of Immanuel Kant. And although Levinas is not exactly a Kantian, nevertheless it is largely the Kantian critical disposition he begins from in setting out his own endeavor. Or more specifically, he begins from the Kantian critical disposition but also seeks to be critical beyond it in a certain way. He is 'critical' *with* Kant insofar as, like Kant, he also sets his own basic project[10] in direct opposition to what Kant had initially formulated and rejected as 'dogmatism' (or what Kant also called 'proud ontology'). Thus, when Levinas says that 'Western philosophy has most often been an ontology',[11] and wants to distance himself from this as a 'first philosophy' that is concerned fundamentally with the '*comprehension* of beings',[12] he is essentially echoing

Kant's position who, as we have seen, begins his *Critique of Pure Reason* by attacking what he sees as a long and pervasive history of 'dogmatism' within philosophy. Dogmatism for Kant, as we have seen in the examples given in Chapter Two,[13] means the natural propensity of reason to overstep its own proper bounds and to claim a kind of possessiveness or authority over areas where it cannot by its own rational means demonstrate any legitimate jurisdiction.

The point of comparison here then is that Levinas is identifying and attacking precisely the same kind of illegitimate overreaching tendency of the cognitive or speculative intellect as Kant is in his critique of 'proud ontology' (i.e. dogmatism), when the former attacks and rejects what he more simply calls 'ontology'. But in the Levinasian critique of it, the ontological disposition now also comes to expression in a unique way, and there are two particular terminological formulations that are especially crucial to it as such. 'Ontology' in Levinas is that particular form of first philosophy which – in its concern for the *'comprehension'* of beings – (a) 'reduces the other to the same' and thereby (b) 'promotes freedom'.[14] We will need therefore to look more carefully at these two formulations, for they are central both to Levinas's general critique of ontology and to his own project of exteriority in response to it.

It is important to recognize in the first place then, that while this term 'the same' has a deeper complexity in Levinas, it can be seen always to appear in one of two basic forms. In its one form, 'the same' means simply any representational object of cognition in phenomenal consciousness. In this first form then, 'the other' is 'reduced to the same' whenever representational consciousness identifies and comprehends something by 'classifying' it in virtue of features it is found to share *in common* with other objects of classification or mental determination. The other is thereby reduced to a likeness or sameness with other things. It is of course true that this 'reduction' through mental classification or thematization is intrinsic to the very nature of representational or phenomenal cognition, which is precisely the 'hegemony' that Levinas is seeking to overcome. At any rate, in this first sense then, 'the same' is always used polemically in Levinas.

But there is another employment of the term that does not necessarily carry these same pejorative connotations, or at least not automatically so. 'The same' is also used to identify *'me'*, as the enquiring self-consciousness perduring through time – or as Levinas calls it, 'the I that is identical in its very alterations'.[15] Here the ontological 'reduction of the other to the same' is not as automatic. Yet it can still occur very easily whenever I (the same) am so oriented as to 'receive nothing in the other but what is already in me'.[16] And it is in this implicit identification of 'the other' with me ('the same') that the 'ontological' disposition thereby also 'promotes freedom' (i.e. promotes *my* freedom with regard to the other). For by viewing the other essentially according to the measurement of his or her 'sameness' with me, the same 'does not allow itself to be alienated by the other'.[17] And the further result of this then, is that by promoting the freedom of the same (the 'I') with regard to the other the ontological disposition also 'forfeits justice'. For justice demands the proper independence of the other from the possessive and controlling demands of the same.

5. Both Kant and Levinas are thus similarly 'critical' in their shared concern to show that representational thinking or cognitive reason must for its own proper integrity be exercised within defined limits. This is deemed necessary especially because of the propensities of representational thinking to claim a kind of ownership or jurisdiction over everything that enters into its field of apprehension. Kant, again, does this by showing that *sensible* reality confronts the intellect with an authority on its *own* causal terms, such that classifying or determining rationality in turn sacrifices its own integrity whenever it seeks to claim a kind of ownership or full jurisdiction over what can only be 'given' to it receptively through the senses via sensible intuition. Indeed, Kant goes even further than this in claiming that 'the *Critique* completely clips dogmatism's wings'[18] by demonstrating that in *all* of reason's activities, even in its most speculative operations, reason must, for its own integrity, be 'directed back to its empirical use'.[19]

But as deep as Levinas's implicit respect is for the Kantian critical project as such, it is for him still insufficient to be able to staunch what he sees as the unrelenting encroachment of dogmatism into even such a critical philosophy. For as the subsequent idealisms of Hegel and Fichte had shown, Kant's own critical principles could be used (even if in the end by again fully abandoning them) to yield even greater and more tautologically self-assured dogmatisms than those of the continental rationalism (and Platonism etc.) which had been the main objects of Kant's polemic. The reason for this, in Levinas's view, is that dogmatism (i.e. the propensity of the cognitive or representational intellect to comprehend everything in its field on its own terms) will *always* find ways of asserting its possessive inclinations whenever there still exists what Levinas calls a '*common frontier*'[20] between the thinking I ('the same') and any 'other' it encounters.

And it is on this specific point that for Levinas the Kantian 'critical' project does not go far enough. For Kant leaves precisely such a 'common frontier' available to cognitive consciousness, in his insistence on the primacy of empirical or sensible reality as the dynamically causal reality of a *shared* human experience. Or to state the contrast more fully, the very same sensible resistance with which the empirically *embodied* 'other' in Kant stands over against the understanding as a 'critical limit' to it: this very same sensible reality provides for Levinas precisely the most basic and final 'common frontier' between the same and the other. And in the availability of this sensible common frontier, the naturally possessive cognitive intellect will again and again, in Levinas's view, ignore the 'Kantian challenge' and 'reduce this other to the same' anyway.

What is required therefore is a 'critical' project that is able to *remove any and every 'common frontier'* between the same (the perduring I) and the other (the not-I). For any common frontier between the same and the other will always be seen by representational cognition as the opportunity for an ontology, which is why Levinas speak of the ontological disposition as 'the permanent possibility of war'.[21] It thus becomes clear why Levinas in the end thinks he must abandon the Kantian critical project and locate himself 'critically' instead within the Husserlian project of a pure phenomenology. For we will recall that this phenomenological project has by its very definition already entirely 'bracketed out' (through the *epoché*) any authority that the causally dynamic world of sensible embodiment in space and time might be able to provide of itself for philosophical reflection.[22] It has confined its operations instead entirely to the level of 'intentional analysis' or *Bedeutungsanalyse* ('meaning analysis') of 'what appears' within pure phenomenal consciousness.

Or to state the required alignment with phenomenology even more specifically, it becomes clear why Levinas thinks he must confine himself to Husserlian 'interiority' as the condition of the possibility of an 'exteriority' which he will seek to formulate differently. For it is only by disallowing what for Levinas amounts to a mere pseudo-exteriority of the empirical world that the last and most basic common frontier (sensible embodiment) can be abolished, by which a relation of totality could be claimed ontologically. This is not of course to say that Levinas does not have a great deal to say about 'sensibility' thematically. But any such discussion occurs always already from within the strict phenomenological confines of 'notions within the horizon of their appearing' in the phenomenal mind. It is never undertaken with a view to the causal dynamism operative on the level of sensible embodiment per se which, apart from the dignity conferred on this as it 'rises to the concept', is seen as at best inert, but more often as something deceptive and sinister.

In fact, there emerges now quite starkly in Levinas a deep distrust, even suspicion, of sensible reality per se, when considered as anything dynamically causal which could speak on its own terms, that is, apart from its prior placement within a phenomenological structure of meaning. Consider the force with which Levinas – and now somewhat ironically with clear dispositional affinities, through Husserl, to what we saw above in Hegel – is willing to express his distaste for any such causal limit. When empirical reality in its causally embodied pressure is seen apart from the meaning-giving clarity and dignity that mentally 'intentional' determination or classificatory recognition bestows on it, it is for Levinas but a 'mocking intention', an 'equivocation' and an 'apparition'; and 'it is as though in this silent and indecisive apparition a lie were perpetrated'. This silent, lying world of sensible appearance and awareness in turn, which has not yet risen to the dignity conferred on it by the intentional determination of the mind, 'is a world that comes to us from the Other, be he an evil genius. Its equivocation is insinuated in a mockery'. Its 'silence is not a simple absence of speech'. Rather 'speech lies in the depths of [this] silence like a laughter perfidiously held back. It is the inverse of language: the interlocutor has given a sign, but has declined every interpretation; this is the silence that terrifies'.[23]

On the basis of these aversions to the causally sensible as an authority for philosophy, it is therefore now entirely from within the cognitive *interiority* of the mental or 'noetic-noematic' confines of pure phenomenology that Levinas must initiate his non-totalizing project of alterity or exteriority. Or in other words, having dispensed with the authority of the empirically causal and sensibly physical for philosophical questioning, Levinas now seeks to locate an exteriority through a phenomenological appeal to what he calls '*meta-physical desire*'.

6. The term 'metaphysics' in Levinas is used quite differently than in its standard philosophical denotation where it usually includes the discipline of ontology. In Levinas by contrast 'metaphysics' stands in a radical opposition to 'ontology'. For whereas ontology, for Levinas, totalizes in seeking to bring everything into its field of visibility or comprehension, the Levinasian project of metaphysics is fed fundamentally instead by a 'desire for the *invisible*'. This 'metaphysical desire', he says, has appeared within the history of thought 'as a movement going forth from a world that is familiar to us ... toward an alien outside-of-oneself, toward a yonder'; it is a desire that is turned quite radically 'toward the "elsewhere" and the "otherwise" and the "other" '.[24] Yet even the term *other* here is not to be understood in any normal sense of a physical or empirical alterity, but rather in an 'eminent' sense. 'No journey, no change of climate or of scenery could satisfy the desire bent toward it.' The metaphysically desired other 'is not "other" like the bread I eat, the land on which I dwell, the landscape I contemplate'. For 'I can "feed" on these realities and to a very great extent satisfy myself, as though I had simply been lacking them. Their alterity is thereby reabsorbed into my own identity as a thinker or a possessor'. In contrast, 'the metaphysical desire tends toward something else entirely, toward the absolutely other'.[25]

   It quickly becomes clear from these statements that the metaphysical 'desire' encountered here is itself something fundamentally different than what any customary analysis of human desire could explain. For under the normal denotation of the term, 'desire' is synonymous with 'appetite' and therefore inevitably with something encountered and experienced as a kind of lack. But metaphysical desire is something which is utterly absent of anything perceivable as a 'lack',[26] such that satisfaction, or completion, or resolution cannot ever even be its aim. Levinas will follow this through resolutely. He will do so not only to the extent of setting metaphysical desire as something fundamentally antithetical to the *will* – which Aquinas, Aristotle and Kant will (as we shall see below) identify as the 'intellectual appetite' or intellectual desire – since for Levinas, 'the other above all alienates the will'.[27] He will, beyond this, go as far as to separate out metaphysical desire even from the purest altruism or *love*, since even love in his view can be 'taken to be the satisfaction of a sublime hunger'.[28] The goal here then is to formulate a relation of the same to the other – where 'the other' is now understood as 'the metaphysically desired' – in which every possibility for self-referentiality has been withdrawn from the same. And it is on the basis of the 'absolute exteriority of the metaphysical term'[29] that this term then qualifies genuinely to be called 'transcendent'. This sense of 'transcendence' as absolute exteriority will then be brought later to bear also on divine transcendence, where it becomes even more radicalized as we shall see.

   All of this can now be drawn together succinctly in a preliminary twofold basic summation of what such a genuine relation of the same to absolute alterity or exteriority most fundamentally involves. What metaphysical desire is seen as providing most essentially in this quest for exteriority, is a 'relation of the same with the other' in which: (a) on the one hand 'the transcendence of the relation does not cut the bonds that a relation implies', and yet (b) on the other 'where these bonds do not unite the same and the other into a whole'.[30]

7. Now the obvious question that immediately arises here, however, is how such a 'transcendent relation' is feasible at all. For it seems impossible that a genuine relation – which analytically entails a relational bond – could be sustained in the face of the 'absolute exteriority' of the metaphysical term (i.e. the other). Or conversely, it seems impossible that the absolute exteriority of the metaphysical term could be held intact in the presence of the bond that a genuine relation implies. Levinas responds to this in a number of ways, but perhaps the most striking and definitive response comes through a new account of what he calls the 'proximity' of the 'other' in the 'face-to-face' relation before the same.

It will already be clear, however, that just as metaphysical desire was something quite different from what we experience as desire in life, so here too the 'proximity' appealed to will have to be quite different than what is normally denoted by that term. In other words, this cannot be a proximity under the usual definitions of an embodied proximity in space and time, that is, not a proximity of real sentient pressure on retina, or auditory nerve, or flesh, since any such embodied proximity would still constitute a sensory 'common frontier'. It must rather be a purely phenomenological account of 'proximity'; for phenomenology, as a science of pure cognitive consciousness, has been able to bracket out any such factors through the *epoché*. And the way that Levinas now seeks to achieve the exteriority of metaphysical desire from *within* the interiority of phenomenology is through the introduction of a certain idea of 'infinity' which thinking can generate from within itself.

In Levinas's words, the true measure of proximity, that is, the proper metaphysical 'distance' of the stranger or the other before me in the exteriority of the face to face, is always only 'the proximity achieved by the idea of infinity'.[31] It is in this 'proximity of infinity' then that we come to the true threshold moment for apprehending 'a relation whose terms do not form a totality'.[32] And while this can be a highly nuanced idea, wherever it comes to expression in Levinas it has its roots specifically in 'the Cartesian idea of infinity', specifically in a certain relation between the Cartesian 'I think' and the idea of infinity, and as such it can be put quite simply as follows.

On the Cartesian formula, all focuses of reflective interest, whether 'things, mathematical or moral notions' or whatever, are 'presented to us by their ideas and are distinct from them. But the idea of infinity is exceptional in that its *ideatum* [i.e. its referent] surpasses its idea'. The essential point here is that 'we could conceivably have accounted for all [other] ideas' by ourselves, but not that of infinity. For infinity is 'an idea whose *ideatum* overflows the capacity of thought', and as such it is 'infinitely removed from its idea, that is, exterior, because it is infinite'.[33] In this capacity, the idea of infinity is then also able to open up further into what Levinas calls a genuinely 'eschatological vision', which is radically opposed to any inherently possessive 'ontological vision', in that it enables the true, transcendent exteriority of the other to be welcomed and encountered entirely on its own terms.

It is in this destination also that we reach the distinctive way that the Levinasian project is 'critical', albeit no longer in the epistemological way as it was in Kant, but now rather 'critical' in what Levinas calls an 'ethical' way. In Levinas's words, the genuinely critical disposition, that is, the genuine 'calling into question of the same' can never 'occur within the egoist spontaneity of the same'. The truly successful critical disposition can rather only be 'brought about by the other'. It is thus 'ethics that accomplishes the critical essence of knowledge'.[34] What the idea of infinity is meant to accomplish here, therefore, is something essentially twofold. It is meant first, and negatively, to remove the possibility of any common frontier by which the relation between same and other could again become possessive. And it is meant secondly, and now positively, to make possible the introduction of a new 'bond' which Levinas calls an '*ethical* bond', one which is 'called out' entirely by the other, and therefore does 'not unite the same and the other into a whole'.

III

8. We have already acknowledged the profound insight and importance of the Levinasian enterprise in many ways, especially in his unique attempt to revive an ethical orientation as fundamental for philosophical questioning. Nevertheless, as a basic outlook, any such radically alterative methodology will show itself inadequate for approaching the question of the transcendence of God. Let me note just two such insufficiencies in Levinas himself, followed by two broader logical observations of the inadequacy of alterity generally for theological requirements, before going on to offer some concluding remarks about what this means for a Christian understanding of transcendence.

The first problem we encounter in Levinas directly is that in order for alterity to be pursued seriously, that is, in the full rigor of its analytical definition as denoting a relation which is devoid of any common frontier: any such alterity must be thoroughly and utterly a *theoretically* engendered one, whereas divine transcendence is not theoretical. Even the 'ethical bond' that Levinas wants to establish here is itself a bond that is a product of a wholly speculative process made possible through the speculative idea of infinity. This concurs exactly with Leora Batnitzky's assessment, voiced from a Jewish perspective, that 'the exteriority of the other is not for Levinas the muddled stuff of culture, history, religion and politics. Rather the exteriority of the other is a *metaphysical principle*'.[35]

A second shortcoming is that the Levinasian orientation to transcendence moves inevitably into something essentially utopian, a result which he himself is willing to acknowledge. It must be granted, however, that the atrocities of the two World Wars and the Jewish horrors of the 1930s and 1940s against the backdrop of which he is writing, give Levinas terrifyingly real reasons for dispensing with the often horrendously brutal and inhuman world of the

causally real as a proper authority for philosophical reflection, or as a qualified source of orientation for either philosophy or attentiveness to revelation.
For it is *this* 'common frontier' more than any other which is indeed always
'the permanent possibility of war'.[36] What is sought instead is what Levinas
calls an 'eschatological vision', a vision from which every common frontier
has been removed through the idea of infinity, and which can thus guarantee
'the certitude of peace'.[37]

But now this eschatological certitude of peace comes at a cost. For in the
first place, it cannot help but be, again, an entirely utopian or idealized certitude of peace. To live in the real world of space and time *just is*, tragically,
to live with the permanent possibility of war. The poverty of alterity for
theology therefore – because alterity must in its maximal magnification
always be an 'ideal' of alterity (accomplished only through the *ideatum* of
infinity) – becomes especially pronounced against the indispensably incarnational demands of Christian transcendence in revelation. For it is into nothing
less than *this* world, this *real* 'fallen' world of the permanent possibility of
war, and precisely not into an 'eschatologically' ideal domain guaranteeing of
the certitude of peace, that Jesus Christ comes as God's self-revelation in a real
human body, and indeed, comes in the likeness of *sinful* man (Rom. 8.3).

This is the difficult and uncompromising meaning of many of the early
passages in Bonhoeffer's *Ethics*, where he is again reflecting Luther's equally
uncompromising incarnational stance on these issues. 'Ecce homo – behold
God become human, the unfathomable mystery of the love of God for the
world. God loves human beings. God loves the world. Not an ideal human but
human beings as they are, not an ideal world, but the real world. What we find
repulsive in their opposition to God, what we shrink back from with pain and
hostility, namely, real human beings, the real world, this is for God the *ground*
of unfathomable love'.[38] But Bonhoeffer does not stop here. He continues on
that it is 'not enough to say that God embraces human beings'. For even
'this affirmation rests on an infinitely deeper one': namely, 'that God, in the
conception and birth of Jesus Christ, has taken on humanity *bodily* ... by
entering as a human being into human life, by taking on and bearing bodily
the nature, essence, guilt and suffering of human beings ... God does not seek
the most perfect human being with whom to be united, but takes on human
nature as it is'.[39]

9. We come on this basis to two broader and more fundamentally logical
shortcomings – two basic illusions in fact – by which all such attempts,
whether through 'exteriority' or 'alterity' are shown to be inadequate for what
is demanded in the transcendence of God. It should be added before proceeding that the basic general dispositions over the next few pages are by no means
new, and they are in agreement, for example, with recent trenchant and much
more elaborate discussions along these lines in books by David Burrell and
Denys Turner.[40] The present treatments, however, proceed from somewhat
different perspectives and are also focused toward somewhat different ends. In
keeping with our own Levinasian focus then, let us look at the general limitations of 'exteriority' first, and then after that also to the general limitations of

'alterity'. To illuminate the former, we can begin from certain insurmountable problems that we encounter in trying to express what is demanded in the relation of God as Creator to his creation.

When we say that as the Creator of everything God 'transcends' the whole created order of what is; and when we say further, following Gen. 1.1, that God's act of creation is the 'beginning' of *all* 'there is', and that this 'in the beginning' is therefore a creation of everything out of nothing, or a creation *ex nihilo*: when we say all of this, we are trying by this word 'transcends' to express something essentially twofold, both aspects of which must initially be put in purely negative terms. We are trying to express firstly that as the Creator of all 'there is', God himself is not merely an element or *constituent within* the 'there is' (as discussed above), but is rather the ground and origin of all 'there is'. And secondly, we are trying to express that God in his eternal livingness and non-finitude is not *comparable to* anything that exists finitely within the created extensive magnitudes or limitations of space and time. 'To whom will you compare me or count me equal? To whom will you liken me that we may be compared?' (Isa. 46.5). So the two negatives intended by the term 'transcendence' then are that God is not *contained within* the created 'there is', nor is God in his transcendence *comparable to* anything created.

But here is where the failures of the language of exteriority begin to emerge. For it is true that when we try to amplify or understand the first point – i.e. that God is not merely a constitutive 'existent' among other existents within the created order, but the Creator of that order – we will find that we have no alternative but to speak of God as outside or 'exterior' to creation. If the reality of God does not originate from 'within' the created universe, then by necessity for human understanding it must be 'outside' it, and any communication or revelation of God to the world must therefore be seen as a disclosure 'from outside'.

Yet when we think this through with proper critical rigor we will recognize that this 'outside' or exteriority has really not expressed God's transcendence at all. For it will quickly become obvious that we will find it impossible to think of this 'exteriority' of the Creator in any other way than once again as a *spatial* exteriority and therefore as a creationally conditioned exteriority. We can see this plainly in the impossibility of thinking something 'beyond' (and thus 'exterior' to) the 'end' of space, or something 'prior to' (and thus 'exterior' to) the beginning of time. For with any 'exteriority' so posited, we will be entirely unable to think of it except to place it *in* a time 'prior' to the 'beginning' of time, and *in* a space 'beyond' the 'end' of space. It is impossible for us to escape this, as any attempt will quickly show.

If therefore we are to deal in full earnestness with the 'in the beginning' of the creational account; that is, if we are to deal in full earnestness with God's *genuine* 'transcendence' of the created order as Creator, and not be satisfied with an illusionary pseudo-transcendence, then we must say that God's genuine transcendence as Creator is no more 'outside' the created order than it is a constitutive element *within* it (including the 'within' of human subjectivity). And we must say this despite the fact that, within the limitations of our discursively cognitive capacities, it is impossible to 'think' it as anything *but* 'outside', which reinforces once again the fundamental inability of our cognitive capacities to understand even analogically what God's transcendence is. For both 'interiority' and 'exteriority' are spatially and temporally determined designations, which God, as the Creator of space and time, transcends, and therefore they cannot apply to God in the way that we have to apply them to him.

10. A similar conundrum faces us when we try to construe God's transcendence of the world in terms of 'alterity' or 'the Wholly Other'. For just as we have seen that 'exteriority', in terms of its very meaning, carries an intrinsically *extensive* or spatio-temporal denotation which cannot apply to God as the Creator of these extensive magnitudes: so also it is clear that 'alterity', by the very meaning of the term, carries an intrinsically *comparative* denotation which cannot apply to God.

It must be granted, however, that the Levinasian project of alterity itself to a certain extent recognizes this limitation and this unavoidable illusion. Yet even while acknowledging it, the project must remain – as an essentially phenomenologically cognitive exercise – and indeed it consciously does remain, fully operative within the illusion. Consider then how Levinas states this when he pushes the exteriority and alterity directed in its 'ethical' focus to even more radical lengths when he speaks of the '*absolute* remoteness' of God's transcendence as 'Other'. In his own words, 'God is not simply the "first other", the "other par excellence", or the "absolutely other", but other than other, other otherwise, other with an alterity prior to the alterity of the other, prior to the ethical bond with another and different from every neighbor, transcendent to the point of absence, to the possible confusion with the stirring of the *there is*'.[41]

Now it is clear from this statement that Levinas is seeking to reject, as theology also must, any understanding of God's 'otherness' as something comparable even to any ethical 'other' within the Heideggerian domain of the 'there is'. Yet the fact remains that by its sheer designation as *other*, 'the other' is unable to sustain its very meaning and intelligibility *as* 'other' except as a *comparative* designation, which in the end always in some way refers back to 'the same'. It is impossible for us to think 'other' otherwise than this because apart from its comparative relation back to the same it loses its inherent meaning. 'The other' is therefore an *intrinsically* comparative designation according to its very analytical meaning, and apart from this is empty. Indeed, Levinas himself has no difficulty admitting this point.[42] But we can push all of this further still, in order to come to the real heart of the problem, by turning analogously again to the demands of the 'in the beginning', that is, of the '*ex nihilo*' in the creational account.

Consider then that one of the most important theological functions of the 'in the beginning' or the 'out of nothing' demand in the creational account, is to ensure that there is no *conjunctive* connection that could bring Creator and creation into a comparative ordering or a comparative continuum. The reason that any conjunctive connection must be rejected is to ensure that the world is never seen pantheistically to be identified with God, or even panentheistically as a kind of appendage of the Creator. (This, even though we must equally be able to say that God in Christ fills everything in every way, which is precisely the problem before us.) Such a theological error of the conjunctive relation between Creator and creation will in general be readily acknowledged and granted. For even though we may occasionally speak loosely of the relation between Creator and creation as a relation between 'God' and 'all that is not God', we cannot mean this in any strictly conjunctive or quantitatively total-izing terms. We cannot mean by this, in other words, that 'on the one hand' there is God, and 'on the other hand' there is all that is not God, such that by combining the two we could reach a quantitative totality of 'what is'. For this would already commit the error of supposing implicitly that something could be 'added' to the non-finite reality of God, as if to yield merely something like an overall increase in 'quantity'. And this of course would already make God not-God for it would implicitly view God from the outset as essentially a quantitative 'existent', and thus as something finite, which is to say, as essen-tially already a component *within* the created order, rather than as the Creator *of* that order. Any 'unity' of God and the world, which we may, for example, speak of as having been achieved through the reconciliation of the world to God in Jesus Christ, can thus never be merely the conjunctive unity of a 'totality'.

But this is only half the matter. For even while the error of the conjunctive connection will as such be readily granted, there is a different kind of mistake that can much more easily befall theological thinking in another direction. For it is exactly in the interests of *avoiding* the error of relating God and the world *con*junctively and pantheistically, that there can be a strong natural tendency to want to speak instead of the relation between Creator and creation in the opposing terms of *dis*junction. Now it is precisely this relation of disjunction which is always at bottom involved in any talk of transcendence as 'the other'. But something important is implicitly forgotten as such. What is forgotten is that disjunction is no less a cognitive mechanism that brings entities into a comparative relation than is conjunction, even if the disjunctive comparison comes to expression in terms of opposition or over-againstness. And as we have seen, this contrastingly comparative or differentiational character of dis-junction is by no means diminished, but is in a way magnified all the more, when it is 'radicalized' through the language of the 'absolutely remote', or the 'otherwise than other', or the 'absolute disjunction', or 'the Wholly Other', and so on. For to 'radicalize' is to exponentialize according to cognitive cri-teria, and thus not to dissolve but indeed to magnify. Or to state this in another way, the mechanism of *dis*junction is no less a function of reason as intrinsically a faculty of coherence, which is to say a faculty of unity, than is *con*junction. For discursive reason will still by its very nature look at disjuncts or opposites as essentially connected and therefore comparable *by virtue* of their disjunction or opposition. And this is why even the disjunctive language of 'the other' or 'trace of the other' still, for all its efforts to the contrary, ultimately collapses inevitably into a totalizing relation, even through a theor-etical idea of infinity.

We must in light of this not only agree with Kierkegaard that 'God is not a "more" ', that is, a quantitative 'more', as if the being of creation and the 'being' of the Creator could simply be added together cognitively as 'commensurate' quantities to yield a summative totality of 'what exists'. We must also take this further and say that God is not a qualitative 'other' either, as if the transcendent reality of God and the reality of creation could be brought together cognitively as merely 'incommensurate' disjuncts.

IV

11. But let us now finally in one further way, through Augustine, try to amplify what is at stake in all of this. And although the particular kind of error that Augustine will implicitly identify in what follows will be found to occur only indirectly in Levinas himself, it will affect him nonetheless and will thus re-emphasize the inadequacy of any cognitive approaches through alterity or exteriority to express a proper disposition to God's transcendence of the world.

When we wish to speak of the transcendent reality of God which is revealed in specificity and with authority first in the law of Moses, but most fully in the incarnation, life, death and resurrection of Jesus Christ, it is crucial, as Augustine says, to begin from, or at least never lose sight of what the transcendent reality of God is not.

> ... when we aspire to that height from this depth, it is a step toward no small bit of knowledge if, before we can know what God is, we can already know what he is not. For assuredly He is neither heaven nor earth, nor like earth and heaven, nor any such thing as we see in the heaven, nor any such thing as we do not see, and is perhaps in the heaven. Even if by the power of your imagination you magnify the light of the sun in your mind as much as you are able, either that it may be greater or that it may be brighter, a thousand times as much or innumerable times, yet even this is not God. Neither as the pure angels are thought of as animating heavenly bodies, changing and making use of them in accordance with the will by which they serve God, neither if all were brought together and became one – and there are thousands and thousands of them – is any such thing God. Nor would it be so, even if you were to think of the same spirits without bodies, which is indeed extremely difficult for our carnal thought.[43]

Now in the recognition of this utter unthinkability and unperceivability of God in his uncreatedness and eternal glory, we will find ourselves unavoidably and indeed quite rightly addressing the question of God's transcendence as one which 'surpasses' all powers of human perceiving and thinking, that is, as surpassing and therefore transcending not only all natural powers of sense perception but also all natural powers of human reason. The scriptures themselves, after all, declare that no one has ever seen God or can see God (Jn 1.18; 1 Tim. 6.16); and this pertains as much to the intellectual vision as it does to the sensible vision. But we must attend carefully to something deeper and more final in what Augustine is saying here, something which implicitly identifies an error which can easily befall us in the otherwise perfectly right and proper considerations of God's transcendence as a surpassingness. Let me try to explain this.

It is a natural propensity for us – indeed, a natural illusion which must constantly stand under correction – when speaking in terms of the 'transcending' or 'surpassing' of the powers of human sense perception and reason, to understand these terms as designating essentially an 'eclipse' *of* these faculties themselves. And when theology proceeds along these lines, it will then find itself inclined, as is often done,[44] further to designate such a transcendence or surpassingness by such terms as 'supra-sensible' (surpassing or transcending sense perception, and thus exterior to its reaches) or 'supra-rational' (surpassing or transcending human reason, and thus exterior to its reaches). However, it is precisely on such an understanding of God's transcendence that another exemplification of the error we are seeking to address takes place.

The point is that when we think of God's transcendence as 'supra-sensible' or 'supra-rational', we must then, by our very definitional understanding of these terms, construe this transcendence as 'occurring' at or beyond a limit at which our sensible and rational capacities are exhausted and surpassed, and therefore as something remote and distant, and utterly exterior to us as such. And the unavoidable implication here (whether we intend this or not, which is precisely its illusion) is that if our sensible and rational powers were only greater, the transcendence by which God surpasses these capacities might then perhaps after all come into view through a magnification of the sensible or intellectual vision. It will be utterly impossible for us, under the usage of such terms, to avoid thinking and 'positing' along these lines, because that is what supra-sensible and supra-rational mean. We must in other words be careful that in any usage of such terms we do not allow ourselves to be led astray by them through making human limitations essentially the measure of God's real transcendence.

The point in short, therefore, is that God's invisibility to and transcendence of our powers of sense perception and rational apprehension (our cognitive powers) *has nothing whatsoever to do with the limitations of these*. For even if, as Augustine says, these powers were able to be 'magnified a thousand times or innumerable times', they would still be entirely unable to afford any glimpse of God in his transcendence. But this now means something even more decisive. It means that these powers by themselves cannot – not even through their own idea of infinity – provide even a proper *orientation* to divine transcendence. And the specific reason for this, as we shall see more fully in a later discussion, is that as cognitive powers they are intrinsically objectifying and thus limiting (determining) powers, whereas God's transcendent reality is not a determinate or even indeterminate cognitive 'object' of any kind.

We can therefore now make a summary statement which may on the face of it seem peculiar and strange. The transcendence of God may not be understood as a 'supra-sensible' transcendence or a 'supra-rational' transcendence at all. That is, God's transcendence may not be understood as either a surpassing *of* our perceiving or a surpassing *of* our thinking at all. This of course is not to make the ludicrous suggestion that God is therefore to be viewed theologically as something sensibly or rationally apprehensible as created things are. It is only to say that God's transcendence of creation may not be measured by or understood merely as an 'infinite' increase of any created magnitude or capacity at all, whether a quantitative magnitude or a qualitative magnitude; and this latter includes exteriority and alterity. As Denys Turner states the same point in different terms, we may not allow ourselves to construe Christian transcendence in 'metaphors of "gaps", even infinitely "big" ones'; or, as we might now add, even infinitely disjunctive ones.[45] Drawing specifically again on Augustine's discussions on these matters, Turner speaks further of God's transcendence as being '*closer* to my creaturehood than it is possible for creatures to be to each other. For creatures are more distinct from each other than God [precisely in his "transcendence" of their creaturehood, and thus also his transcendence of their creaturely "distance"] can possibly be from any of them'.[46]

None of this is to question that when in prayer and worship and action we address God as an I addressing a Thou, we do of course, in a perfectly trustworthy and critically unreflected way, meet God as 'not-me' and therefore, in a perfectly innocent and untroubled exercise of the imagination, as 'other' than me. We are saying only that under rigorous theological scrutiny this 'Thou' may not be seen as being addressed essentially as a cognitive radical alterity or exteriority (or for that matter as merely the interiority of human 'inwardness' either as we shall discuss further below). We will see the more exact reasons for this later on as we begin to express ourselves positively on these matters. But for now we might just conclude by saying that we are trying to take Martin Buber's insight more seriously than Levinas allowed himself to do – because of the self-admitted confinement of his whole philosophical project to the analysis of 'notions in the horizon of their appearing'[47] – that 'the life of human beings is not passed in the sphere of transitive verbs alone'.[48]

It should be added, therefore, that what is *not* being suggested in the rejection here of the language of alterity (as much as that of ontology) is that alterity-language, or even incommensurability-language, is somehow *too* 'radical' or *overly* severe for fundamental theological questioning with regard to God's transcendence. To the contrary, the point is that even in its radicality it is *in*adequate to it. Or to state the point more correctly, the question itself as such will be shown to be essentially ill-formed for the demands of the transcendence of God, thus yielding answers which can be neither true nor false but simply empty. It is ill-formed and empty in an analogous way that, for example, to speak of the second law of thermodynamics or Shakespeare's *Hamlet* as being thirty miles from Chicago is neither true nor false but simply empty.

We will in subsequent chapters see that God's transcendence as disclosed in revelation demands to be encountered at its communicative origin or threshold as something quite separated out from any such approaches, and indeed engaged theologically through a different use of reason. And it is to this other use of reason that we now turn, in preparation for that.

Notes

1 While the term itself etymologically is Greek, it first appears in the Latin form of *ontologia* in the sixteenth and early seventeenth centuries, for example, in *Ogdoas Scholastica* by Jacob Lorhard (1606) or the *Lexicon Philosophicum* by Rudolf Göckel (1613).
2 *Being and Time* (New York: Harper and Row, 1962), p. 21.
3 *Being and Time*, p. 26.
4 'There is no God in the domain of the "there is" ', Bonhoeffer, *Akt und Sein*, DBW 2 (Gütersloh: Christian Kaiser Verlag, 1998), p. 112.
5 Levinas, *Totality and Infinity*, p. 42 (hereafter *TI*).
6 See pp. 31–4 above
7 Levinas, *Otherwise Than Being* (Pittsburgh: Duquesne University Press, 1998), p. 183 (hereafter *OTB*); see also e.g. *TI*, pp. 28–9, 44–5.
8 *OTB* p. 183, emphasis added.
9 See e.g. *TI* pp. 42–8.
10 In *Totality and Infinity*, for example.
11 *TI* p. 43.
12 *TI* p. 42, emphasis added.
13 See p. 27.
14 *TI* p. 42.
15 *TI* p. 36.
16 *TI* p. 43.
17 *TI* p. 41.
18 Kant, 'What is Orientation in Thinking?' in H. S. Reiss (ed.), *Kant: Political Writings* (second edition) (Cambridge: Cambridge University Press, 1991), pp. 237–49, 11.
19 Kant, *Critique of Pure Reason* (Cambridge: Cambridge University Press, 1998), A672–3/B700–1.
20 *TI* p. 39.
21 *TI* p. 21.
22 See pp. 31–2 above.
23 *TI* pp. 90–1.
24 *TI* p. 33.
25 *TI* p. 33.
26 *TI* p. 299.
27 *TI* p. 240.
28 *TI* p. 34.
29 *TI* p. 35.
30 *TI* p. 48.
31 *TI* p. 50; see also especially Chapter 3 in *Otherwise Than Being*: 'Sensibility and Proximity', pp. 61–97.
32 *TI* p. 39.
33 *TI* p. 49.
34 *TI* p. 43.
35 Leora Batnitzky, *Leo Strauss and Emmanuel Levinas: Philosophy and the Politics of Revelation* (Cambridge: Cambridge University Press, 2006), p. 89, original emphasis. Batnitzky's book makes important and innovative moves deserving careful attention for the question of the relation of revelation and reason, and her basic orientations in this regard will resonate strongly with our own in later chapters.
36 *TI* p. 21.
37 *TI* p. 22.

38 DBW 6, p. 84.
39 DBW 6, pp. 84–5.
40 David Burrell, *Knowing the Unknowable God* (Notre Dame: University of Notre Dame Press, 1986); Denys Turner, *The Darkness of God* (Cambridge, New York: Cambridge University Press, 1995).
41 Levinas, *Collected Philosophical Papers* (The Hague: M. Nijhoff, 1987), pp. 165–6.
42 See e.g. *In the Time of the Nations* (Bloomington: Indiana University Press, 1994), pp. 181–2. I am indebted to Leora Batnitzky's *Leo Strauss and Emmanuel Levinas* (Cambridge: Cambridge University Press, 2006) for directing me to this reference.
43 Augustine, *On the Trinity*, Bk. 8, Ch. 2, (3) (Cambridge: Cambridge University Press, 2002), p. 6.
44 See e.g. Friedrich Schleiermacher, *The Christian Faith* (Edinburgh: T&T Clark, 1948), pp. 62–8.
45 Denys Turner, *Faith, Reason and the Existence of God* (Cambridge: Cambridge University Press, 2004), p. 214.
46 *Faith, Reason and the Existence of God*, p. 214, original emphasis.
47 *OTB* p. 183, emphasis added.
48 Martin Buber, *I and Thou* (New York: Charles Scribner's Sons), p. 4.

CHAPTER 5

APPETITION, MOTION AND REASON

I

1. When we try to take human rationality itself as a focus of scrutiny, the single most basic and defining character we will eventually arrive at is that it is fundamentally, as Aristotle first formulated it, a 'faculty of judgment'. This means essentially that it is a faculty of organized reflection which is able to hold before itself certain subjects of focus, whether to gain insight into them through observation or analysis, or to weigh and adjudicate between them comparatively, or again to orient them towards certain desired ends or whatever, but always by bringing the subjects of focus to reflective connection within some mechanism of ordering. And this implies further that as a faculty of judgment reason is intrinsically also a faculty of ordered connectedness or relatedness.

Now it is often taken as virtually axiomatic today that because human reason is expressed intrinsically as a *mental* exercise, that therefore when we speak of human reason as the 'judging faculty' we are dealing essentially and exclusively in the domain of *cognition*. And by the domain of cognition we mean the domain of thinking and perceiving, language and logic, grammar and interpretation, representation and reference, or in short, the domain of discourse. Within the cognitive domain as such the formal exercise of reason can of course manifest itself in a wide variety of ways. It is exercised quite differently, for example, in elementary formal logic or pure mathematics where it must confine its judgments entirely to the internal calculative functions of the intellect per se, or to the relations of ideas within reason itself, than it is in the strongly empirical disciplines of meteorology or ornithology, which bring the judging faculty to bear for the ordering of what is encountered predominantly through sensible observation. Or again, it is exercised quite differently in the discipline of literary theory, where the judging faculty is brought to bear on the semantic and syntactic relations within texts, than it is in the discipline of ethics, where the cognitive judging faculty is focused on issues arising out of moral consciousness or ought-consciousness.

But for all their differences, all of these remain essentially discursively cognitive disciplines, that is disciplines which exercise themselves most fundamentally within the interpretive and explanatory structures thinking and perceiving, representation and reference, language and grammar and so on, with a view to an expansion of understanding and knowledge or at least a deepening of insight for their given purposes. And again, to repeat the earlier statement, it is often understood as virtually axiomatic today that because all reasoning is mental, that it must as such be at bottom cognitive or discursively interpretive in these ways.

But this is in fact incorrect. For we also find ourselves using reason as the judging faculty in a quite fundamentally different way. This other use of reason is one which so suffuses and grounds any and every aspect of conscious human life that we are constantly employing it even when we may not be cognitively aware of doing so. What most basically distinguishes this other use of reason from the discursive or cognitive use is that the judging faculty is not used in the ordering of *percepts* and *concepts* for thinking, but rather in the ordering of *appetites* (or desires) and *motives* for bodily action. It is a use of reason which, when fully explained, will be quite easily distinguishable from cognitive or discursive reason, which is why its separate treatment from the latter has, unlike today, been a virtual commonplace throughout much of our intellectual history and heritage, as we shall see in what follows.

What I am speaking of has in the past has been treated under the designation 'practical reason', i.e. reason relating to matters of 'praxis' or action in space. But it is better for our purposes to call it 'motive reasoning' – where 'motive' is to be understood in both its 'motivational' and (physically) 'motional' aspects – because the term 'practical reason' has today often come to be thought of as virtually synonymous with what we currently call 'ethics'. And ethics as we understand it today is not engaged through practical reasoning. The discipline of ethics in any of its current forms (whether metaethics, prescriptive ethics or even applied ethics) is no less exclusively an exercise of the discursive or cognitive understanding – even though it takes issues of 'praxis' or right action as its essential 'subject matter' – as are any of the physical or human sciences. This is not to overlook the rather unique place of ethics among the academic disciplines. It is only to say that ethics per se is not engaged through motive reason or practical reason – nor indeed should it try to be – but rather through cognitive reason, as will become clear.

True practical reasoning as motive reasoning has all but disappeared as a genuine source of orientation from the currently predominating academic discussions, including moral ones. And the reasons for its disappearance are related directly to what, under the currently prevailing cognitivist monovisional mindset, we saw in Chapter Two to be the subsumption of causally embodied authority under the lordship of the cognitively 'determining' mind. The direct correlation between the loss of attentiveness to the authority of causal reality there, and the loss of attentiveness to motive reasoning here, is quite simple and straightforward. For once the full subordination of embodied causal reality in space and time under the sovereignty of cognitive or 'meaning-giving' consciousness has been allowed to occur, it is entirely inevitable that motive or practical reasoning should also be subsumed under cognitive jurisdiction. The reason for this is that motive reasoning or practical reasoning

just is reasoning for motivated *bodily movement in space*. It is nothing
else than a use of reason for real embodied action in space, that is, for
real *causal agency* in the world. And once the natural causal processes occurring dynamically in the world have been denied any independent 'reality' and
authority apart from the dignity and 'meaning' conferred on them by cognitive
'determination', it is then inevitable that questions of human causal agency
in the world – where humans are not only sensible receptors of causal
processes but become themselves causal agents of dynamic change in the
world – should also become subsumed entirely under the authority of the
cognitive.

We cannot here go into a depth-discussion of this to the extent that we did
in Chapter Two, and in any case many of the lines traced there will apply here
as well, given the focus of both around causal dynamism. It will suffice only to
say, first, that Hegel is again perhaps the most obvious and influential example
of the subsumption of practical or motive reason under theoretical or discursive reason. Anyone who is acquainted with Hegel will know that one of
the most decisive aspects of his whole program is an assimilation of action into
cognition, and of practical reason into theoretical reason, or more accurately
that 'the absolute idea . . . is the identity of the theoretical and practical idea'.[1]
But essentially the same collapse reigns in the other manifestations of the
cognitivist mono-visional approaches today as well, whether in phenomenology, or in the many approaches associated with the 'linguistic turn', or also
in prominent strains of Anglo-American analytical philosophy, even if it
is approached differently there. In this last case, for example, desires and
motivations are brought under ultimate conceptual jurisdiction in the reduction of these to the cognitive status of 'intentional attitudes', or as this is
expressed with even more explicit conceptual discursivity, 'propositional attitudes'; and phenomenology does something similar through its own 'eidetic
reductions' of desires and motives to cognitive or phenomenal 'value-objects'
and 'value-complexes'.[2]

In the present chapter I want to lay the groundwork for showing later that a
reinvigoration of genuine motive and practical attentiveness is indispensable
not only for a reasoned attentiveness to the present reality of the transcendent
God in revelation, but also for any philosophical endeavor which is concerned
to address itself to the center of life.

2. Throughout most of our intellectual heritage, reason, understood as the
human 'judging power', has been seen as exercising itself in two essentially
different ways, pertaining specifically to two fundamentally different human
faculties on which reason can bring its ordering judgment to bear. This double
function or use of reason has come to expression most rigorously and clearly
in the Aristotelian, Thomist and Kantian traditions, but it is also prevalent
elsewhere whether explicitly or implicitly.

At any rate, the first of these two basic faculties on which reason as the
judging power can be brought to bear is *the faculty of cognition* or cognitive
apprehension. And this term 'cognition', in all three thinkers, is meant to
include both 'concepts' which can be generated from within thinking itself,

and 'percepts' which come to thought through sensible encounter. Or in Aristotle's exact words, it is meant to include both 'thinking and perceiving'.[3] The second is *the faculty of appetition* (i.e. having to do with appetites or desires). These two faculties come to expression in Kant as *Erkenntnis* (cognition) and *Begehrungsvermögen* (appetition or desire). Kant himself dedicates entirely separate treatises to a critical study of the use of reason for each faculty differently. The faculty of cognition is the central focus of Kant's first *Critique* (the *Critique of Pure Reason*, i.e. where the 'pure reason' being critiqued is pure discursive or cognitive reason, or also 'speculative' reason as discussed above). And the faculty of appetition or desire is the central focus of his second *Critique* (the *Critique of Practical Reason*). Exactly the same focuses and distinctions come to expression in Aquinas, whose Latin terminology is more directly reflective of our own, as the distinction between *cognitiva* and *appetitiva*. Indeed, this distinction is an entirely indispensable one if not the central methodological one in Thomas's whole treatise on human nature, and it bears importantly as such on some of his theological treatments as well, such as those on faith and grace.[4]

It is important to recognize firstly that in all three thinkers appetitions (or desires) are shown to be quite fundamentally different than cognitions (concepts and percepts), and this not only in their origin and manifestation in life, but also accordingly in their logical definitions. Indeed, Aristotle goes out of his way to put an especially pronounced emphasis on the entirely distinct status of appetition or desire compared to all other human capacities. In *On the Soul*, for example, after having dealt at length with what he sees to be all the other capacities and faculties found in human life – the cognitive, the nutritive, the sensible and the imaginative and so on – in coming after this to the appetitive nature, Aristotle deems this 'to be distinct both in definition and in power from all the hitherto enumerated'.[5] Its distinctness 'in definition' means its distinctness logically or analytically in terms of its meaning (based on experience); and its distinctness 'in power' means what we shall see is its distinctiveness as the *sole motivating power* for generating reasoned movement or action in space. (As we shall see in the final chapter, the appetitive and motive faculty will come to expression with a whole new intensification for theological concerns also in the work of Søren Kierkegaard, who will speak of it as the 'passional' nature.)

But secondly, not only are these faculties themselves essentially different, but the use of reason with respect to each is also essentially different. More fully, because the intrinsic activity and function of cognition (perceiving and conceiving) will be found to be fundamentally different than the intrinsic activity and function of appetition (desiring), so also reason in turn will order each differently to reflect their own separate intrinsic activities and functions. Let me try to make this somewhat clearer generally before going into greater specifics.

The essential difference is that the faculty of cognition will be found to operate most fundamentally and intrinsically as what Aristotle calls the '*discriminating power*' of human beings for *thinking and perceiving*. Whereas the faculty of appetition will be found to operate most fundamentally and intrinsically as the *'motive* power' of human beings for *'originating local movement in space'*.[6] It is important here, especially for purposes of initial clarification, not to confuse or identify either of these two powers yet with *reason*. In all three of our interlocutors, reason as the single *'judging* power' is in a way seen to be a 'higher' faculty which can bring its judging or ordering activity to bear on both the 'discriminating power' (cognition) and the 'motive power' (appetition).

When we speak of 'reason', therefore, we are always implicitly speaking of a certain *use* of reason as the judging power. Either reason will bring its judging or ordering power to bear on linguistically defined concepts and sensible percepts for questions of right thinking and understanding; or it will bring its judging power to bear on appetites (desires) and motives for questions of appropriate action in space. The former use of reason is called the cognitive use of reason (or also the 'discursive' use of reason because it is concerned with matters of thinking and linguistic discourse). And the latter use of reason is called the 'motive' or also the 'practical' use of reason because it is concerned with matters of motivation and motion in space, or action, which is to say 'praxis'.

Before commencing with a full exploration of this, however, we need to clarify something which might be somewhat perplexing about the relation between 'thinking' and 'reason'. The point is that we may be inclined to suppose uncritically that 'thought' or 'thinking' – because it occurs necessarily or intrinsically 'in the mind' – is thereby already automatically 'rational'. But this would be to jump too quickly into the term 'rational' without sufficient attention to what it demands. For thoughts are indeed always *mental* or *conceptual*, but they are not yet for that reason alone already *rational*, since thoughts or conceptual procedures themselves can of course also be irrational or incoherent. In order to qualify as rational, the thinking and conceptual procedures must themselves be brought under the ordering scrutiny of reason as the judging power in order to ensure the correct exercise of thinking. The same ordering authority of cognitive reason can be brought to bear on percepts. For example, sensible percepts can be illusionary or inexact, as when the moon appears larger on the horizon than it does overhead. And the judging faculty of reason can also be brought to bear on this as it investigates it empirically and inductively, so that I am not misled by the illusion even though I cannot escape it.

This then is an initial account, in the simplest of terms, of how reason can be a judging faculty equally but differently for both the cognitive faculty (including concepts and percepts) and for the appetitive faculty. For just as in the one exercise it brings percepts and concepts to a rational ordering, so in the other exercise it brings appetites and motivations to a rational ordering.

3. In what follows we will be focusing primarily on the motive or appetitive use of reason since we will already be quite familiar with the basic operations of the cognitive or discursive use, and the latter will come to discussion mainly for comparative purposes. And we can thus proceed with the task at hand along three ascending focuses. We will look first more exactly at how the

appetitive and cognitive *faculties themselves* are different; secondly, more exactly at how the *use of reason* as the 'judging power' with respect to each is also different; and then finally at how reason in its practical or motive exercise can be *genuinely principled* within itself in a way that anything qualifying as reason must be.

We can begin with the first focus by observing initially something fundamentally different in the basic *constitutive structures* of 'cognitions' (concepts and percepts) versus 'desires' as we experience them. With regard to the former it will be clear, as Thomas states it, that what we mean by 'cognition' or the 'cognizing' of something *just is* the 'apprehending' of something. The cognitive faculty, in other words, is intrinsically a kind of 'visional' or envisioning faculty, whether this takes place through sensible vision or a purely intellectual vision, as when, for example, after having had the logic of a difficult mathematical theorem explained to us, we come to 'see' the truth of it. Or another way of expressing this inherently 'visional' character of cognition is to say that its concepts and percepts are intrinsically always thoughts *about* X or perceptions *of* X. In other words, it is impossible to have a thought or perception without such an 'aboutness' (or what philosophy calls the 'intentionality' of thought), even if the apprehended idea is intrinsically problematic, such as the idea of infinity or the mathematical constant π. And this means further that a cognition as an 'apprehension' is always in a basic mental 'possession' of its object, whether a conceptual or perceptual object. This inherently possessive character of cognition has already been discussed extensively above through Levinas.

But now desires as appetites are fundamentally different than this. Let us take, for example, on the simplest sensible level, the desire for food or nourishment in a state of hunger. We find that such a desire springs up within us in the character of a want or a need without the presence of any sensibly perceived or conceptually imagined object, for example, when hunger pangs arise suddenly during the course of a busy workday without any particular thought of food. Of course a desire can also be for a *particular* object as well (in fact, many are). But even here it is essential to the intrinsic character of a desire that it *lacks* its 'object', for if it had it, the desire would be satisfied and would disappear *as* desire. So the initial difference then, in simple terms, is that concepts and percepts are intrinsically in (mental) possession of their objects, whereas desires intrinsically lack their 'objects'.

This brings us directly to the second distinction between the cognitive and appetitive faculties themselves, which concerns the fundamentally *different orientations* they express as they *relate* to their objects. For example, I may think conceptually of the recliner chair in my study, or I may, in sensibly perceiving it, recognize it for what it is by classifying it mentally under the category of a kind of chair. Or again, I may further analyze it cognitively in terms of the quality of its construction, the softness of its cushions, or its tattered appearance. But the cognitive relation expressed here is one of a fundamentally different kind than out of exhaustion to desire it as a place of sleep or as a means to gaining a much-needed rest. Or again, I might apprehend a glass of water on the table before me, whereby I implicitly recognize it as the real signified 'referent' or real empirical object of my mental image or representation of it. And from here I might also find myself making further judgments about it, for example, as to the murkiness or clarity of its fluid contents. But all of this expresses a fundamentally different kind of relation than to be physically thirsty and out of that physical need to desire the same glass of water as a means to satiation or assuagement.

The basic point in all of this is that to *want* something is to *relate* to that 'something' in a quite different way than simply to perceive it or to think about it. The latter, cognitive relation is that of a mental *representation* to its objective *referent* for purposes of description, explanation or meaningful analysis in thought. But the relation of desire or appetition to its object is fundamentally different than this. And here we come to what will prove to be one of the really crucial differences for rationally methodological and procedural questions. For a desire is not in the least concerned with understanding or analyzing its object in terms of its descriptive meaning. It is not, in other words, concerned with its object simply as the 'referent' which relates to its mental image. It is rather concerned with this object fundamentally as a *means* to an *end*, or more exactly, as a means to achieving a real desired end.

But at this juncture an even deeper point of difference emerges in the relations of cognitive and appetitive consciousness to their objects. And in fact, as both Aristotle and Kant lay this out, I have already misspoken in a certain way in my construal of the 'object' of desire. We can express what is meant here by returning to the previous example. If I relate to the glass of water before me, not merely as an object of representational reference within some mental framework of description or explanation, but as a focus of desire through *thirst*: here the real 'object' of my desire is not actually the physical object per se; not really the glass of water itself. Rather, when we attend with greater care to what the desire is really *for*, it will become clear that the actual 'object' which is desired is more correctly the *reality* of being *relieved of thirst*. The glass of water itself is merely a means to achieving this desired end. And it is this desired end which is the real 'object' or destination being sought. Moreover, such an 'object', that is, such a desired end, cannot be achieved or encountered except by an *action*, through which the desired object (being relieved if thirst) *becomes* a reality. Or to use Kant's precise words (which echo Aristotle exactly): 'an object (matter) of the faculty of desire . . . [is] an object whose *reality* is desired'.[7] Or again, to be an object of desire signifies the relation of that desire 'to the action by which it . . . would be *made real*'.[8]

4. Having thus considered briefly how the faculties of cognition and appetition themselves are different, we must now also look further at how the use of reason for each is different. And we should begin this with an important clarification, specifically with regard to the status of thinking in motive or practical reason. For on the face of things, it will surely seem odd to suggest, as we are, that motive or practical reason is not at bottom or fundamentally a conceptualizing or 'thinking' use of reason at all (or perhaps better, not a use of reason *for* thinking at all), but rather a practical one, that is, a use of reason *for* motivated action. For how, it might legitimately be asked, can desires

become a focus of the judging faculty of motive reason at all without being *thought of* as such? How, in other words, can the various options open to me in weighing and adjudicating between means for achieving desired ends be dealt with rationally in any other way than by thinking about them in cognition?

In order to answer this, we must first be entirely clear on what is being claimed here exactly. We will come to some clarificatory examples in a moment, but let me first make just two general comments. In the first place, what is not being claimed is that the percepts and concepts, which are the subject matter of thinking, are not or may not be *present* at all in motive or practical reason. Or more precisely, it does not mean that percepts and concepts aren't themselves *used* by motive or practical reason, just as they are also used in cognitive or discursive reason. We may not forget, in other words, as we have seen above, that the merely mental status of thinking (through concepts and percepts) does not yet make thoughts and thought processes rational, for thoughts and thought processes can be irrational. It is the cognitive *use* of reason which is required to ensure they are appropriately ordered, with regard to questions of referential truth, knowledge or meaningful insight. Similarly, in the practical or motive use of reason for action, it is not again that thoughts (concepts and percepts) are absent, but simply that they are *used* by this exercise of reason, albeit not now for a deepening of knowledge or analytical insight, but as means to achieving real desired ends in life. We can clarify this through some examples.

I may, after hearing of delays on the London Underground, choose to take the bus to Paddington Station instead, in my desire not to miss the 9 a.m. express to Heathrow. Now when I reason to this choice or decision, I do of course have the thought or mental image of 'bus' and 'underground' or 'tube' before me, and I understand their basic meanings as such. But I am not in the least concerned with a phenomenological or semantic analysis of the concepts of 'bus' or 'tube', nor with a scientific analysis of their physical constitution or make-up as moving vehicles. I am rather in my motive reasoning concerned with them entirely as means to achieving real ends in life.

Or when a student after much deliberation chooses one university over another to work toward a medical degree, both the thoughtful deliberation toward that decision and the decision itself are always motivated in accordance with the fulfillment or the making real of certain kinds of desires. These may be, for example, choosing a university close to home because of travel and financial concerns, or because it has an especially distinguished faculty in the student's area of interest, or again because it has good housing facilities for a student with a family, etc.

More than this, even though over the seven- or ten-year period of study all of the student's rational activity in study will indeed be primarily and fundamentally cognitive in nature, nevertheless even all this cognitive activity – when it is genuinely *organized* or reasoned cognitive activity and not just stream-of-consciousness thought – will *always* itself be undertaken on the basis of some underlying motivating desire. Perhaps it will be a desire to go on to specialize in oncology because a family member has recently died of cancer; or perhaps to please one's parents, who have always wanted a medical doctor in the family; or perhaps just for the sheer joy or love or passion for medical science itself, for intellectual curiosity, for discovery, for learning; or perhaps again in the shorter term, just the desire to achieve a good grade on the next day's weekly quiz. What begins to emerge here is that motive or practical reasoning is something more primary than discursive or cognitive reasoning. For *every* actual act of cognitive reasoning – if it is really *organized reasoning* and not just daydreaming – is organized on the basis of some motivating desire.

None of this is to suggest that academic disciplines must for their legitimacy and value all have some 'practical' application. Nor does it mean that the value of a discipline should be measured according to the degree of such a practical application. For many purely theoretical ventures can have different kinds of value even when it may be difficult to find exact practical reasons for engaging in them. It is only to say that all structured reasoning, no matter how purely theoretical or abstract, will always be undertaken on the basis of some motivating impulse or desire. For every single rationally organized thought that we can have will be traceable ultimately to a motivation for such organization, and every such motivation has its roots further in a desire or appetite. And it is *these* motivating desires which ground *all* reflected action, including any action of organized thinking, which are the subject matter or constituents of practical reason.

It may be clear by now what all of this is inevitably pointing to. The domain of motive or practical reasoning, that is, the domain of reasoning from means to real desired ends, the domain of reasoned decision and action in which all other (cognitive) rational endeavor is grounded: this domain of motive reasoning or practical reason is nothing less than our reasoning at the center of life. For practical or motive reason is the 'deciding reason' which in large part defines the very course of our lives. It is the reasoning by which we live and move and decide our becoming.

II

5. The foregoing discussion by itself, however, while perhaps enabling us initially to expand our focus with regard to the activity of reason, does not yet help us forward constructively in the way that it must. For while it may explain, along roughly Kantian, Aristotelian or Thomist lines, how motive or practical reason operates differently than cognitive reason, it has not yet shown how this motive use of reason can be something genuinely *principled* of itself in a robust way that fully merits the designation 'reason'. And we must now turn our attention to that.

The best way to pursue this will be to begin from a certain basic similarity between the cognitive and appetitive faculties, despite their differences. The point is that just as the faculty of cognition, as we have seen in Chapter Two, has both a sensible and an intellective component (through perception and conception), so also the faculty of appetition has a sensible and an intellectual component.

To refresh our memory of the two components first with regard to the cognitive, let us for purely heuristic purposes picture a spectrum between the two poles of 'sensibility' on the one side and 'intellection' on the other, in between which each of the cognitive academic disciplines can be roughly positioned. Pure formal logic, pure mathematics and certain kinds of calculus, for example, operate properly only when they divest themselves of all empirical or sensible influences, and they will therefore fall on or near the intellective pole. Quantum physics likewise is much nearer the intellective pole than the sensible since most of its operations are mathematical. But it is not *purely* intellective, or it is not *pure* mathematics, because as physics it always depends on some component of sensible observation. It would therefore not fall directly at the intellective pole as will formal logic or pure mathematics, although it would be near to it. By contrast, the largely observational sciences of meteorology or ornithology would fall much nearer the sensibility pole since they depend primarily on sensible encounter, bringing intellectively organizational factors to bear on that. Other disciplines would fall in between.

In the same way we can look at the 'sensible' and the 'intellective' as two poles between which all appetitional or motive (practical) consciousness takes place. On the one end of the spectrum there would be the purely sensible appetites which have to do entirely with physical need. And at the other end of the spectrum is what Aquinas (and Kant with him in different words) calls the 'intellectual appetite' or 'intellectual desire', which is to say, 'the will'.[9] Moreover, specifically in Aquinas, it is because the response of love for God and neighbor is expressed from the purest depths of desire through the motive intellect (and not the cognitively speculative intellect) that Thomas, along with the predominance of the theological tradition, and following scriptural directives, speaks of the will or intellective desire also as 'the heart'.[10] It is to be strongly emphasized as such, however, that neither the heart nor the response of love which springs from it ceases to be genuinely rational for Aquinas and the tradition, or to require a committed exercise of the intellect. Its rationality, however, is located fundamentally and originally in the domain of the motive or practical use of reason, which is reason governing desires and motivated action, and not in the speculative use of reason, which is reason governing thinking and cognition.

Before going on to explore the 'principledness' of the motive or practical use of reason, however, which is the main task remaining in this chapter, it will be important to pause briefly to consider the relation specifically between 'the will' on the one hand and 'practical reason' on the other, especially because this relation is treated somewhat differently in Aquinas (following Aristotle) than it is in Kant. For Kant, 'the will' and 'practical reason' are seen at bottom as essentially one and the same thing. In Kant's own words, 'Everything in nature works in accordance with laws. Only a rational being has the capacity to act in accordance with the representation of laws, that is, in accordance with principles, or has a *will*. Since *reason* is required for the derivation of actions from laws, *the will is nothing other than practical reason*.'[11] 'The will' and 'practical reason' are thus in Kant essentially identified, and there is a rigorous logic underlying this identification of which we shall see intimations in later paragraphs.

In Aquinas, however, although indeed 'the will is a *rational* power since it is in the reason',[12] it is not as explicitly identified with practical reason as it is in Kant. One might say that the basic difference between the two accounts is as follows. In Aquinas, the will is seen as in certain ways separated out from practical reason insofar as it is a power of choice and freedom that the practical use of reason prompts and guides by providing the principled *ends* for willing: ends which, as reasoned goals or ideals, are seen to be provisions of practical reason and not of the will per se.[13] We will in a moment see somewhat more exactly what this involves. For Kant, by comparison, the will, *as* rational, carries its rational principledness *within itself* through 'imperatives' which are intrinsic to the very nature of the will as a faculty of rational decision and action. These imperatives, in other words, as we shall see more fully below, are for Kant not provided by practical reason as anything foreign to the will, or as some end or ideal outside of its exercise, but are rather among the constitutive elements or endowments which make the will what it is as the intellectual appetite, or without which it could not be what it is as the power of free rational choice and enacted decision.

Granted, this is all highly compacted, and the reader should not be concerned at this point if the relation between will and practical reason on these two accounts is not entirely clear. And in any case, at the present juncture it does not matter whether we follow Aquinas or Kant on this. The important point for now is only that in both accounts, as in Aristotle, the will is understood as a thoroughly rational power. And in fact we will begin to understand all of this better as we move out of this brief excursus and back to the central question at hand, which has to do with the question of a 'principledness' for the practical or motive use of reason.

We have said that just as the faculty of cognition has both a sensible and an intellective component (as just reviewed), so also the faculty of appetition has a sensible and an intellectual component. At the far end of the sensible appetite would be what Aristotle and Aquinas call the 'nutritive' desires which, as the term suggests, relate entirely to the basic nutritionally physical needs of all organic life. Our own simple illustrations given above, relating to hunger, thirst and bodily fatigue, turn out therefore to be essentially of this kind. As we make our way towards the middle of the spectrum, between the sensible appetite and the intellectual appetite (the will), we would find what for Aquinas and Aristotle would still qualify fully as 'bodily' or 'sensible passions', yet which as such are not merely nutritive in character, but which begin to contain elements of a motivation associated with the will or the intellectual appetite.

Different kinds of examples here might be: the desire for the success of a certain business enterprise, the desire to gain entry into medical school, the desire to meet and embrace a loved one after a long absence, or lusting after one's neighbor's wife, or again the desire to be free of a painful and debilitating illness. All of these, while springing essentially from sensible desire, nevertheless also to one degree or another involve a reasoning from means to ends governed by the will. The last kind of desire in these examples (to be free of a painful illness) relates to what Aquinas calls the 'irascible' appetites, by which is meant those passions or desires whose basic character is that of a natural *avoidance*, such as of pain or fear. By contrast, all of the prior examples relate to what Thomas calls the 'concupiscible' appetites which, as the name suggests, designate passions whose basic character is that of a natural *attraction*, such as those experienced in the physical pleasures. The concupiscible appetites in other words are not to be thought of as concupiscent appetites. That is, they do not all relate to lust or covetousness (although they include these), but rather signify more simply again appetites or desires of attraction as opposed to appetites or desires of repulsion. Indeed, love itself – even the love for God – is thus in Aquinas placed as the highest and purest among the concupiscible appetites.

But now as we come to the other end of the appetitive spectrum, what exactly is meant by a purely 'intellectual appetite' in the will? Or what is meant by a desire that proceeds purely intellectively from the will alone? It was easy enough to picture this pole at the one end of the cognitive spectrum, where the purely intellective academic disciplines such as elementary formal logic, pure mathematics, or certain kinds of calculus provided ready examples of cognitive activity which in its proper exercise is absent of all empirical or sensible factors and is *purely* 'speculative'. But it seems much more difficult, at least initially, to envisage what a purely intellectual desire or appetite could be. And the reason for this initial difficulty, once again, is that we will always be inclined, especially today, to imagine that anything *purely* 'intellectual' would have to be cognitive.

So what then is the status of a purely intellectual desire as found in Aristotle, Aquinas or Kant? In order to approach this correctly, it is indispensable to re-emphasize first that what even all of the previously discussed sensible passional desires most essentially *are*, or what they most essentially serve as, are not *significations for meaning* but rather *motivations for action*. Once this is recognized, what is meant by a purely 'intellectual appetite' becomes much easier to demonstrate, at least in definition. A purely intellectual appetite, or a desire which springs entirely from the rational activity of the will, would be quite simply one which is able to *motivate to action from purely intellective sources*. It would be an entirely rational motivation or impetus, in other words, one which is able to motivate to action apart from the influence of any sensible passions, and indeed in a way that often runs counter to these.

In order to illustrate in a preliminary way what this involves, let me just cite two simple intermediate examples here. I call them 'intermediate' because the examples will involve an activity of practical reason focused through the will that will not yet be purified entirely of sensible components, but they will be able to serve nonetheless as examples of how the practical intellect through the will can motivate to action in a way that runs counter to bodily passional desires. Conserving scarce food supplies even when I am hungry, for example, involves an activity of the motive intellect by which I am able through a reasoned exercise of the will (i.e. through motive or practical reason) to be able to give precedence to the desire to have sufficient for tomorrow even though this runs counter to my sensible desire to have my present hunger fully satisfied today. Or likewise, a student for example may, through a reasoned activity of the will, continue to study in preparation for an important examination even though every immediately present sensible desire – exhaustion, mental fatigue, frustration – runs counter to this.

Now to be sure, in these examples the practical or motive intellect still motivates itself through the will in accordance with a more distant sensible desire: the desire to stay alive bodily in the first example, or in the second, the desire to succeed as a student in order to pursue a career in medicine or whatever. However, a *purely* intellectual appetite in Aristotle, Aquinas and Kant contains no such sensibly motivating component whatsoever, but is rather a motivation which proceeds from the intellect alone. (Justice, for example, will be one such purely rational motivation for Aristotle and Aquinas, as we shall see.) And it is in such a purely intellectual motivation that we come finally to what all three figures see as the possibility of a genuine and indeed universal 'principledness' for practical or motive reason. Or in other words, just as any principledness for the cognitive use of reason is impossible without its own purely intellective foundational principles (e.g. such as those of 'non-contradiction' and 'identity') so also the practical or motive use of reason must be able to supply its own basic principledness if it is to qualify genuinely as reason. So let us start to look more closely at what such a principledness could be.

6. To begin with, it will already be clear to some readers that what we are describing in such a purely intellectual motivation is exactly the most fundamental definition of what Kant means by the principledness of a 'categorical imperative'. For what the term 'categorical' essentially denotes here is nothing else than a motivating imperative which can be recognized in, or derived from, the purely rational 'categories' which for Kant can be found in the motive or practical intellect *alone*, that is, apart from any sensible component whatsoever. The practical intellect, in its concern for ordering means to desired ends through enacted decision, in other words, can for Kant be found to contain its own purely rational principles and categories, just as the cognitive intellect can in its concern with ordering concepts and percepts for questions of referential truth. We cannot go into what these categories are here except to say again that it is only in such a purely intellectual motivating source – i.e. in the ability of the appetitive intellect (i.e. the will) to motivate *itself* entirely through principles and maxims that can be found within the practical intellect – that, for Kant, we will be able to find a principledness for practical reason which is truly 'objective' or universally authoritative, and hence fully 'rational'.

We will return to the import of the Kantian practical endeavor in a moment, where we will discover both an important achievement in it and also, especially for theology, an equally important shortcoming. But let us look first at Aristotle and Aquinas, who will likewise orient their considerations of a principledness for practical reason ultimately in this purely intellective way. The essential difference will be that the principledness in these two will not come to expression as a *purely intellectual imperative* (i.e. categorical imperative) as it is in Kant, but rather in the form of *purely intellectual virtues*. The Aristotelian–Thomist picture, however, will in the end be found to be inherently problematic in a specific way, a problem which Kant implicitly discovers and seeks to correct. So let us review this briefly before returning to what are somewhat different Kantian destinations.

A 'virtue' for motive or practical reason, and thus a virtue for action, is described further by Aristotle as an 'excellence' or a 'perfection' for action and also for dispositions to action. Or more broadly speaking, as Thomas says, a virtue as an excellence is that which 'perfects' any power which human beings have.[14] And while there are a great many individual virtues, Aquinas, following both Aristotle and Ambrose, as well as what he shows to be scriptural sources, identifies four among these that are the 'cardinal virtues': two for the sensible–passional component of the appetitive faculty, and two for the intellective component of the appetitive faculty. The two cardinal virtues perfecting the sensible–passional component are temperance and courage (or fortitude), and the two cardinal virtues perfecting the intellective component of the appetitive nature are justice and prudence (*prudentia*, i.e. 'practical wisdom').[15] All other virtues for the appetitive faculty are seen as in one way or another subordinate to these. The principledness afforded by the virtues can be approached here in either an ascending way (from the 'lower' sensible virtues upward) or in a descending way, but it is clearer and fairer to Aristotle and Aquinas to approach it ascendingly.

Now normally when we think of an excellence or a perfection of anything, we consider it in the sense of a destination of maximal magnification, or as the extreme or the ultimate point and thus the 'ideal' of any endeavor. But the excellence of the virtues, at least the sensible virtues, and as anyone familiar with Aristotle will know, is of an importantly different character. What gives the sensible virtues their unique character in Aristotle is that the perfection or excellence sought in these virtues is not an excellence in the sense of an ultimate or a pinnacle, but rather an excellence in the sense of a 'mean', that is, of an intermediate or equilibrium. Courage, for example, is the mean or excellence between cowardice and rashness; temperance, the mean or excellence between self-indulgence and insensibility, and so on with all the virtues. In all cases, the virtues or excellences are 'destroyed by excess and defect, and preserved by the mean'.[16]

But now the question that immediately arises here is: how is it possible for a virtue as a mean or intermediate to provide a genuine principledness? Or how is such a mean not inherently relative to cultural and situational factors? In other words, where do these virtues themselves come from, or how can they be grounded in a way that allows for a genuine principledness?

Aristotle's initial answer to this is on the face of it somewhat ambivalent and seemingly circular. For he begins by simply locating the grounding principledness of these sensibly passional virtues in the cultivation of what he calls empirical 'habits' which express them. Thus courage emerges and is identified as the virtue that it is, only insofar as it is actually cultivated as a habit in life, i.e. in finding the 'mean' between cowardice and rashness through the cultivation of this mean; and likewise for temperance, as the habit that is found simply in its cultivation as the 'mean' between self-indulgence and insensibility. Now there is a long-standing debate in both Aristotelian and Thomist scholarship about what appears to be an inherently question-begging or circular status in the basic justification of these virtues as habits. For in the one direction, it is argued, the 'origin' and principledness of the virtue of courage or temperance – having been defined as a 'habit' – is found solely in the *cultivation* of this habit through the practice of it. That is, the origin of the virtue is found only in the 'acquisition' of it through the 'practice' of the habit which the virtue *is*. Yet likewise in the other direction, the 'practice' of the habit is itself made possible only through the cultivation of it.[17] The justification of the sensible virtues therefore seems to be based in a vicious circle, which as such seems incapable of providing any robust principledness.

However, before one advances too hastily to the charge of circularity here, what may not be forgotten is that for Aristotle and Aquinas these sensible virtues as habits are themselves rooted in and made subservient to two higher cardinal virtues which are the purely intellective ones: i.e. justice and prudence (*prudentia*). And justice and *prudentia* themselves here turn out not to be grounded or acquired in the cultivation of habits, but, as Aristotle and Aquinas claim, are knowable entirely from the nature of the practical intellect itself. Aquinas, for example, maintains that the virtue of justice can be understood as supplying its own purely rational principledness for the appetitive faculty in that, unlike courage or temperance, what justice demands for action can be known purely intellectively and thus objectively from its analytical definition alone.

The basic rationale here is as follows. It can be known from the very definition of justice, as we are aware of it in the mind, that its essential concern is for 'due action between equals'. And once it is recognized in this definition, its binding principledness as such can be recognized as something necessary for the right relation of means to ends in the purely intellective consideration of *any* equal 'other'. In other words, its principledness as such can be known from reason alone, on the basis of its rational definition, prior to and apart from any sensible encounter with any particular embodied human other in space and time, or apart from the cultivation of it as an empirical habit. *Prudentia* ('practical wisdom') is likewise deemed a purely intellectual virtue for the appetitive faculty (and indeed the principal virtue for this faculty) because it designates the very 'form' in which practical reasoning occurs – i.e. it is the 'form' of reasoning concerned with the right ordering of means to rightly desired ends.

However, at this juncture we encounter a difficulty which seems to echo back to the analytical insufficiencies discussed earlier on in the book. For if we look carefully at the principledness established in these last two virtues we will see that it is grounded in an argument which, at least initially, appears to be just as circular as the principledness of the sensible virtues in the cultivation of habits was circular. For the argument for the principledness of *prudentia* is, in the one direction, simply defined as the 'perfection' of the practical exercise of reason as it operates 'rightly' according to its first principles; and in the other direction it is again *prudentia* itself which *supplies* these first principles. And likewise, the argument for justice is simply grounded in the analytical definition of justice as 'due action between equals', whereupon its rational principledness can be guaranteed as a conceptual tautology.

But once again, one may not be too hasty with the judgment of this as something fully circular or self-guaranteeing. For both Aristotle and Aquinas will seek to locate an even more ultimate ground or principledness for these practical intellectual virtues by appealing to something still higher and final. Yet while in this ultimate appeal they will indeed avoid the charge of circularity, they will find themselves faced with a new and equally vexing shortcoming, which Kant implicitly recognizes. To explain this, it must be understood first that the virtues for Aristotle and Aquinas are not limited only to the practical or motive domain of action, but find an even higher expression, and a more ultimate principledness, back in the speculative domain of cognitive reason. The virtue of 'practical wisdom' (*prudentia* in Aquinas, *phronesis* in Aristotle), which is the principal one for the appetitive faculty, is always rooted more ultimately in what is seen as the higher virtue of 'speculative wisdom' (*sapientia* in Aquinas, *sophia* in Aristotle), which is the principal one for the cognitive faculty.

And this brings us to the vital point. The genuine and ultimate principledness of practical reason will not be found in what practical reason itself can provide, but will rather ultimately be found in something truly final and quintessentially 'objective' which only speculative reason can provide, something which is outside the domain of practical reason. What then is this speculative 'ultimate' to which even practical reason must orient itself for its principledness? It is the metaphysical appeal to the speculative idea of 'the good' or the ideal of 'the good'. It is in the speculatively intellectual appeal to the ideal of the good, in other words, that even justice and *prudentia* as the highest virtues of the appetitive intellect, are ultimately grounded. And through the appeal to this purely speculatively apprehended ideal, which rests securely unto itself within a postulated metaphysical domain of pure essences or being, the charge of circularity can be finally overcome, because a real external and immutable 'reference' and grounding can ostensibly be claimed.

Kant, however, will implicitly see two problems with this. The first is that any such attempted 'reification'[18] of a speculative idea into a real objective metaphysical 'essence' is what both he and Levinas have shown to be the rationally unsustainable error of dogmatism.[19] In other words, even though such a reification is putatively undertaken under the guidance of the speculative understanding, it is a move that speculative reason itself cannot justify, and is thus, by the measure of speculative reason itself, an irrational move. But as Kant implicitly sees, there is beyond this another, methodologically even more basic oversight that occurs here. The point is that such an ultimately *cognitive* appeal to purely speculative metaphysics for practical principledness is already an explicit *abandonment* of the whole *practical* project of reason itself. And it thus fails to supply the genuinely practical principledness for motive reason that this use of reason must have if it is to qualify genuinely as reason. If such a genuine principledness for motivated action is to be found, in other words, it must be one which the practical exercise of reason is able to supply for itself. So let us turn to what Kant offers differently as he seeks to correct this.

III

7. It will have been noted, perhaps as a matter of some curiosity, that in the whole discussion of practical reason thus far, virtually nothing has yet been said about any *moral* component in all of this. And the reason this absence has been possible is that although moral reasoning is indeed a *kind* of practical or motive reasoning, in that it is concerned most fundamentally with reasoning for right action or praxis, it nevertheless comprises only a subset or a particular portion of motive reasoning more broadly. It will be clear, for instance, that none of the simple practical examples given so far have yet contained a moral component. For they have been concerned only with subjective desires (subjective needs and wants), together with the expediencies, pragmatics and practicalities of fulfilling these or realizing them with a view to their natural satisfaction, which is to say with a view to happiness. To return to a prior example, if through an exercise of practical reason I decide to take the city bus to the rail station rather than my usual route on the underground, because I have discovered there are delays on the underground today that will likely make me late for the morning train, I have then indeed made a practical decision but I have not yet made one with any real moral import. That is, I have not yet made a decision in which any question about the goodness as opposed to the evilness of such a decision has been able to arise.

What then is this moral component for practical consciousness or motive reason exactly, or where does it originate? We will be exploring this question in the next chapter, especially in view of something decisive that the Bible itself will be found to pronounce on it. But we can begin with a very simple and basic point of clarification. The origination of our awareness of this moral element is located in an irremediably mysterious presence or emergence within our appetitive or motive faculty of an '*ought*-awareness'.

We will address somewhat more fully as we proceed why this ought-consciousness must be seen as inherently 'mysterious'. But for present concerns, we can begin from something rudimentary. We have seen thus far in Aristotle and Aquinas that desires, whether sensible or intellective, are the sole motivating influences to reasoned action in the fulfillment of an appetite (need or want). And what is initially already mysterious about ought-consciousness in this light is that although, like a desire, it emerges unannounced and immediately within us in the nature of a *motivating* awareness: nevertheless its motivating impulse as such is not toward the practical fulfillment of *any* subjective need or want at all. It announces itself rather in the character of what we ineluctably experience as the authority of an *objective obligation* or demand, or a 'must'.

Indeed, what is even more peculiar about this 'ought' is that although, as a motivation, it seems to emerge from *within* desiring consciousness, nevertheless it announces itself often in a way that runs directly *counter* to the interests of the subjective desires or wants we may be experiencing at the time. We encounter this 'ought' of course most rudimentarily in what we call 'conscience' which, in Barth's words, 'as with a blare of trumpets from another world',[20] declares itself without warning from within us, precisely in condemnation or censure of a subjective want. Now it is true that in its immediate and unreflected origin in conscience, this 'ought' can appear as something often inchoate and unprincipled, and we will address this further in a moment. But it raises its voice of 'ought' nonetheless, and the crucial point as such to be made at this juncture is the following simple and obvious one. It is most fundamentally in virtue of this mysterious ought-consciousness that the very possibility of questions of what is morally good and morally evil can even arise in us. We can have utterly no consciousness of good and evil apart from the consciousness of a moral 'ought'. Or to state this more forcefully in the other direction, the consciousness of the moral ought *just is* the consciousness of good and evil.

We will say much more about this in the next chapter. But the reason for raising it here is to mark what is the really decisive point of departure between the Aristotelian–Thomist and Kantian pictures with regard to the principled-ness of practical or motive reason. For what the Aristotelian–Thomist 'dog-matic' appeal to the metaphysical ideal of 'the good' most essentially leads to in this regard is a very strange result. It leads to the unavoidable result that moral consciousness as ought-consciousness – that is the consciousness of good and evil – itself effectively *derives from* the exercise of practical reason, as this use of reason orients itself ultimately to the metaphysical ideal of 'the good'. (There is an obvious echo here of the Platonic and Augustinian position that the consciousness of evil is derived from the idea of the good, as most essentially a privation of the good.) Or at the very least there is the supposition that moral consciousness acquires its integrity and validity as ought-consciousness, only as this consciousness is secured in and by cognitive reason through the speculative idea of the good.

But as Kant recognizes, the Aristotelian–Thomist supposition that moral consciousness thus derives from the speculative idea of 'the good' in no way accords either with the reality of human moral awareness itself or with anything that reason can justify (which is exactly why it is a dogmatism). For in the awareness of the 'ought', I am aware of the consciousness of good and evil within myself *immediately* and non-derivatively. I am aware of it immediately no less than I am aware of the power to think in mental images as a power that does not derive from an idea but is immediate to me. Or again, I am aware of it immediately no less than I am aware of the power to move in space immediately, that is, in the very constitution of my human being. We can look again to conscience as a witness to the truth of the 'underivedness' of moral consciousness as ought-consciousness. For the point is that we precisely do not encounter conscience within ourselves originally as something that emerges through careful deliberation on the first principles of pure practical reason or of pure speculative reason. We encounter ought-consciousness rather as that which condemns and commends immediately, on its own terms, and often precisely in a way that persists uncomfortably even in the face of the most elegant rationalizations.

We have no choice, therefore, but to make the following crucial observation. Moral consciousness confronts us with the immediacy of something like *a law within us*, even if this law in its most rudimentary form (e.g. in conscience) is inchoate and unprincipled. It is a law, moreover, which speaks from within us, never as something unifying, as reason does, but intrinsically and always as something dividing, that is, as something which always discriminates as it immediately either commends or condemns. Moral consciousness is therefore a third human faculty or power beyond Aristotle's two (of cognition and appetition), inasmuch as it does not itself *derive* from a rational 'right ordering of thoughts' or from 'the right ordering of desires', but in fact already stands in immediate judgment of many desires without the aid of rational reflection, condemning some as vices and commending others as virtuous. We will see in the next chapter that the Bible addresses this law directly and gives a specific name to it.

But let us just note finally here that it is exactly on this point that Kant's *Critique of Practical Reason* departs fundamentally from the Aristotelian–Thomist picture. For far from seeing moral consciousness or ought-consciousness as deriving from a speculative ideal of the good, Kant seeks a general principledness for practical reason precisely by focusing on ought-consciousness *as* an irremediable mystery immediately at the center of our being. Indeed, we might say that in the moral question of ought-consciousness we encounter something no less irremediably mysterious than the age-old cosmological question, as formulated for example by Leibniz, is also irremediably mysterious: 'Why is there something rather than nothing?' (or also the similar one: 'What is a beginning in time?'). It is these two philosophically ultimate and entirely separate natural mysteries which form the basis of Kant's well-known statement: 'Two things fill the mind with ever new and increasing admiration and reverence, the more often and more steadily one reflects on them: The starry heavens above me and the moral law within me.'[21]

This then brings us to Kant's vital insight in the *Critique of Practical Reason*. And we must take at least this one insight very seriously, even though it will be impossible for theology to follow many other aspects of the second *Critique*, including basic features of its destination in the categorical imperative. But the one vital insight is this. The practical or motive use of reason does not find its principledness outside of itself in speculatively and dogmatically postulated *ideals for thinking*, but rather in *imperatives for action* which are known directly from within ought-consciousness per se.

What is especially unique about these imperatives is that their intrinsic rightness or obligatoriness is shown to be *immediately* visible to ought-consciousness or moral consciousness itself. And what 'immediate' means here is that their goodness or necessity as imperatives or obligations is not known 'mediately' through any rational demonstration, and indeed *cannot* be rationally demonstrated. Or in other words, what we perceive as their intrinsic goodness and necessity as imperatives for action is not known through the demonstration of *any further reason* for their obligatoriness, by reasoning from 'means to obligatory ends'. They are rather directly or immediately apprehended in ought-consciousness as *ends in themselves*.

For example, the goodness or rightness of the obligation never to treat fellow human beings solely as means to ends – i.e. never solely as objects to be used – but always with the dignity that befits them as fellow subjects, cannot be demonstrated or proven by any amount of moral reasoning. We do indeed recognize this as an obligation or imperative, but we recognize it precisely as an obligation which needs no further reason to justify its rightness. It is known immediately as a 'reason in itself' or an 'end in itself'. These imperatives, then, are not the *products* of moral reasoning but are rather, together with other 'moral endowments', the very basis of moral consciousness as ought-consciousness.[22]

We cannot here get into the specifics of how Kant develops this as a philosophical system. Nor will we be able to follow him through to his conclusions that practical reason can be genuinely rational and principled only when it orients itself to the imperatives or demands on action *that it can know from within itself*, as the condition of its own possibility. Nevertheless the one vital insight which remains intact is that when we allow practical reason to operate fully in its own integrity through the will, without surreptitiously taking refuge in the quasi-securities of a dogmatically exercised speculative reason, we will find that it orients itself fundamentally and intrinsically always to *imperatives or commands for action* which are apprehended immediately within ought-consciousness, as the condition of the possibility of this consciousness, and not to speculatively posited *ideals for thinking*. We shall in the next chapter begin to see, through attentiveness to the scriptures, and in a way that departs significantly from Kant, how exactly an imperative for motive reason announces its authority in a fundamentally different way than an ideal for speculatively cognitive reason.

Notes

1 Hegel, *Science of Logic*, tr. A. V. Miller (London: Allen & Unwin, 1969), p. 824.
2 Edmund Husserl, *Ideas: General Introduction to Pure Phenomenology*, tr. W. R. Boyce (New York: Macmillan, 1931), pp. 230–1.
3 *On the Soul*, III.3, in *The Complete Works of Aristotle*, ed. Jonathan Barnes (Princeton: Princeton University Press, 1984), vol. 1, pp. 641–92.
4 See *Summa Theologica* Ia Q79–Q83; Ia IIae Q22–48; Ia IIae Q55–Q76 (New York: Benzinger Brothers, 1911), hereafter *ST*.
5 *On the Soul*, III.9.
6 *On the Soul*, III.9.
7 *Critique of Practical Reason*, in Mary J. Gregor (ed.) *Immanuel Kant, Practical Philosophy* (Cambridge: Cambridge University Press, 1996), 5:21, p. 155, emphasis added (hereafter *CPrR*). See also e.g. Aristotle, *On the Soul*, III. 10.
8 *CPrR* 5:57, p. 186, emphasis added.
9 See e.g. *ST* Ia Q9 A1; Q80 A2; Ia II ae Q22 A3; Q24 A3.

10 *ST* Ia IIae Q24 A3. The scriptures themselves consistently identify the heart as the seat of desire: e.g. 1 Chron. 29.18; Pss. 20.4; 37.4; Eccl. 2.10; Isa. 26.8; Rom. 1.24.

11 Kant, *Groundwork for the Metaphysics of Morals* in Mary J. Gregor (ed.) *Immanuel Kant, Practical Philosophy* (Cambridge: Cambridge University Press, 1996), 4:413, p. 66, emphasis altered.

12 Ia IIae Q10 A2, emphasis added; see also e.g. Ia IIae Q9 A5, 6; Ia Q82 A1, 5.

13 In fact, the relation here is considerably more complex than this, in that the practical intellect is said to motivate the will in one way (as providing the 'end' to which the will exercises itself); and the will is said to motivate the practical intellect in another way (as providing the 'agency' by which the practical intellect is engaged in this way or that; see *ST* Ia Q82 A4). The will as the intellectual appetite is also further said to be able to motivate or 'move' *itself* as well as being motivated or moved by the sensible appetite (see *ST* Ia IIae Q9 A2, 3).

14 *ST* Ia IIae Q 56 A 1.

15 *ST* Ia IIae Q61.

16 *Nicomachean Ethics*, Book II.2.20–5; II.7.9–10, in *The Complete Works of Aristotle*, vol. 2, pp. 1729–867 (hereafter *NE*).

17 See *NE*, Book II.5.33–8.

18 To 'reify' means to convert into a real thing, or in this case to convert a mere idea of reason into a really existing or objectively 'subsisting' metaphysical entity.

19 See pp. 27, 63.

20 Karl Barth, *The Word of God and the Word of Man* (London: Hodder and Stoughton, 1928), p. 10.

21 *CPrR* 5:162.

22 See e.g. Kant, *The Metaphysics of Morals* 6:399 in *Immanuel Kant, Practical Philosophy* (Cambridge: Cambridge University Press, 1996); see also p. xiv in the same volume.

Chapter 6

Rational Integrity, Finitude and Sin

I

1. We have throughout this book been concerned with a single defining and motivating theological question or task. We are seeking to attend to, and in the full integrity of reason to become accountable to, the present reality of God at the center of life as testified by the scriptures and as witnessed and affirmed with assurance in faith. This can be called a 'theologically apologetical' venture because it is concerned to go beyond doctrinal questions of description and interpretive meanings – as these doctrinal questions themselves are pushed further to their own ground in the reality of God on which they depend – to giving an explanatory account of the truth of these meanings in life and embodied history.

We have seen also, however, that under the impact of an array of powerful idealistic, analytical, phenomenological, literary and other influences, this kind of questioning has to a large degree disappeared as a primary focus of theological concern. Theology (and Christian philosophy) has instead become quite broadly content to defend its 'validity' and integrity as an intellectual discipline within the conceptually self-guaranteeing securities of linguistic, phenomenological and epistemological theory: whether (a) by confining itself to the interpretive analysis of texts as 'end-stations' of enquiry; or (b) by reconfiguring revelation itself as something essentially conceptual which is 'given' directly within cognitively discursive domains; or (c) by effectively ignoring divine revelation and restricting its focus instead to the internal epistemological warrantability of 'Christian belief' and so on. Theology has thereby in its fundamental questioning often become something conceptually mono-visional. If, however, revelation is indeed disclosed at the center of life and not in theory, then theology must become attentive again to all of the ways that human beings know and relate to the reality in which they find themselves alive, and not just one.

One of the central focuses we are seeking to reinvigorate here as such is an attentiveness to revelation as a causally dynamic disclosure in life, generating real effects in life, as it has predominantly been viewed in the past, rather than as something pre-eminently conceptual or phenomenological which is

'communicated' directly to discursive cognition. We have seen the fundamental inadequacy of these latter kinds of approaches in being able to orient
themselves in any conceptually sustainable way even to God's transcendence,
whether through ontological questioning or through addressing God's transcendence as 'the Wholly Other'. The question remains therefore how theology as a discipline of the intellect orients itself with rational accountability
to its ground as something presently living and real, which is to say as causally
dynamic in life. This question must be approached differently today than it
often has been in the past, however. Within a pre-modern cosmology, for
example, theology still had available to it certain kinds of substantialist
metaphysical appeals for addressing such questions, appeals which are no
longer tenable today.

It is to this end that I want now and for the remainder of this book to begin
applying to our problem the findings of the last chapter, where it was shown
that beyond the cognitive use of reason we also find ourselves rationally
engaged in life in a quite fundamentally different way, through the motive and
appetitive use of reason (which is to say the 'practical' use of reason). Indeed,
we saw that although this employment of reason has become largely over-
looked as a focus of critical study, it is nevertheless a use of reason which so
suffuses and grounds any and every aspect of conscious human life that we are
constantly employing it even when we may not notice we are doing so. What
most basically distinguishes this use of reason from the discursive or cognitive
use is that in its judging activity it is concerned not with percepts and concepts
for questions of meaning in thinking, but with appetitions (desires) and
motivations for the making real of desired ends through action.

An important part of what we will be seeking to demonstrate from here
on, therefore, is that whenever theology seeks to be attentive to its ground in
the present reality of God – or when it seeks to account for the truth of its
meanings, not analytically in theory but really in life – it must focus its
endeavors fundamentally or originally through the appetitive and motive
('practical') use of reason, and not most fundamentally the discursive use. This
is not, however, to say that the predominance of actual doctrinal or apologetical activity will not still remain essentially cognitive or discursive. Nor as
such is it to diminish the indispensability and importance for theology of
interpretation, hermeneutics, textual criticism and so on, for this is again
predominantly what theology is and does. It is only to say that when theology
wants to ask about the truth or reality of what it is considering – the revealed
reality in which theology is grounded and on which it depends – its questioning must be focused and oriented fundamentally through motive or appetitive
reasoning and not fundamentally through discursive or cognitive.

2. As a way into commencing with the task of demonstrating and explaining
this, however, some further specific backdrop will have to be laid with regard
to the question of 'revelation and reason'. We will be interested especially
in the often implicit perception today that divine grace itself becomes active in
the very thinking processes of the believer in the consideration of this question. Let me commence toward that end then with some observations about

the activity of the theologian per se as he or she engages in the exercise of doing theology under the common definition of it as a discipline of 'faith seeking understanding'.

To begin with, even if we assume, as at least under the foregoing definition we would need to, that grace must infuse and undergird the task of theological thinking – since the revealed 'subject matter' in relation to which the theologian seeks understanding is encountered and recognized first through faith and by grace – even so, this infusing and undergirding of the theological endeavor by grace must not be misunderstood. What I mean by this is that there is an increasingly common implicit assumption in many discussions today that because theology's 'subject matter' is 'God', that therefore the normal and naturally exacting rigors, limitations and critically defining functions of reason can be adjusted, expanded or even dispensed with when required, by appeal to God himself, who ostensibly authorizes this.

This can be done in an array of ways, several of which we have already seen evidence of above. But speaking specifically now to the present context, it can be done in one way when theological thinking, under the guidance of grace, is seen as generating new levels of cognitive expansion through 'prophetic' gifts of illumination which grant esthetic and philological insight into 'subterranean' levels of truth.[1] On such a view, it is theology which under the guidance of grace 'saves reason and fulfils and preserves philosophy' whereas philosophic reason 'left to itself, brings itself . . . to its own end'.[2] It can also be done in another way, as we shall discuss more fully in a moment where, under the exercise of grace, God himself is found to 'commandeer' the theologian's own cognitively rational processes against their normal functions. Through such a commandeering, the most basic and intrinsic constraints and axioms of reason in its 'natural' usage are supernaturally lifted, so as to ensure that theology can accomplish its purposes as 'talk about God'. Or it can be done in yet other ways, for example, through neoplatonist calls for an 'expansion' of reason to its full 'grandeur' within a 'universe of reason', a universe which is seen to contain the revealed Logos (understood as 'Word and reason') of God within it as its apogee.[3] The considerable variety and prominence of confessional perspectives from which such views have recently come to be disseminated have then filtered through to a more general blurring of critical distinctions between revelation and reason. And one finds them reflected much more broadly where the following kinds of statements are not uncommon: 'intellectual activity is itself sacred and a form of worship', or 'reason is employed, directed and improved by religious commitment', or again, 'Christ provides the justification for human powers of reasoning because he is the cosmic and indwelling Logos'.[4]

All of this, however, also has another side to it in that it has contributed to what can be seen as the emergence of new a kind of obscurantism in theological discourse. This new manifestation is not like the more obvious forms, which declare themselves openly as anti-rational (e.g. Foucault, Rorty),[5] but rather comes to expression in a more subtle form. Indeed it claims to uphold reason in '*truer*' and more comprehensive ways, and it typically supports this claim on the basis of a two-stage rationale. It first declares that the really rigorous and critically exacting yet fundamentally *defining* demands of rational integrity are too 'narrow' to accommodate Christian transcendence or revelation, and it dismisses these demands as such. It then secondly replaces this 'narrow' and genuinely rigorous version with a new, kinder and gentler rendition of 'reason', which has been redefined specifically to accommodate the content and purposes of the particular field of discourse it is meant to serve. Whereupon it is able to decree, without perceiving any further obligation to account rationally for this decree (since it has already removed itself from the rigors of any normal or truly public accountability), that this is indeed the 'higher' and 'more comprehensive' form of reason, because it can accommodate transcendence with a kind of effortlessness that 'narrow' reason, with its unwavering commitments to clarity, logical consistency, public accountability and genuine circumspection cannot, or can only do with difficulty.[6] But all that has really happened here is that the problem itself has been deflated. Or to return to the earlier quotation from Donald MacKinnon, the problem here has simply been converted into a solution and as such into a convenient 'recipe for dissolving a multitude of problems'.[7]

Now it may seem unfair or unjustified to bring Barthian theology back into discussion in this context, especially since the Barthian attention to critical rigor and internal consistency is not only exemplary but often formidable. Nevertheless, several key moves are made right at the heart of its fundamental methodology (i.e. in the relation of revelation and reason) which exemplify perfectly the kinds of anti-rational measures theology will be forced to adopt – an anti-reason which will be 'justified' under appeal to the authority of grace – when it orients itself to revelation as a 'communication' occurring originally and pre-eminently in cognitive domains. The compromises that Barth will eventually be allowing with regard to rational procedure in theology are already signaled in his dictum that 'revelation is the self interpretation of God'.[8] But in order to put into a proper perspective what needs to be said here, let us revisit briefly the discussions in Chapter Four, where we spoke of the inadequacies of the language of alterity for theological questioning about God.

3. It is well known that Barth, like Levinas, although now from a thoroughly theological perspective, is especially forceful in his rejection of the propriety of 'ontological' language for fundamental theological questioning about God. And Barth too therefore moves to the language of alterity, speaking frequently instead, especially in his early work, of God's transcendence as the transcendence of 'the WHOLLY OTHER'.[9] It is true that he backs away from this exact kind of language later on as he begins the *Church Dogmatics*. But the language he will use to replace it – for example, in speaking of God as 'indissolubly subject' – remains in its fundamentals committed with the same force to these basic kinds of orientations.

Now there are many ways in which what Barth offers here is of great value and power in articulating a proper orientation to God's transcendence in revelation. The importance and value of Barth's development of the view that the 'being' of God may not be considered as an 'existent' in the universe of the 'there is' comes to an especially forceful expression, for example, in his celebrated treatment of 'The Hiddenness of God'.[10] The hiddenness of God's 'being' cannot for Barth be seen as merely a hiddenness *to* human objective viewing, roughly along the lines of 'the Platonic or Kantian [understanding of] a rational idea withdrawn from all perception and understanding'.[11] God's true hiddenness, in other words, is not primarily a hiddenness *to* or hiddenness *from* human beings or human capacities; rather, 'God's hiddenness is the hiddenness *of God*. It is one of His properties.'[12] What Barth means by this can be shown from his treatment of the doctrine of the Trinity. The point made there is that God in his eternal unconditionedness and freedom is not limited by any 'form' at all, not even a form which we might classify as 'being' (see e.g. Deut. 4.15–18). And it is exactly in virtue of God's having no such 'form' that his hiddenness 'is one of his properties'. Barth makes clear as such that the revelation of God, especially in the incarnation of Jesus Christ, is not therefore to be seen as a 'change' in the 'form' of God, but rather as the '*taking* form' of him who in his utter freedom is not constrained by any 'form'. For Barth no less than for Aquinas then, God's 'being' cannot be 'included' in any totalizing language of 'all there is'.

Nevertheless, Barth now encounters difficulties which did not face Aquinas in the same way. For having diagnosed revelation, as we have seen above, as a 'communication' which by its analytical definition occurs as an event of God in conceptual cognition, Barth has restricted himself entirely – and here not unlike Husserl, or for that matter, Levinas – to the essentially phenomenological domain of subject and object, subject and predicate, representation and reference, same and other, for the further theological treatment of God's transcendence. This means that, having rightly rejected any 'objectification' or 'ontologization' of God, Barth is therefore left with no choice but to move to the opposite phenomenological pole, and like Hegel to take up the language instead of 'subject' and 'subjectivity' in speaking of God. And the divine subjectivity as such must be the subjectivity of a 'wholly other'. Or in Barth's words, God is 'the one . . . who is subject, indeed indissolubly subject', even in His self-revelation.[13] Indeed, the radical otherness of the divine subjectivity – which is to say with Levinas, the required absence of any objectifiable 'common frontier' between divine and human subjectivity – is fortified further in Barth's insistence that 'the divine subjectivity [must not be] sucked up into human subjectivity nor may we seek to find even any analogy of being between the two'.[14]

Yet already here, the first signs of more deeply rooted methodological inconsistencies and failings begin to emerge. For even though he insists that the divine subjectivity is incomparable, even through analogy, to human subjectivity, it is nevertheless quite clear that we can have utterly no idea what such a statement about God's subjectivity could possibly mean except by analogy to our own subjectivity. Indeed, Barth himself must mean that there is *some* purchase to be gained theologically from the normal human understanding of the term 'subjectivity', otherwise he would surely have used an entirely different term, and thus avoided any confusion altogether. But let us set this aside and begin to look at the basic kind of questioning that Barth sees as now necessary in light of the radical otherness or non-objectifiability of the 'indissolubly subject'.

Because God in his self-revelation confronts theology not as any 'ontologizable' objective being, but as the one 'who is subject, and indeed indissolubly subject in his revelation', therefore now the *first* question of theology must be formulated in a certain way. The first question of theology can no longer be 'Does God exist?' or 'What is God?' or 'How do we know God?'[15] For all such questions are intrinsically objectifying and ontologizing within the domain of the 'there is'. The first and only proper question, therefore, with which all theology must begin, as it stands before this God who is 'indissolubly subject', is the question '*Who is* God in revelation? . . . *Who is* the self-revealing God?'[16] Only the question 'who?' addresses subjectivity *as* subjectivity, for every other question – especially the predominantly operative philosophical questions of 'how?' and 'what?' – are objectifying questions which treat their sources of concern as objects of 'interest' to be 'comprehended' (in Levinas's language) and therefore grasped or possessed.

We know this even from human relationality. For it is only in the recognition that the human being before us is 'another I', that is, another rationally self-aware and self-determining subject, that we see fit to address the human person as a 'who' in his or her own right as such, and never merely as an object. However, as Bonhoeffer will later say (and the resonance with Levinas will be especially clear here), it is impossible for us to address the fellow human being genuinely and wholly as 'who?' – that is, in an entirely dispossessive way – without the unavoidable presence, even in this 'who?' address, of the possessively objectifying demands also of the 'how?' and 'what?' And Barth's point in this light is that God, as '*indissolubly* subject' – i.e. as the one whose 'being' contains nothing objectifiable – is utterly immune from any such objectification, contrary to the way in which human subjects are still able to be objectified.

It is here, however, that certain insurmountable theological problems begin to surface in the Barthian project. The specific problem that Barth knowingly faces is this. Barth fully acknowledges that as theology goes about its tasks, which are in their essential constitution cognitive and conceptual, it *must* engage even with this 'who?' as a 'subject matter' of its own conceptually thematic questioning, and therefore unavoidably as an 'object' of its questioning. And it is at this juncture that we come to a development in Barth that moves into the anti-rational, in that the authority of revelation will be used to 'commandeer' reason against itself for theological purposes. The move runs to the methodological and revelational heart of what Bonhoeffer would later criticize as Barth's 'positivism of revelation' as discussed above, or to what I am also calling a self-guaranteeing tauto-theology.

The point is that after having fully excluded the admissibility of *any* objectifying language for addressing God as 'indissolubly subject', Barth then not only goes on to allow it anyway, but to declare that the objectification of God is indispensable. Eberhard Jüngel, one of Barth's most distinguished followers, expresses succinctly what will turn out to be the highly conflicted and rationally unsustainable position Barth is forced to adopt here. In Jüngel's words, even though God's 'being' as indissolubly subject entirely prohibits any objectification whatsoever, nevertheless 'insofar as the knowing man is the *subject* of the knowledge of God, God must be spoken of as the *object* of this knowledge. In this sense talk about God's "being-as-object" is indispensable' (original emphasis).[17] Or as Jüngel continues, now quoting Barth directly, Barth 'makes clear that the problem of the knowledge of God and that of God's objectivity "is itself already a part of the doctrine of God because it can definitely consist only in a representation of the being and activity of God" '.[18] Or in other words, God's objectivity is already part of the dictum that revelation 'interprets *itself*' within doctrine, as the theologian remains open to the work of grace in his or her logical intellect. To be sure, as Barth's own words now further make clear, 'the objectivity of the divine . . . is not one object in the series of other objects of man's cognizance';[19] and 'certainly we have God as an object but not in the same way we have other objects';[20] and again, he insists that he hereby in no way intends to 'commend some kind of realism or objectivism'.[21]

Nevertheless, it is exactly in these denials that Barth himself fully recognizes that he has left us here with two explicit contradictions, and in his characteristic rigor he knows he must reconcile them. The first apparent contradiction is that although, on the one hand, any objectifying talk of God is declared to be entirely disallowed, it is, on the other hand, declared to be mandatory. The second is that although, on the one hand, the divine 'objectivity' is stipulated as being removed from all comparative and determinative demands of normal objectivity, yet, on the other hand, it must be recognized as 'object' nonetheless.

And it is specifically in the way that Barth undertakes to reconcile these apparent contradictions that brings us to one of the centerpoints of what makes his work in these areas not only tauto-theological but also at this fundamental point anti-rational. For Barth now goes on to 'resolve' the opposites in these apparently explicit contradictions by appealing to a 'miracle'[22] which the Holy Spirit works in the processes of reason itself, that is, in the hiddenness and privacy of the individual's phenomenal consciousness, by grace through faith. And the way that this (ir)rational miracle is seen as working exactly is as follows. The intrinsically objectifying or representational reason of the believing theologian is, in Barth's words, miraculously 'exempted'[23] by the Holy Spirit from its own most basic and defining integrities, constraints and rigors, so as to allow God, who is not an object, to be brought permissibly into objective consideration after all, since theology as a discipline of the human intellect must operate in these terms. Or Barth will speak likewise in terms of a 'sanctification' of the reasoning capacities of the believing theologian, a sanctification which unilaterally alters these capacities (as they are exercised under grace in faith), so as to make theology as theo-logy possible. In Barth's own words (as Jüngel also quotes him): 'God "*exempts*" himself as well as the . . . man' from the defining operations of the discursive intellect's representational and objectifying structure and 'makes himself known as separated from all other objects. At the same time he also sanctifies man in his relationship to himself, i.e. puts him into a separated position'.[24]

Now again, there is indeed a theologically self-guaranteeing security which can be gained by such 'exempting' appeals to revelation. But beyond the fact that these procedures themselves must by any normal measure be seen as entirely anti-rational procedures, the result here is also deeply conflicted in another way. The point is that it is utterly impossible for us, in the actual task of *doing* theology, to 'think' God as 'object' *except* as an object of *thought*, and thus inescapably as an object among other objects. We need only to try this once or twice to assure ourselves of its futility. In other words, the miraculous 'exempting' which is posited here in pure theory can never be actually efficacious in the real work of doing theology. It is therefore a miraculous 'exempting' which can have a bearing only in a pure posited theory of dogmatical procedure within itself, and not in the actual reflective task of the theologian per se. And a 'miracle in theory' is just as much a contradiction in terms and therefore meaningless, as a 'theoretical act of kindness' is a contradiction in terms and meaningless.

4. But let us in light of all of this return to our original premise, and to the initial observation that followed from it, in order to approach the issue at hand in a different way. We have been asking about the activity of the theologian per se, engaging in the discipline of theology under the common definition as an exercise in 'faith seeking understanding'. And we have said above that even if we assume, as at least on such a definition we would need to, that grace must infuse and undergird the task of theological thinking – since the revealed 'subject matter' in relation to which the theologian seeks understanding is encountered and recognized first through faith and by grace – even so, this infusing and undergirding of the theological endeavor by grace must not be misunderstood. For as we have now seen, and as any practicing theologian knows full well, it quite obviously cannot mean that the way that grace through faith makes itself effective for me as a theologian is by miraculously 'exempting' my cognitive processes from the normal and natural rigors of cognitive or representational reason, in the way that Barth suggests, and as implied in different degrees also by the other related views noted more briefly above.

The undergirding gift of special grace here, in other words, is not a gift which would then allow the engraced theologian, alone among all other thinkers, to overcome the natural rigors or limitations inherent in and demanded by critical thinking (limitations under which other disciplines would by implication then still 'suffer'), for the theological purposes of allowing God, who is not a determinable object, to become a determinable object for cognition or discursive consciousness after all, as this kind of consciousness requires it. Any such 'positing' of an exemption from the normal demands of cognitive reason for theology would not only impute to the believing theologian a kind of superhuman intellectual capacity, a capacity which any theologian, in the actual practice of doing theology, will be all too aware that he or she does not possess. It would also make theology in its roots an entirely anti-rational endeavor by any visibly normative measure of reason.

This brings us to a vital threshold of distinction. The point is that there are two completely different kinds of 'limitations' which confront theological questioning in such considerations, two limitations which must be carefully distinguished and not conflated. One set of limitations is the fully natural one which we are subject to simply in virtue of the inherent *finitude* of our human existence as creatures in space and time. The other is a fundamentally different 'limitation' which according to the scriptures comes about through the entry of sin, which is to say through a radical alienation from God by a corruption of desire. We will discuss the difference between these in greater depth below. But the important point here is to recognize that we may not confuse the work of grace which is given to redeem us from the blindness and alienation incurred through the entry of sin and to restore an utterly broken communion, to mean also an overcoming of the natural integrities, constraints and limitations which define us by virtue of the finiteness of our creaturely being in space and time. Indeed, if we were to expect that the believing theologian, through the decision of faith and by grace, becomes exempt from what are the natural defining constraints and finite capacities of created reasoning or cognitive consciousness, including what Kant shows are the natural illusions of this consciousness:[25] then we might just as well expect that the believing theologian also thereby becomes exempt from the natural constraints and illusions of sensible or empirical consciousness. Or we might just as well expect, for example, that for the believer the moon should no longer appear larger on the horizon than it does overhead.

Let us then try to frame what is at stake here in somewhat different terms. When the scriptures speak of the 'renewing of the mind' through faith which brings a transformation in the life of a believer (Rom. 12.2), what is quite clearly meant or demanded here is not a renewal of the mind with respect to its capacity for cognitive apprehension, whether empirically and causally with regard to percepts, or logically and inferentially with regard to concepts. The renewing of the mind by the Holy Spirit is neither an expansion of the capacities of logical reasoning nor an exemption from the natural rigors of logical reasoning. Nothing of this sort is intended. Rather, as Ephesians takes up this same theme – and here we will see the importance of the distinctions made in the last chapter beginning to emerge – the injunction here explicitly is 'to put off your old self which is being corrupted by its deceitful *desires*' so as in *this* way 'to be made new in the attitude of your minds', and then from there 'to put on the new self, created to be like God in true righteousness and holiness' (Eph. 4.23, 24). In other words, even if we set aside the theologically unsustainable idea of an 'exemption' from the rigors of reason by faith, even excepting this, the 'renewal of the mind' intended here is not one which makes the theologian a sharper logical thinker. It is rather the desiring and motive intellect which is primarily addressed in the renewal of the mind. And in order to understand the ground of this renewal which revelation offers, we will need to turn our attention to a focus on this 'old self' whose desires, according to Ephesians, are 'deceitful'.

II

5. That human beings are presently in a state of alienation from God through
the entry of sin is a central tenet of Christian theology, and the origins of this
alienation are traced back to an event which theology thematizes as 'the fall'
away from God. Now it is reasonably safe to say that Christian treatments of
the fall can by and large be seen as taking one of two basic kinds of orienting
directions on what it is meant to signify. These two orientations are sometimes
distinguished in terms of the basic difference between what can roughly be
called an Augustinian account and an Irenaean account of the fall, which is to
say the fall seen either as a specific and real historical event, or as something
contained in the unfolding of the creational process itself.

But this question cannot and need not be our concern here. What is
important is that in whichever of the two basic directions it is understood, it
is seen as integral to the essential character of this movement into alienation
that it is a fall away from an unbroken communion with the living reality of
God or with the very 'being' of God. 'Prelapsarian' human beings, in other
words, enjoy unbroken and unhindered communion with the reality of God,
or with God in his very 'being'. My interest in what follows is not to engage
in a deeper doctrinal discussion on the theological treatise of sin or of the fall.
I am interested only in what can and must be said about the basic character of
this 'alienation' itself, for the purposes of coming back later to illuminate
through it our own central concern, which is the present reality of God at
the center of life in the revelation of Jesus Christ. For the revelation of Jesus
Christ is given precisely for the redemption and reconciliation of the world
to God, which is to say it is given in grace for the purposes of restoring the
relation and communion that was severed through the entry of sin. And the
point is that if we are to understand the nature of revelation properly in its
present reality as that which effects the restoration, then we must also seek
to understand the basic nature of the alienation itself. For again, the redemption and reconciliation offered by God in Jesus Christ are addressed precisely
to the heart of that alienation.

What I wish to do then in order to illuminate this is to ask just two basic
questions, one with regard to the divine nature and one with regard to human
nature, which are as follows. Firstly, is it possible from the scriptures to identify anything of the *divine* nature, or anything of the 'being' of God, which
the fall away from God through sin is an alienation *from*? And secondly, is
there anything that can be said from the scriptural testimony about what it
is in *human* nature, or in the human created constitution per se, which precipi-
tates or effects the alienation from perfect communion with God?

Let us begin with the first of these questions. It is generally agreed that
whatever else we can say theologically about God in terms of his 'attributes'
(e.g. omnipotence, omniscience, omnipresence), what God *is* in his very 'being'
or reality, in a way which cannot be numbered among the attributes, is
divine righteousness or holiness, and divine love. As Barth states this in
Trinitarian terms, God's most intrinsic nature (or 'essence' as he puts it) must

be understood as 'the threeness of God's holiness, mercy and love'.[26] Echoing Schleiermacher, Barth goes on to say that 'all the attributes we can assign to God' do not relate 'to his essence as such' (i.e. not to his essence as holiness, mercy and love) but rather to 'his acts' of revelation to the world.[27]

What this importantly implies is that we may not see God's 'being' or reality merely in any sense of 'pure being' or 'supreme being', but always as already consisting in divine righteousness and love. For as Isaiah says, 'the holy God will show himself holy by his righteousness' (Isa. 5.16); and as John says, 'God is love' (1 Jn 4.8). Indeed, it is because God loves *in* righteousness that Barth, speaking specifically of the righteousness of God, is willing to say that 'whoever understands him on this point understands him wholly'.[28] For God is the one who alone is the 'Holy One' (1 Sam. 2.2), the 'Righteous One' (Isa. 24.16); the ground on which Moses meets God is 'holy ground'; the signet on Aaron's forehead is inscribed with the words 'HOLY TO THE LORD' (Exod. 28.36; 39.30); and again, 'The holy God will show himself holy by his righteousness' (Isa. 5.16).

It must immediately be added here, however, that the holiness or righteousness of God that is declared here has nothing whatsoever to do with any human ideal of 'the good', not even analogically, whether such an ideal is posited philosophically or 'theologically'. For as Barth rightly says, even – and indeed especially – in all of our highest ideals of the good or righteousness 'we suffer from unrighteousness'.[29] How it is therefore even possible to know what we are speaking of in the divine righteousness, if it is wholly incomparable to any human righteousness, will be discussed in greater depth in the next chapter. But for our present concerns, the important finding that now begins to emerge from the above is this.

It is the divine righteousness and not the divine love against which our alienation from God's very 'being' or reality must be defined. For according to Romans 8, nothing in all creation, not even 'demons', nor indeed even death which is the ultimate fruit of sin, can separate us from the love of God. We will find below how this alienation from God – as most essentially an alienation from divine righteousness – comes to be mirrored in revelation as a restoration of the divine righteousness, both in revelation as law and in the revelation of Jesus Christ.

But let us turn to our second question, which was to ask whether there is anything identifiable in human nature, or in the constitution of the human creature per se, through which the alienation originally comes. And here we will indeed find something stated clearly and consistently in the Bible, something which echoes what we have already seen implied above in the character of the 'renewed mind'. What will become clear from the scriptures as we proceed is that the alienation from God occurs originally and fundamentally as a corruption of *desire*, that is, a corruption originating in the appetitive and motive powers and not originally as something coming through a misperception or misconception in the cognitive powers.

But this needs to be explained, and in order to do that, let us turn directly to the creation narrative itself to see what can be gleaned more broadly there with respect to these two faculties. In doing so, we will find firstly that several things that can be inferred about Adam's cognitive faculties even prior to the entry of sin. And in order to make this clear we will need now to amplify further the important distinction noted only briefly above between the natural limitations of Adam in virtue of his created finitude, and the radically new and fundamentally different limitations that come to Adam through sin.

6. To begin with then, there are natural constraints and limitations – i.e. natural *capacities* – within which Adam even before the entry of sin is confined by virtue of his very createdness. In other words, 'capacities', as the term itself already stipulates, are *limitations* as much as they are *powers*. Created embodied powers, as finite powers, are always specific powers, constituted as specific abilities and capacities, and are therefore limited powers. The visual capacities of the eye cannot hear, the aural capacities of the ear cannot see, and the discriminating powers of the mind cannot move physical objects and so on. In short, Adam's capacities as a finite being are the capacities they are, precisely in their confined constitution *as* those powers and not other powers.

Even more than this, it is precisely by Adam's creaturely confinement to *human* capacities that he is also precisely *defined* as a human being, or more exactly, that he is defined within the limits of what it is to be a human being. In other words, these are limitations that Adam has in his very constitution as a finite creature, and which as such do not result from the entry of sin. Far from that, they are rather limitations within which he already exists in the very *perfection* and integrity of his createdness as a human being (i.e. his perfection and integrity as a man and not as an angel or a camel or a tree). And this also means that Adam's cognitively perceptual and conceptual faculties, which in part constitute or define his human being, are likewise, in the very perfection of their integrity as such, finite and limited faculties.

But this in turn now points further to something crucial. For it is precisely in virtue of their finite character as intrinsically *limited*, that the conceptual and perceptual faculties are also, as finite, intrinsically *limiting*. We can see this, for example, in the way that the conceptualizing intellect engages with the images that are brought to it through sensible perception. For the intellect, in the very act of cognition (or re-cognition), naturally classifies these images in identifying or 'determining' them for what they are and not something else. We can see this at work even in the Genesis narrative, where after God has 'formed out of the ground all the beasts of the field and all the birds of the air', he brings them 'to the man to see what he will name them' (Gen. 2.19). Naming is an identification by classification or thematization, and therefore inherently a limitation of its object within conceptually determined definitions. In short then, through the very perfection and integrity of their limitedness or finiteness they are inherently also limiting or finitizing faculties.

But these two results now bring us to the really vital concern for our own purposes, especially with regard to something that follows from this with respect to Adam's perfect communion with God and knowledge of God. The point is that even in its perfected and sinless state, Adam's original communion with and knowledge of the 'being' or reality of God may not, in light of the above, be seen as anything like the perceptual and conceptual communion or relation or knowledge he has with respect to created things. It will, for example, be obvious from other scriptural sources that we may not simply group what Adam heard as 'the sound of the Lord God as he was walking in the garden in the cool of the day' (Gen. 3.8) together with the sounds that any of the named animals might be making as they might also be walking in the garden in the evening breeze. And this means explicitly that we do not understand Adam's awareness of and communion with God to be at its origin an awareness and communion through the same sensibly perceiving and conceptually determining cognition by which he is able to name the animals that come before him.

The reason this is excluded is twofold. First, as we have seen, both Adam's perceptual and conceptual capacities are in their finite perfection and integrity inherently objectifying and therefore finitizing faculties, whereas God permits of no finitization or objectification. Or conversely, there is nothing in God which could become visible to these cognitive faculties of perceiving and conceiving anyway. For God is from eternity the one who is invisible, the one who lives in unapproachable light, the one whom no one has ever seen or can see (Col. 1.15; 1 Tim. 1.17; 6.16). God is the one who from eternity permits of no human 'naming', permits of no setting within a perceptual or conceptual cognitive ordering of 'identification' (Exod. 3.14; Deut. 4.15–19). This in turn means something important, both for our understanding of what the alienation from God through the entry of sin involves and, as we shall see later, also for our understanding of the present redemptive reality of God in revelation. For the foregoing considerations now make it quite clear that the fall away from God cannot be seen as a fall from a state in which God was 'visible' to finite human *cognition* into a state where God is no longer visible as such, either as a perceptual object, or as a purely speculative contemplative 'object'. We must therefore look elsewhere to seek to understand what, from a human standpoint, the alienation from God involves.

And on this question the scriptures, not only the creation narrative but also elsewhere, will give an answer which is quite clear and consistent. The Genesis narrative itself depicts the descent away from God not originally as a failure in the faculty of the cognitive understanding, that is, not originally as merely a cognitive lapse consisting in some kind of empirical misperception or logical misconception. The fall into sin as already intimated is rather depicted consistently as most essentially or originally a *corruption of desire*. Before proceeding to amplify this, it is important to remember that this means a corruption of that faculty by which we find ourselves capable of being motivated to action through a reasoned assessment of means to desired ends. And indeed, we will find as such that all three aspects of the Thomist account of the appetitive or desiring nature – nutritive, sensitive and intellective – can be seen as present in the Genesis account.[30] For as Gen. 3.6 states now explicitly: it was 'when the woman saw that the tree was good for food' (that is, desired through the 'nutritive' appetite), 'and that it was a delight to the eyes' (that is, desired through the 'sensitive' appetite), 'and that it was to be desired to make one wise' (that is, desired through the 'intellectual' appetite, or the desire to have one's 'eyes opened' in gaining an understanding of 'knowing good and evil – i.e. the "wisdom" sought), that "she *took* of its fruit and *ate*".

All three of these, in other words, are motivating factors to the reasoned action undertaken as means to attaining their desired ends. And what is especially vital for our own broader purposes is to recognize that the mental 'interest' expressed in all three of these relations is not merely the representational interest of a 'signifier' to a 'signified' for cognitive apprehension. It is not merely one of a perceiving subject to a perceived object, i.e. not merely a relation of 'noesis' to 'noema' (for the tree is perceived or mentally re-presented in Eve as such before it comes to be desired in illicit ways). Far from the relation merely of a representation for *signification* or cognitive apprehension, it is rather a relation of *temptation* in which the fruit of the tree is seen as the means to gaining certain illicitly desired ends, which, when brought to its completion in the enacted decision, results in the disobedience of sin. That the descent into sin and alienation therefore come through a corruption of the motive nature with respect to desire, and not through an error of cognitive apprehension with respect to percepts and concepts, is corroborated exactly again, for example, in the James epistle: 'each one is tempted when, by his own evil desire, he is dragged away and enticed. Then, after desire has conceived, it gives birth to sin; and sin, when it is full-grown, gives birth to death' (Jas 1.14–15).

It is not necessary, for the purposes this chapter is seeking to achieve, to enter into a debate with those views which hold that the cognitive (perceiving and thinking) intellect is somehow also corrupted by the fall into sin.[31] We can, however, venture some brief comments on just two basic difficulties which such views must encounter. Firstly, it is difficult to cite any direct scriptural support for such a view. For as we have seen, the Bible makes it quite clear that sin enters only where temptation and disobedience are possible. It is entirely impossible either to be tempted or to disobey in thinking per se or in perceiving per se, that is, according simply to the cognitive structures of subject and predicate, representation and reference, perception-noesis and perception-noema, and so on. Temptation and disobedience are possible only with respect to desires and motivated action and never simply with respect to cognition and thinking. Even when we speak of having 'evil thoughts', it is not the content of the thoughts per se, no matter how shockingly shameful they may be, that constitutes the badness of the evil thought itself. To think of, or to witness the horrible evils of child pornography, for example, as a law officer might have to do in gathering evidence for a court case, or less drastically, to think or conceive of an act of embezzlement, is not yet to have an 'evil thought'. It is only when such thoughts are informed and motivated by a wretchedly perverted kind of lust or by a premeditated motivation of greed, as means to satisfying desired evil ends, that they become evil thoughts. It is therefore again first and foremost with respect to the faculty of desire and motive reasoning that the temptation and disobedience which precipitate and constitute the entry of sin and alienation originally arise.

A second difficulty is a logical one. It is clear that in the absence of any direct scriptural instruction in its support, such a position that holds to the inherent corruption of the cognitive intellect must be sustained through rational argumentation. And the problem here is then a self-defeating one. For if discursive or cognitive reason is indeed inherently corrupted, and thus incapable of any genuine and binding integrity of its own, then any cognitive argument about the fallenness of reason is itself susceptible to that fallenness and as such is unreliable. At any rate we cannot get into these debates any further here, and I recognize that rejoinders have been brought especially to the latter of the two difficulties just mentioned. Our own main point has been only to try to make clear that it is through a corruption of the desiring and motive nature that the alienation originally comes, in preparation for showing later that revelation itself, which is given to restore communion, is directed precisely to that nature by which sin came into the world.

7. But finally, we have also discovered something else, something of immense import with regard to what the alienation from God through sin actually is, even though this point has thus far been stated only indirectly. It is something that will turn out to be especially crucial for the question of the origin within us of moral consciousness as ought-consciousness, a consciousness whose origins, as we have seen, remain mysterious and unsatisfactorily accounted for by any philosophical endeavor past or present. The crucial point is this.

Whatever else the human fall away from God might also involve in a derivative or secondary way, what it *is* most fundamentally in its primal origin, according to the scriptural narrative itself, is a fall into 'the knowledge of good and evil' (Gen. 2.9, 17; 3.5, 22). And this means that at its origin the alienation from God through the entry of sin is precisely and nothing else than *a fall into ought-consciousness*, that is, *a fall into moral consciousness*. The Genesis narrative makes quite clear that the fall is not most essentially and simply a descent from a 'good' state into an 'evil' state. It is rather the descent into the knowledge of good and evil, which is again to say a descent into moral consciousness or 'ought' consciousness. This of course is no new thought and has been widely recognized. But its full ramifications for theology and especially for the disclosive character of revelation have often not been followed through. We can quote Barth here, for example, who, along with an array of others before and after him, including Luther, Maimonides and Bonhoeffer, recognizes exactly this in saying that 'when [Adam] sinned . . . he became ethical man' or better 'moral man'.[32]

Bonhoeffer too speaks of the fall as a descent from the perfect unity and simplicity of the origin (*Ursprung*) into a state of endless 'ethical conflict' such that the human being is now, in the knowledge of good and evil, 'the person of perpetual conflict' or also the person of 'irremediable conflict'.[33] The onset of 'ethical conflict' as the primal origin (*Urphänomen*) of moral consciousness through the fall into the knowledge of good and evil, 'is itself the contradiction of human beings against God'.[34]

But the full implications of this need to be followed through. And when this is done, we will be led to a summary statement that may seem somewhat jarring as it stands and which will need further explanation in order that it not be misunderstood. What the foregoing means most essentially is that to be morally conscious *just is* to be 'in sin'; or inversely, to be 'in sin' *just is* to be morally conscious. This may at first seem strange since we usually think of a robust moral consciousness as what we use to *avoid* 'sinning'. But the identification of moral consciousness here with 'being in sin' is not meant in that way. Or it does not mean that simply in virtue of our nature as morally conscious beings we are yet guilty of actual individual acts of sin. Just as little of course does it by any means suggest that the moral questions of good and evil are not still vitally important and utterly central for the Christian life or for theology. Indeed, moral questions will become a fundamental focus below in the final chapter. It means rather, in ways to be explained below, that our moral consciousness as ought-consciousness is the most fundamental *mark* or sign in us of what theology calls 'original sin' or also 'hereditary sin'. Or even more to the point, *moral consciousness*, as the knowledge of good and evil, *is the mark we bear immediately within us* and at the center of our being, *of our alienation from God*. Again, we will explore more fully what this involves below. But in order to draw the present discussion to a conclusion, let us ask just one further question.

What is it exactly *about* this moral consciousness, as the consciousness of good and evil, by which it constitutes 'original sin'? Or what is it about this consciousness exactly by which and through which we are deemed to be in a state of sin? It will be found to be two things above all others. It is firstly that in the fall away from God into the knowledge of good and evil through a corruption of desire we have become *a law unto ourselves*. This law unto ourselves which we have become, in other words, is an autonomous (self-regulating) moral law by which we bear our own measure of righteousness irremediably within us, in the immediacy of our desiring and motivating intellect for the question of how we shall live.

But there is also something else, a second thing which is decisive about this mark. For the tree of the knowledge of good and evil, which stands alongside the tree of life at the center of the garden, is also the tree of death because it carries the sentence of death. ('You must not eat from the tree of the knowledge of good and evil, for when you eat of it you will surely die': Gen. 2.17.) And what is most decisive about this mark, therefore, is that as morally conscious beings, humans alone among earthly creatures have the knowledge of their earthly life as being lived towards death. Or inversely, to know oneself to be living towards one's own death, and therefore as being oriented to death, is integral to what it is to be morally conscious.

We can sum up these two by reference to a central declaration of Romans. It is (a) because the fall into sin is a descent into the knowledge of good and evil by which we have become a law unto ourselves, and (b) because the knowledge of this law is at the same time the knowledge of living our lives towards death, that the New Testament also gives a specific name to this morally conscious law. It calls it 'the law of sin and death' (Rom. 8.2).

We will explore this further in the next chapter, but it is vitally important to understand even here that the scriptures entirely prohibit any misinterpretation of the law of sin and death to mean the Mosaic law. This as we shall see is disallowed not only because, as Rom. 5.12–14 says, sin and death reigned even before the law, but much more so because the Mosaic law itself is declared explicitly to be 'holy, righteous and good' (Rom. 7.12). And indeed, faith itself will be declared to be not a nullification of the law but a full upholding of it (Rom. 3.31). The law of sin and death is rather the law of good and evil, the human moral law into which we have fallen through a corruption of desire, and by which we have become a law unto ourselves.

A final point to be added at this juncture relates to the nature of the 'corruption of desire' itself by which alienation comes. According to Rom. 7.8, what the corruption of desire of Gen. 3 most essentially involves is a falling away from the desire of perfect love for God in perfect communion with God, and into 'covetous desire', or self-seeking desire. We might say therefore that moral consciousness, or the law of sin and death, by which we now seek to distinguish good from evil and to do good instead of evil, is most essentially the law within us by which we seek to regulate '*covetous* desire'. Whereas Adam in his origin knows nothing of covetous desire, and therefore nothing either of good in distinction from evil,[35] but only the desire of perfect love for God.

All of this brings us to a crucial destination which will serve as an important point of departure for the rest of the book.

8. It is therefore now no 'accident' – i.e., it is not merely a divine arbitrariness or occasionalism – but rather testimony to the eternal wisdom made visible in the grace of God, that when the revelation of God is given through Moses, it comes as *law*. That is, it comes in the imperative form of command addressed immediately to the motive and desiring understanding, and not in the indicative form of a concept addressed mediately through representation to the cognitive and discursive understanding. Or more fully, it is by the wisdom of the grace of God in the visible *telos* of redemption – and not merely by a peremptorily voluntaristic and thus utterly unaccountable decree, which might be supported in pure theory through dubious human definitions of God's 'freedom' – that when the first revelation comes through Moses, it declares itself not with the authority and character of a '*there is*' to the cognitive nature, but rather with the authority and character of a '*thou shalt*' directly to the motive and desiring nature, which is to say to precisely that nature by which the alienation from God occurs. The revelation of God in the Mosaic law is therefore shown to be already utterly a command of unmerited grace and a command of love. For in the wisdom and visible design of his grace, working in harmony with the fallen creation he loves, God addresses exactly the depths of that into which we have fallen in our appetitive and motive nature – and not some supposed residual 'grandeur' of our cognitive or speculative natures, by which we might still through a kind of rational illusion consider ourselves capable of aspiring to Godly heights – as he to declares himself in the form of law.

Moreover, this original character of revelation as command and summons or call, addressed directly to the motive understanding, will prove to be indispensable also for a proper attentiveness to the revelation of the Logos of God in Jesus Christ. For by his own testimony as recorded in the Gospels, and by the further fundamental development of this in the Pauline epistles, Christ does not declare himself as the fulfillment of a quintessence of onto-logical 'being', or as the fulfillment of an ideal of esthetic sublimity, but rather as nothing less than the fulfillment of the law (Mt. 5.17–20; Rom 8.3–4): a fulfillment moreover which he achieves 'in the likeness of sinful flesh'.

The central aim of the next chapter will therefore be to explore what is demanded for a Christian understanding of divine transcendence in revelation in light of the following two scriptural stipulations: one, that the first revela-tion in the Mosaic law comes in the imperative form of a 'thou shalt' for motive and appetitive consciousness, and not in the indicative form of a 'there is' for conceptually discursive consciousness; and two, that the revela-tion of God in Jesus Christ is declared to be the fulfillment of this law and not its abolishment.

Notes

1 See e.g. John Milbank, 'The Theological Critique of Philosophy in Hamann and Jacobi' in John Milbank *et al.* (eds), *Radical Orthodoxy* (London: Routledge, 1999), pp. 27–9.
2 Milbank, 'The Theological Critique of Philosophy', p. 37.
3 Benedict XVI, 'Faith, Reason and the University, Memories and Reflections', Address at the University of Regensburg, 12 September 2006; see also below pp. 154–5.
4 Louise Hickman, *Conversations in Theology*, vol. 3, issue 2, November 2005.
5 See my discussions of this in *God, the Mind's Desire* (Cambridge: Cambridge University Press, 2004), Chapter 2.
6 For a fuller discussion on this, see my essay 'Radical Orthodoxy and the New Culture of Obscurantism', in *Modern Theology* 20:3 (Oxford: Blackwell, July 2004), pp. 363–405.
7 MacKinnon, *Explorations in Theology* (London: SCM, 1979), p. 150.
8 *CD* I.1 p. 311.
9 See e.g. *The Epistle to the Romans* (London: Oxford University Press, 1965), pp. 444–5.
10 *CD* 2.1 pp. 179ff.
11 *CD* 2.1 p. 183.
12 *CD* 2.1 pp. 183–4, emphasis added.
13 *CD* 1.1 p. 382.
14 *CD* 1.1 p. 382.
15 *CD* 1.1 p. 301.
16 *CD* 1.1 pp. 297–303.
17 Eberhard Jüngel, *The Doctrine of the Trinity* (Grand Rapids: Eerdmans, 1976), p. 42.
18 Jüngel, *Trinity*, p. 42.
19 *CD* 2.1 p. 15; Jüngel, *Trinity*, p. 43.
20 *CD* 2.1 p. 21.
21 *CD* 2.1 p. 13; Jüngel, *Trinity*, p. 43.
22 See e.g. *CD* I.1 p. 331.
23 *CD* 2.1 p. 15.
24 *CD* 2.1 p. 15; Jüngel, *Trinity*, p. 44, emphasis added.

25 See discussion p. 27 above.

26 *CD* I.1, p. 361.

27 *CD* I.1, p. 371; see also Friedrich Schleiermacher, *The Christian Faith* (Edinburgh: T&T Clark, 1948), pp. 194ff.

28 Karl Barth, *The Word of God and the Word of Man* (London: Hodder and Staughton, 1928), p. 13.

29 *The Word of God and the Word of Man*, p. 11.

30 See discussion above pp. 89–91.

31 See e.g. Alvin Plantinga, 'The Reformed Objection to Natural Theology', in *Christian Scholar's Review* 11, no. 3 (1982) 187–98.

32 Karl Barth, *CD* 2.2 p. 517; Moses Maimonides, *The Guide of the Perplexed* (Chicago: University of Chicago Press, 1963), Bk 1, Ch. 2, pp. 23–6; Dietrich Bonhoeffer, *Ethik*, vol. VI in Dietrich Bonhoeffer Werke, 16 vols (Gütersloh: Christian Kaiser Verlag, 1998), p. 302.

33 *Ethik*, pp. 43, 48, 299.

34 *Nachfolge*, DBW 4, (Gütersloh: Christian Kaiser Verlag, 1994), p. 61.

35 See e.g. Maimonides, *The Guide of the Perplexed*, p. 24.

Chapter 7

Reason, Law and Revelation

I

1. In a summarization of the conclusions of the previous chapter we can begin here from the following threefold premise: (i) If the revelation of God as given in the Mosaic law declares itself originally with the authority of an imperative demanding a motive response through action, and not originally with the authority of an indicative which grants a conceptually representational or speculative illumination for thinking; and (ii) if the revelation of God in Jesus Christ is truly the fulfillment of this law through something which is actually accomplished or achieved 'causally' in embodied history and not merely asserted discursively as the denouement of a story in a textual narrative: then (iii) this calls for a critical re-evaluation of the way that the theological question of the relation of 'revelation and reason' must be understood and asked. The present chapter and the next will offer such a re-evaluation in two stages: first, through some closer attention to the revealed Mosaic law itself which Christ fulfils in his mortal life; and on that basis, secondly, through a return to the earlier questions left open with regard to the reality, efficacy and meaning of divine causality at the center of embodied life. These two together will then finally also require a critical re-examination of the basic character of faith. But we must begin with such a re-evaluation of the relation of revelation and reason from the Mosaic law itself, which as revealed law is transcendent law, in order to prepare the way to ask later what it means to say that Jesus Christ in embodied history is its fulfillment.

We can commence by noting two stipulations preliminarily. The first will be amplified momentarily by way of the particular Jewish thought of Franz Rosenzweig; but before getting to the specifics of that amplification, let me just state the stipulation itself in general terms. The point is that we never 'hear' *any* law or injunction, even just a human one, truly as an *imperative* or command in the fully authoritative sense of this term as declaring an obligation for action, unless we hear it in the immediacy of our own motive and appetitive consciousness as a demand on this consciousness. It is entirely possible and indeed proper – as we do for example in jurisprudence or legal history – to set a group of laws as 'commands' before ourselves indicatively and representationally for conceptual scrutiny or for cognitive evaluation and weighing, without really 'hearing' these as imperatives demanding action in a way that evokes the response of an obligation in the will of the hearer which motivates to causal agency.

Rosenzweig recognizes exactly this stipulation for what is required in a Jewish understanding of a genuine encounter with the Judaic law as revealed law. In his words, the command is properly attended to as a genuine imperative only when it is heard in the immediacy of an 'absolutely pure present'.[1] When the 'thou shalt' of the command is encountered merely as an 'indicative'[2] – that is, when it is *first* brought under the cognitive gaze (i.e. in the character of a 'there is') – it then assumes a representational or codified 'objectivity', through which its immediacy as a genuine imperative is lost. And by this objectivity or indicativity, it automatically comes to be heard, in Rosenzweig's words, no longer in the immediacy of the pure present, but as something with a 'past' and a 'future'. Indeed, Karl Barth is pointing toward precisely the same (motively) immediate character of the command when he states that ' "*there is*" no command of God'; or more fully when he insists that 'the proposition: "*There is* a command of God" is quite inadequate as a description of what concerns us' in the command.[3] We may then, in light of the discussions of the last two chapters, summarize this first point preliminarily as follows. The divine 'thou shalt' which is declared as imperative to the motive understanding is entirely emptied of its force when viewed first as an indicative 'there is' under the cognitive gaze, where it loses the immediacy or the 'pure presence' of obligation and conviction and assumes the representational aloofness of a past and a future.

In contrast to such an indicative hearing, as Rosenzweig now continues, 'the imperative of the commandment makes no forecast for the future', nor any claims on the past; for 'it can imagine only the immediacy of obedience'.[4] When the law is heard originally as something objectively (cognitively) codified, it then 'counts on periods of time, on a future, on duration'. The commandment heard as a genuine imperative, however, 'knows only the moment: it waits for the outcome right within the moment of its growing audible' in which alone it 'possesses the spell of the genuine tone of a commandment'.[5]

Two important points follow from this. First, it will be fully clear from the above that when we use the term 'imperative' here, this is by no means to be understood merely in the sense of another grammatical 'mood', along with the other grammatical moods of the indicative, subjunctive, vocative, optative and so on. To hear the authority of the imperative as such a 'mood' is already to hear it first as something representationally thematized and classified and thus fundamentally to mishear it.

Even more importantly, what we may take Rosenzweig to mean is that the Mosaic law is never heard genuinely in the immediacy of the imperative if it is heard most essentially as a *moral code*. For it is precisely in its cognitively objective codification as a moral code that the commandment assumes the status of an indicative inhabiting a past and a future. Indeed, we can amplify this requirement beyond even what Rosenzweig is saying, by drawing on the discussions of the previous chapter. The methodologically more basic reason that the Mosaic law may not be heard most essentially as a moral code is that *any* moral code – by its very definition as a *moral* code – is already a code falling *within* the authoritative jurisdiction of our own moral consciousness, which is to say within our own knowledge of good and evil. And this means that any and every 'moral code' – as a *moral* code – is already a code of righteousness based exactly on that knowledge by which we have become *alienated* from God through a corruption of desire.

Now it is precisely such a misapprehension of the Mosaic law as essentially a moral code that Paul is addressing in the epistle to the Romans, where he often speaks in two quite radically opposing and seemingly contradictory voices about the law. On the one hand, Romans says explicitly that 'the law is holy, and the commandment is holy, righteous and good' (Rom. 7.12). Indeed, it declares that even faith itself – through which the righteous requirements of the law are met – is not a nullification of the law but a full *upholding* of the Mosaic law (3.31). Yet on the other hand, and in a way which can seem prima facie to run against this directly, Romans also states just as forcefully that 'no one will be declared righteous in [God's] sight by observing the law' (3.20); and likewise that true justification by faith comes entirely '*apart* from observing the law' (3.28). The answer to this seeming discrepancy, in agreement with Rosenzweig, hinges exactly around this matter of whether or not the Mosaic law is heard fundamentally or primarily as the provision of a moral code. For on the one hand, it is when its commands are encountered genuinely as the communication of a divine imperative in the immediacy of the motive nature that the Mosaic law is indeed holy, righteous and good, and that its righteous requirements as such are fully met in faith. But to hear its commandments originally in the indicative or cognitive structure of a moral code, brings them back to within a human measure of righteousness, by which 'no one will be declared righteous in God's sight'.

There is, however, a deeper, and unavoidably subtle, further dynamic at work in all of this. It is an aspect by which the inherent *telos* of revelation in the Mosaic law will be found to mirror importantly the divine *telos* in the revelation of Jesus Christ. And what needs to be said here as such is this. The reason that the Mosaic law can indeed be so easily misread as essentially a moral code is that *as* revealed or divine law it *discloses* itself by taking on the 'form' of a moral code. In other words, the divine law through Moses comes hidden in the likeness of a human moral code, just as the divine Logos in Jesus Christ comes 'hidden in the likeness of sinful flesh' (Rom. 8.3). Or more fully, the divine law through Moses takes its form precisely *in* a particular moral code – complete with all the cultural, historical, geographic, ethnic and ritual customs and expressions of a real and particular historical people – just as the divine Logos in Jesus Christ takes form in a particular mortal body, who lives and expresses himself also within the political, ethnic and ritual customs of a particular historical age and culture.

There is a theologically subtle point waiting to be made here, yet one which despite its subtlety is entirely indispensable and fundamental for a proper understanding of divine revelation, either through Moses or in Jesus Christ.

The point is that in both forms it assumes – whether the moral code or the mortal flesh – both of these essentially 'fallen' forms of divine revelation at the center of human life are intrinsic to and inextricable from the very *reality* of revelation as *divine* revelation. And they therefore constitute what both Luther and Bonhoeffer treat thematically as the constitutive and *inalienable* 'weakness' and vulnerability of divine revelation wherever it is disclosed as the 'weak Word' (1 Cor. 15.43, 2 Cor. 12.9; 13.4, Heb. 4.15; 5.2). The taking on of this weakness is the cost and essence of its grace in revelation, for it meets us unmeritedly directly in the center of our own alienation. And part of the essential weakness and vulnerability of revelation as such is that in both these forms it is always susceptible to humanization, legalization, codification and blindness; susceptible to misinterpretation as a great moral law to be observed, or as a great human example to be emulated.

But in either case, the indispensable point is that it is impossible to 'extract' revelation from these fallen human forms, so as to render it 'pure' and 'strong' and no longer weak. For again, its weakness in taking on these forms just is its grace and its revelation, and thereby its redemptive strength and power. But the inalienability of revelation from the weakness of these alienated forms must be pushed even more forcefully. The divine law may not even be seen as something *other* than, or separated from, the moral code in which it takes form (it is not a heteronomous law), or something from which revelation in its 'authenticity' must be theologically extracted. The revelation of the divine and holy law can no more be extracted or abstracted from the weakness of the moral code in which it takes form than the revelation of the eternal Logos in Jesus Christ can be extracted or abstracted from his the weakness of mortal body in which it takes form. It is here again that we see the same *telos* of revelation in the divine law as we see in the divine Logos. It is a *telos* through which the Mosaic law is shown to be entirely a command of grace, as God by unmerited favor works in harmony with a fallen creation. For in taking on the form of a moral code – that is, in taking form as a code within the consciousness of good and evil which is the law of sin and death – the divine law (which is from eternity holy, righteous and good: Rom. 7.12) clothes itself in precisely that which most fundamentally defines our own unrighteousness and fallenness.

We will below return to these themes in a somewhat different context. But the basic summary point to be re-emphasized at this juncture, especially in light of what has been established in the foregoing two chapters, is the following one. A command can be encountered in the fully authoritative and immediate sense as a genuine imperative only if it comes to be 'heard' as command in our *motive* and appetitive understanding, where *alone* we can become conscious of it as carrying the force of a genuine obligation for action. In other words, the divine command is not heard rightly – i.e. we do not genuinely become 'hearers of the word' in this instance at all – unless we hear it as an imperative addressed directly, and in the immediacy of our own present, to the appetitive and motive nature, that is, as a direct call or summons to obedience.

2. We have said above that the central aim of this chapter in light of the previous is to explore what is demanded for reason in a Christian understanding of divine transcendence or revelation in view of the following two scriptural stipulations: (a) that the first revelation in the Mosaic law comes in the imperative form of a 'thou shalt' for motive and appetitive consciousness, and not in the indicative form of a 'there is' for conceptually discursive consciousness; and (b) that the revelation of God in Jesus Christ is declared to be the fulfillment of this law and not its abolishment. We can now, however, on the basis of the preceding paragraphs, restate this aim in a somewhat more 'apologetical' mode as follows.

What we are searching for is a reasoned understanding or 'account' of divine transcendence in revelation, the 'threshold' or the 'passing-over' of whose communication is no longer located *originally* at the frontiers of the discursive understanding. For this use of reason operates inherently within the grammatical and phenomenological oppositions intrinsic to the cognitive gaze: oppositions of subject and predicate, subject and object, representation and reference, same and other, and so on. And under this cognitive gaze – when it is made foundational or pre-eminent – revelation as divine transcendence then unavoidably takes on the representationally mediated character of an indicated 'referent' or 'ideatum', where the primary interests in turn are those of evaluating the *signification* of this ideatum for meaning-oriented consciousness. Instead of this, we are now searching rather for a reasoned 'account' of revelation and divine transcendence, the 'threshold' or the 'passing-over' of whose communication occurs originally at the frontiers of the appetitive and motive (motivational and motional) understanding. For as we have seen in Chapter Five, only this use of reason, which operates intrinsically according to the purposes of means to ends, is able to be open to the immediacy of the imperative, where the primary attentiveness is to *obligation* for action-oriented consciousness.

What this means exactly is as yet far from clear, and it will need to be explained much more fully as we proceed. But we must first address the second of what we said above are two preliminary stipulations. The point is that even if, in following the first stipulation, we do bring ourselves to hearing this law genuinely as an imperative, still we do not hear it aright unless we hear it genuinely as a divine imperative and not as a human one. The really crucial question therefore is: how is the Mosaic law heard genuinely as divine law and not merely human law? For it must be admitted that much of the Judaic law can indeed be read as a set of rules and regulations which might be human in origin. So by what mark or marks exactly does the Mosaic law declare and authenticate itself as divine law?

Here we must say, in attention to both Jewish and Christian sources, that there is above all one single, primary and definitively authoritative such mark. It is a mark which, as we shall see also in Rosenzweig, is inalienably connected to something distinctive in the 'commandment of commandments', or in what Jesus himself in the gospels calls 'the greatest commandment' in which all of the law and the prophets are summed up. To quote Rosenzweig directly, this greatest commandment is 'the one commandment which is not only the highest of the commandments, but is really the only one, the sense and essence of all the commandments that ever may have come out of God's mouth'. It is the commandment to which 'millions of lips testify … evening and morning: "You shall love the Eternal your God with all your heart and with all your soul and with all your might." '[6]

However, we are not here yet speaking to this commandment of commandments itself. We are rather asking about the particular *mark* it contains or generates through which the Mosaic law is able to authenticate itself as divine law.

What then exactly is this 'mark' generated by the greatest commandment through which the Mosaic law is heard genuinely as divine law and not merely a human one? As stated explicitly in Romans it is this: 'through the law we become conscious of sin' (Rom. 3.20). We return again then unavoidably to the subject of sin, although now with a quite different focus than in the previous chapter. And I must candidly confess that for the essentially methodological or critically epistemological goals of this chapter, I attempted in all kinds of ways to avoid returning to the reference to sin at this stage altogether, for two basic reasons. The first is that any mention of the consciousness of sin will almost automatically be read as a statement primarily about the consciousness of human corruption and guilt, which as we shall see it is not, at least not primarily. The second has to do with the way that the term has often come to be invoked today, at least in my view, as a license for epistemological shortcuts. Such short-cuts use the concept of sin as an opportunity to redefine the limits and parameters of reason in arbitrary ways, which do indeed make some basic theological problems easier to answer in theory, yet which compromise theology's indispensable commitment to critical rational rigor. However, it became entirely impossible to avoid coming back to the term, precisely *for* reasons of rational rigor, as I hope to show.

At any rate, we will seek to pay special attention also to a Jewish voice on this momentarily through Rosenzweig. But let us begin by focusing for now on the Romans statement itself, where the first thing to be noted is that what we are dealing with in this context is specifically the question of the *consciousness* of sin, and not the question of the reality or real presence of sin itself in the world. We need therefore to consider briefly what is meant by the distinction between the *reality* of being in sin on the one hand (i.e. the reality which we inhabit through our very existence from Adam in the knowledge of good and evil), and the *consciousness* of being in this state on the other.

Romans itself make this distinction explicit, as it is already implied in Genesis, in saying that before the law was given in Moses, sin and death real-ly reigned in the world through Adam in actual human existence, even though prior to the Mosaic law there was no *recognition* of sin as such. Or as Romans states it exactly, in Adam 'sin entered into the world through one man, and death through sin, and in this way death came to all' (Rom. 5.12); and this means that even 'before the law was given, sin was in the world' (4.13). However, as the same passage goes on to say, there was no consciousness of being in sin as such, despite its reality in the world, since 'sin is not taken into account when there is no law' (4.13). It is the revealed law, therefore, which according to Romans awakens the awareness of being in sin: 'through the law we become conscious of sin (3.20). Or as Romans 7 amplifies this, 'I would not have known what sin is except through the law' (7.7).

To illustrate analogously this distinction between the reality of being in sin and the consciousness of it, consider that there are many things that may be really occurring in the present with respect to my own life-reality even though I may not be conscious of them. There may really be a benign tumor in my abdomen even though I am not conscious of it. Or suppose that a casual acquaintance in my past, upon whom I have for some reason left a good impression, has unbeknownst to me just died and left me a sizeable portion of his estate. In such a case the bequeathed property is now actually or legally in my possession even though I am not yet aware of it. In fact this latter example illustrates aptly what theological treatments of sin often speak of as 'hereditary sin'. 'Hereditary sin', in other words, is what we spoke of previously as the 'original sin' inherited from Adam. And it is this which Romans speaks of as the sin which really reigns in the world whether humans have come to a consciousness of it or not.

Indeed, as Kierkegaard especially makes clear, what the descent into original sin through a corruption of desire essentially involves in its very nature as sin, is precisely a fall into the unconsciousness of it or into the ignorance of it. And while this may initially seem paradoxical, it has a fully transparent logic to it. For what the fall into sin most fundamentally denotes is an entry into a state where human beings – in their own knowledge of good and evil – have become an autonomous and self-governing law of righteousness unto themselves. And it is the very character of any autonomous or self-sufficient law that it does not and cannot recognize accountability or responsibility to the judgment of an alien law. For as soon as it would recognize such an accountability beyond itself, it would thereby precisely cease to be an autonomous or self-sufficient law. It is in this way that human beings, in their own autonomous law of righteousness, have become blind to the original law of divine righteousness from which they are really alienated in the knowledge of good and evil. And they have thereby precisely become unconscious of their alienation from the original righteousness, which is to say unconscious of their being 'in sin'.

In sum then, it is exactly this blindness to the reality of being in sin – which is *not* to say a blindness to the reality of *evil* as we shall see, for we know that through the consciousness of good and evil – that Paul is addressing in Romans in saying that 'through the law we become conscious of sin'. Or in other words, it is a blindness that the divine command in the Mosaic law restores to sight. The question of how the law does this as revelation remains to be addressed. But it should be noted importantly here again in passing that all of this further reinforces the point made earlier that the 'law of sin and death' of which Romans speaks is *by no means* the Mosaic law, which is itself 'holy, and the commandment is holy, righteous and good' (Rom. 7.12). The law of sin and death is rather the moral law within us – the knowledge of good and evil – by which we have become our own measure of righteousness and a law unto ourselves. Quite radically to the contrary, the divine command in the Mosaic law – *as* that which *generates* in us the consciousness of sin – is shown to be precisely *that by which we become aware* that our *own* knowledge of good and evil in the moral law *is* 'the law of sin and death'.

3. But having made these preliminary observations, we now come to the central point at issue, which has specifically to do with the 'consciousness' of sin that the law is able to generate in us. As intimated above, the misfortunate but unavoidable theological difficulty we face in engaging with the question of the consciousness of sin is that it will usually, and almost as a matter of automatic reflex, be understood as virtually synonymous with the consciousness of human 'corruption', 'evil' and 'badness', and thereby also derivatively understood as a consciousness of moral guilt and shame. And while the consciousness of sin is indeed also the consciousness of a kind of corruption – and while its character as this may by no means be diluted or diminished (although even here it will need its proper contextualization as we shall see, for it will not be the kind of corruption we might naturally expect) – nevertheless it will be shown to be something essentially derivative and secondary as such. Or it will be shown in its character as a corruption to be consequent on something more primary, something which in its primal origin has nothing whatsoever to do with corruption but with the grace of divine revelation.

At any rate, it is already fully evident from the Romans statement itself that what cannot be meant here is that through the law we become conscious of evil or of moral corruption, or of our own moral wrongdoing. For in the first place, not only does the Romans passage not say that 'through the law we become conscious of *evil*', but rather that 'through the law we become conscious of *sin*'; but additionally, and on the basis of the previous chapter, something else is also entirely clear. The point is that we are by ourselves, through the knowledge of good and evil, and quite apart from the Mosaic law, already aware, and indeed often all too tragically and unspeakably aware, of the reality of evil and moral corruption in the world, including the reality of our own moral wrongdoing.

What must be said instead therefore is this. The consciousness of sin is not in its *origin* a consciousness of human corruption, but rather first and foremost, as Kierkegaard says (and as Rosenzweig will agree), the first consciousness of being 'before God'.[7] The consciousness of sin, in other words, is not genuinely the consciousness of *sin* unless it is only derivatively a consciousness of something in 'me' as I stand 'before God'. Far from being in its origin the consciousness of a corruption therefore, the consciousness of being in sin is most truly – in its genuine *origination as* a 'consciousness' – the first consciousness of divine *revelation*, and thus also the first genuine consciousness of divine transcendence.[8]

Now of course none of this can be properly addressed without reference to faith, for the self-revelation of God is known only through faith; and we will in the next chapter argue to certain conclusions with regard to the essential character of faith in light of this and preceding discussions. But let me just say here for present clarification that when, with Kierkegaard and Rosenzweig (in the discussion to follow), we speak specifically of the '*first*' consciousness of being 'before God'; or when we speak of revelation encountered in faith at its *origin*, we are speaking simply of a certain passage from a state where the awareness of God in revelation was not present in the believer through faith, to one where it is. In other words, we are not yet speaking more broadly about continuing in the life of faith itself (which is a distinction that the scriptures make frequently, e.g. 'Just as you received Christ Jesus as Lord, continue to live in him': Col. 2.6), even though the observations made here will hold there as well. We are rather speaking only about the threshold at which revelation passes-over into a genuine communication in the first awakening of faith in the believer, in order later to make certain necessary dispositional observations about the theological orientation to the transcendence of God more broadly. And the preliminary point here (which remains to be explained fully) is that this 'threshold' at which the transcendence of divine revelation is received is inalienably one which passes through and involves the consciousness of sin. And therefore any theologically apologetical account of divine transcendence must unavoidably be focused through this.[9]

But before commencing with that explanatory task, it will be important to look in some greater depth at what the consciousness of sin essentially means in the first awareness of revelation. To that end, we can turn again to Rosenzweig who likewise, from a Jewish perspective, expresses with especial eloquence the character of the first awareness of God in the commandment as inalienably also an awareness of being 'in sin'. More specifically, he sees the encounter with God and the consciousness of sin as occurring concomitantly in the 'moment of confession' at which the commandment 'Thou Shalt Love' is heard genuinely in the immediacy of an imperative. As Rosenzweig puts it, in this 'moment of confession' before the command 'the soul meets with difficulties'.[10] The 'difficulties' here stem from a double and conflicting kind of awareness. On the one hand, as the soul comes before God in the moment of this first confession, there is an immediate and overwhelming awareness of being loved by God. Yet at the very same time, and conflicting with this, 'it is hard to confess that one was without love in the past'. And it is the 'jolting' and 'startling'[11] recognition of the soul's emptiness of this love in its past, and therefore the awareness that in the command one has encountered something radically new, that for Rosenzweig is the consciousness of being in sin. Or as he goes on to describe this exactly: as the soul becomes aware of God in the commandment of commandments, its simultaneous recognition of having been without the consciousness of the love of God in the past, manifests itself in a sense of shame over this lack. In his words 'the soul is ashamed of its past Self and of not having, with its own strength, broken the spell whose captive it was'. Or more fully, 'the soul is ashamed of confessing its love to God who calls out to it his commandment of love; for it can acknowledge its love only by also acknowledging its weakness, and by replying to God's "Thou Shalt Love": I have sinned'.[12] Now in the first instance, as Rosenzweig continues, this 'I have sinned means: I was a sinner'. Yet also, 'with this confession of the past sin, the soul clears the way for the confession: I am a sinner'. However, 'this second step is already a full confession of love'. For 'it casts afar the constraint of shame and fully surrenders to love'.[13]

We shall return to Rosenzweig briefly below, where we will find that this particular account needs also to be amplified in a certain way. But on the basis of the foregoing we must now continue to push all of this further with regard to the real question before us which remains unanswered. For while we have seen from both Jewish and Christian perspectives that the first consciousness of being before God is also the consciousness of being in sin, we have yet to address with explanatory rigor what it is *about* the law, and specifically about the commandment of commandments, that *brings about* the consciousness of sin, and thus the first genuine consciousness of revelation and divine transcendence.

II

4. Let me commence this sharpened explanatory task by repeating one of our basic premises as already stated above, but amplified now through a particular connection between law and gospel.

Just as in the revelation of the divine Logos in Jesus Christ there is a single point of maximal dynamism through which the divine power is manifested absolutely and with utter finality as not a human but a divine power: the resurrection from the dead (1 Cor. 15.17); so also in the revelation of the divine law in Moses there is a single point of maximal dynamism through which the divine command is manifested absolutely and with utter finality as not a human but a divine command. This, as we have seen, is the command at the heart of the Jewish *Shema*, the command that Jesus also names as the first and greatest commandment on which 'all the Law and the Prophets hang' (Mt. 22.40), and through which they must be heard. 'Hear, O Israel: The LORD our God, the LORD is one. Love the LORD your God with all your heart and with all your soul and with all your strength' (Deut. 6.4–5). Just as nothing in the Christian gospel can be heard as divine gospel unless it is 'heard' through the resurrection of the crucified Christ from the dead, so also nothing in the Mosaic law can be 'heard' genuinely as divine law unless it is heard through this command.

Now the greatest commandment has an entirely unique character which will not only bring us to the really vital center for understanding what it means theologically to say that 'through the law we become conscious of sin', but which will also, on the basis of that, demand a re-evaluation of the theological approach to the question of divine transcendence itself. Let us continue by exploring the first of these two questions.

We commence with a puzzle. It is fully clear that, on the one hand, the great commandment is expressed in the form of an imperative to be obeyed, which is to say in a form that seeks to elicit in us the awareness of an 'obligation' or 'duty' before it. Yet on the other hand, as we shall explain fully in a moment, it is utterly impossible that the 'obligation' it demands or seeks to elicit can be recognized *as* obligatory through any capacity or mechanism of our own *moral* awareness and reasoning. And this already immediately brings us before a conundrum, since it is only in and through moral consciousness as ought-consciousness that we ourselves can have *any* awareness of 'obligation' for action at all. Human obligational awareness as ought-awareness, whenever this is encountered genuinely with the force of a 'must' or a duty, *just is* moral awareness and never anything but this. We will address this problem itself in a moment, but the important preliminary point of emphasis at present is simply to say that the 'obligation' expressed in the commandment of commandments *cannot be a moral obligation*. Let me try to explain this.

It is recognized as self-evident in any moral discourse or normative moral framework that no demand, no matter how urgent, can count as issuing an obligation for me if I lack all means of addressing it or responding to it. For example, we may today fully recognize and abhor the evils of the slave trade in America and Britain in the eighteenth and nineteenth centuries, but we cannot be seen to have a moral obligation to do everything we can to stop those atrocities because we have no means to do so. Or to take a hypothetical contemporaneous example: if while walking along the beach on an ocean-side holiday I come across a person who is drowning, I have an obligation to come to that person's aid. But if I am sitting at my desk or teaching a class in London while this is happening, the same moral obligation does not arise for me, despite its unaltered urgency, because I lack any means to address it. Or as Kant summarizes succinctly, something that is analytically understood in all moral discourse as intrinsic to the essential meaning of any moral obligation: 'ought implies can'. No genuine 'must' with the weight of moral responsibility and culpability attached to it can arise with regard to an urgency, no matter how great, which I have no means of addressing or responding to.

Now while these are poor and inept examples, because the 'absence of means' they exemplify has essentially to do with temporal and spatial distance, nevertheless they can help to show us analogously that the obligation encountered in the greatest commandment cannot be a moral obligation. We are indeed capable of following other individual commands in the Mosaic law. In fact, there are some commandments in the Decalogue that we may manage not to break (at least not through real action) throughout our entire lives: murder or adultery, for example. The one that is perhaps most difficult not to break is the last one: covetousness. And the reason for this, as we have seen earlier, is that human desire, in its intrinsic nature, has in the alienation from God through its own corruption become most essentially 'covetous desire' (Rom. 7.8; Jas 1.14, 15). Nevertheless we may perhaps manage for short periods of time even to obey this command.

But in the commandment of commandments, through which all others must be heard, we are confronted with an imperative and obligation which we utterly lack the means of obeying even for just one moment of our lives. The impossibility of the command to 'love the LORD your God with all your heart and with all your soul and with all your strength', is echoed again in the parallel Levitical command, repeated in 1 Peter, to 'be holy, because I the LORD your God am holy' (Lev. 19.1; 11.44–45; 1 Pet. 1.15), and yet again in Jesus's own command to 'be perfect even as your Father in heaven is perfect' (Mt. 5.48). It is because of our utter inability even for one moment of our lives to obey these impossible commands that the Psalmist, and Paul in Romans along with him, can declare as unequivocally as they do that, according to the measure of righteousness issued in the great command, 'there is no one righteous, not even one'; or again that the Psalmist can say 'no one living is righteous before you'; or even more forcefully from Isaiah that 'all our righteous acts are like filthy rags' (Pss. 14.1; 53.1; Rom. 3.9–12; Ps. 143.2; Isa. 64.6). Any recognition of an obligation to obey these 'impossible commands' cannot therefore be that of a moral obligation carrying a moral culpability. For again, it is impossible for our moral nature to recognize itself rationally and culpably as duty-bound when it lacks every means of responding to a demand, no matter how urgent.

But this now brings us to the real issue at hand. For the fact remains that Christian and Jewish believers do indeed claim to recognize this command as an imperative that carries the authority of an obligation and a summons to obedience, despite the impossibility of obeying it. And they claim to recognize this moreover as a call and summons which is by no means just a subjective 'call of conscience' issuing in an existential *Schuld* and *Sorge* associated with a longing for a unity of 'Being', as it is in Heidegger, but rather as the summons and call of the love and righteousness of God himself, expressed in the commandment.

5. What we begin to see emerging here as such, in the problem of transcendence encountered as an 'impossible imperative' for the obligational or motive understanding, is a kind of parallel to the problem of transcendence envisioned as an 'impossible referent' for the cognitive or speculative understanding.

Now the problem of an impossible imperative will demand a fundamentally different kind of approach to divine transcendence than the problem of an impossible referent or ideatum, as we shall see. But the initial critically apologetical question that confronts us in the impossible imperative is the following one. How can this morally impossible obligational response which is generated in believers by the revealed commandment be theologically 'accounted for' or 'defended' as a genuine *obligation* in the revelation of the command if it is not a *moral* obligation? For again, human obligational awareness as ought-awareness *just is* moral awareness and never anything but this.

We will in the concluding chapter offer an affirmative answer to this question. But at this stage of the argument, and in preparation for that, we will need to look somewhat more carefully at the basic character of this 'impossibility' that we meet in the command. For the impossibility that confronts us here, as an impossibility which is issued in the form of a command or imperative to the motive understanding, is fundamentally different than the impossibilities or apparent impossibilities which can be expressed representationally and referentially in the form of conceptual indicatives or ideas for the speculative understanding.

In order to amplify what is at stake here we can helpfully draw attention to a particular debate in contemporary political theology that has gained a certain prominence especially in North America over recent decades. It is a debate that takes place around what is called the 'ethics of Jesus' and which is likewise centered on what such 'impossible commands' – as found in the greatest commandment and in many other commands of Jesus himself – must be understood to convey.

On the one side of the debate is what might be called broadly a Niebuhrian view,[14] which construes the 'impossible commands' of Jesus given in the Gospels as essentially 'ideals' which, despite their impossibility, can still be 'relevant' sources of guidance for Christian political and moral discourse and exchange, as this seeks to engage in the political and cultural dynamics of the real world. On the other side is what can be called broadly a Yoderian view,[15] which speaks likewise of these impossible commands as in a way issuing a kind of 'ideal' for Christian political and moral discourse. Yet it understands their guidance as such not in terms of their 'relevance' with respect to worldly or secular discussions at all, but rather as 'eschatological' statements (in an other-worldly sense of eschatological) whose main aim is to 'subvert' what are seen as essentially polluted and corrupted worldly or natural discussions in politics and ethics, with a view to exposing them as false or ill-formed.

We cannot get further into the details of this debate itself, except to say that it has become paradigmatic of two much more broadly cast opposing basic dispositions, the one or the other of which underlies a great deal of political theological discussion today. What is most vital for our purposes, however, is not to seek to adjudicate between them in any way but rather to point to a basic oversight which occurs on both sides of this debate in light of our own discussions above. I do not mean through what follows to suggest that this oversight renders these discussions moot or valueless, but only that, having failed to acknowledge what the impossible commands are in their primary force, both sides are in an important way diminished in their effectiveness even as secondary discussions.

The oversight is that by having from the outset construed the impossible commands as essentially impossible *ideals* for interpretative application in a conceptual system of 'Christian ethics' – whether for purposes of 'relevance' or 'subversion' – both positions have already 'heard' the impossible commands as essentially 'indicative' points of cognitive guidance for political theory. And they have thereby entirely missed the real force of what they really are as *imperatives* addressed immediately to motive consciousness as commands to be obeyed.

But the even more specific error in this elision is that *what* is impossible in the impossible command, as a revealed or transcendent command, has been fundamentally misunderstood. For *what* is impossible in the revealed command is not that it confronts the *discursive* understanding with the transcendence of a *conceptually impossible ideality* which, while setting an impossible 'standard', is understood as still being 'applicable' in the construction of a Christian political or ethical theory, whether subversively or relevantly. No, what is really impossible and transcendent in the command, when it is heard genuinely as revelation, is that it awakens in the *motive* understanding the awareness of a *morally impossible culpability* in the consciousness of sin before a morally impossible obligation to be obeyed. And what is especially unique about *this* transcendence as encountered in the command, is precisely that it is not, like the transcendence of the ideal, encountered as something utterly unreachable and remotely exterior beyond the margins of the speculative understanding. Far from this, as Deuteronomy now states in speaking specifically about the commandment of commandments (and Romans with it in declaring Christ as its fulfilment): 'It is not up in heaven, so that you have to ask, "Who will ascend into heaven to get it and proclaim it to us so that we may obey it?" Nor is it beyond the sea, so that you have to ask, "Who will cross the sea to get it and proclaim it to us, so that we may obey it?" No, the word is very near you; it is in your heart and in your mouth that so that you may obey it' (Deut. 30.11–14; Rom. 10.6–7).

In this 'conundrum' of an impossible culpability before the command, therefore, we can see an amplification of what Rosenzweig also calls the 'difficulties' which are encountered by the soul in the 'confession of love' before the command. The 'difficulty' there specifically, remember, arose in the recognition that the confession and embrace of divine love are unavoidably at the same time also the confession: 'I am a sinner'. And the 'amplification' I mean here is that although in the confession of the command 'Thou Shalt Love' the soul does indeed find itself before the *love* of God which 'casts afar the constraint of shame': it at the same time also finds itself before the *righteousness* of God, a righteousness before which moreover, even in the obliteration of all such shame, it still remains culpable in the face of what the command actually commands. For even in the confession of love before the command, the soul nevertheless remains utterly incapable of actually fulfilling the righteous requirements of this command.

III

6. Let us now in light of all of this come finally to the summative point and ask the following question: how are we to understand Jesus's own statement as recorded in the Gospels that he came to fulfill and to accomplish the law and not to abolish it (Mt. 5.17)? Or what kind of truth are Jesus's further words in that context meant to convey: 'I tell you the truth, until heaven and earth disappear, not the smallest letter, not the least stroke of the pen, will by any means disappear from the law until everything is accomplished' (Mt. 5.18)? Or again, how are we to understand the statement that Christ is indeed 'the end of the law so that there may be righteousness for everyone who believes' (Rom. 10.4), but that in light of both Romans and the Gospels he is its end in the sense of its accomplishment, its realization, its full implementation, and not in the sense of its annulment or termination? Or to sum this up, how are we to understand the truth of the Romans declaration that '*what the law was powerless to do* because it was weakened by the sinful nature, God [*himself*] *did* by sending his own Son in the likeness of sinful man to be a sin offering', and that God thereby 'condemned sin in sinful man in order that *the righteous requirements of the law* might be fully met in us' (Rom. 8.3–4)?

In order to address these questions properly with regard to our own apologetical concerns, it will be necessary to cast them in a broader way and to ask two more basic questions. In the final chapter we will return again to the question of revelation as divine causality where we will ask, with a more apologetically 'explanatory' focus, what *actually happens in the world* when the reality of God enters into the reality of the world in the man Jesus Christ in history. But prior to coming to that causally 'explanatory' task, and in order to ensure that the question is framed there in the right way, we must first ask a question with a more doctrinally 'descriptive' focus. We must ask what, according to the scriptures, the revelation of the reality of God in Jesus Christ *actually is*, or what it is most fundamentally proclaimed to be the revelation *of* in the incarnation, life, death and resurrection of Jesus Christ in history.

It will be clear to begin with that even in the days of his mortal life, *what* was revealed in Jesus Christ was not just his human 'flesh', but rather something final of the reality and fullness of the divine nature *in* the flesh. In the man Jesus Christ we are said to encounter not only a great prophet who points the way to God, but rather the very reality and 'being' of God himself. In Jesus Christ we encounter the self-revelation of God 'in whom all the fullness of the Deity lives in bodily form' (Col. 2.9). But what is the fullness of this divine 'being' or revealed reality exactly? In response to this we could of course say many different things. But for theological apologetical concerns – that is, for questioning which seeks to give an account of the present reality of the living God at the center of life and of theology's relation to this as its ground – there is one double-sided answer that will emerge as paramount.

To introduce this properly we should recall from previous discussions that in the alienation from God through the entry of sin, what we have become alienated from is not the love of God, from which nothing can separate us. We have rather become alienated from the righteousness of God, through having become our own measure of righteousness in the knowledge of good and evil. In this light we can state the first of the two interweaving answers to the question of what the revelation of God in Jesus Christ most essentially *is*, as the fulfillment of the law.

For the scriptures will in fact say something final and definitive here about what the gospel is the gospel *of*, or what the good news in the gospel is news *of*, something which is as unmistakable in its consistency as in its clarity. To begin with the language of Romans, where it is a predominating declaration: 'In the gospel *a righteousness from God* is revealed, a righteousness that is by faith from first to last' (Rom. 1.17). Or again, in Jesus Christ 'a righteousness from God, apart from the law, has been made known, to which the Law and the Prophets testify' (Rom. 3.21, 22; see also Rom. 10.3; Phil. 3.9). What is this testimony of the prophets exactly? In Isaiah it is this: 'Listen to me . . . you who are far from righteousness. I am bringing my righteousness near, it is not far away; and my salvation will not be delayed' (Isa. 46.12–13). Or again in Jeremiah, prophesying the 'righteous branch' that will be raised up for David, it is this: 'This is the name by which he will be called: The Lord Our Righteousness' (Jer. 23.6). This name is echoed repeatedly in the New Testament. The epistle to the Hebrews speaks of Jesus Christ, as prefigured in Melchizedek, as none other than 'first, by translation of his name, "king of righteousness" ' (Heb. 7.2); and again as a king 'the scepter of [whose] kingdom' is described as 'the scepter of righteousness' (Heb. 1.8). Even more directly, Acts 17.52 speaks of the advent of Jesus Christ himself as 'the coming of the Righteous One' (see also Acts 3.14). And Paul's own account in Acts of his commissioning by Ananias is described as having the specific purpose that Paul might come to 'see the Righteous One and to hear the words of his mouth' (Acts 22.14). This is echoed again in the first Johannine Epistle, that 'the one who speaks to the Father in our defense [is] Jesus Christ, the Righteous One' (1 John 2.1). The book of Acts speaks likewise of Jesus Christ as 'the Holy and Righteous One' (Acts 3.14) and as the fulfillment of what the prophets had predicted in 'the coming of the Righteous One' (7.52). Further, in Romans 5, 'God's abundant provision of grace' is described as 'the gift of righteousness', a gift given so that 'grace might reign through righteousness' (Rom. 5.17, 21). Indeed, in 2 Peter 'the new heaven and the new earth' itself comes to be identified, with ultimate finality, as nothing less than 'the home of righteousness' (2 Pet. 3.13). What must be said first and foremost therefore is that the 'being' or reality of God revealed in Jesus Christ is nothing less than the re-advent of the original righteousness of God from which we have become alienated.

Yet having said all of this, it is important to re-emphasize that even in this term 'righteousness' we come up against the same problem that confronts theology in any language it uses of God, a problem that we have encountered repeatedly and in several different ways in previous chapters. For although the term 'righteousness' or 'holiness' is used ('The holy God will show himself holy by his righteousness': Isa. 5.16), yet we must acknowledge at the same time that we can have no cognitive or conceptual 'idea' of what the righteousness of God *means*, in any way that would compare with human righteousness, not even analogously to human righteousness. This is not only because God transcends creation as its Creator but especially because the divine righteousness is precisely that reality in God from which we have become alienated through having become our own law of righteousness in the consciousness of good and evil.

This is why Luther speaks of the righteousness of God as an 'alien right-eousness'.[16] But this is not to be misunderstood again as merely an 'other' righteousness for cognitive conception. That is, it is not to be understood as something that could be set 'over-against' my own righteousness compara-tively, not even in 'radical disjunction' from my own righteousness, whether by methods of 'hyper-negation' or 'absolute alterity' or 'incommensurability' or whatever. For all such assessments, as we have seen,[17] are still intrinsically comparative, even and especially in their either/or disjunction, and thus ultimately cognitively unifying. On the contrary: 'To whom will you compare me or count me equal? To whom will you liken me that we may be compared?' (Isa 46.5).

We will be able to address this difficulty fully only in the next chapter where we will find that the righteousness of God is indeed made present to us, although not originally within any conceptually comparative framework of 'meaning' at all, but rather as a righteousness which is actually *accomplished* and enacted causally by God himself in embodied history in the real world. But even at this juncture we can catch a glimpse of what is to come. For if, in the light of the foregoing scriptural declarations, we must affirm that what the revelation of God in Jesus Christ most essentially *is*, is the re-advent of the original righteousness of God; and if, as we have seen, the righteousness or holiness of God is not just a 'predicate' that theology can assign to God but belongs to the reality of his very 'being': then we must equally on the scriptural witness affirm something else with which this declaration of divine righteousness in Jesus Christ is inalienably interwoven.

This 'something else' will once and for all show the full futility of supposing that by any magnification of the human idea of 'the good' we could have caught any glimpse of the divine righteousness. For the revelation of the righteousness of God is precisely not announced in the perfection of a highest speculative, phenomenological or philological ideal. To the contrary, 'the coming of the Righteous One' is a coming 'in the likeness of sinful flesh' (Acts 7.52; Rom. 8.3). Or as 2 Corinthians repeats this with force: 'God made him who had no sin to be sin for us, so that in him we might become the righteousness of God' (2 Cor. 5.21).

It is this twofold inalienably interwoven scriptural stipulation, therefore – (i) that Jesus Christ is the revelation of 'the righteousness which comes from God', and (ii) that he *is* the revelation of divine righteousness 'in the likeness of sinful flesh' – that describes for us definitively what it means to say that Jesus Christ is the fulfillment of the law. Or to repeat this summarily again in the language of Romans: what the righteous and holy law itself 'was powerless to do in that it was weakened by the sinful nature,[18] God [himself] did* by sending his own Son in the likeness of sinful man to be a sin offering . . . in order that the righteous requirements of the law might be fully met in us' (Rom. 8.3).

We may not stop here, however, but must push all of this further. Or more fully, we may not, through having addressed doctrinally or narratively the question of what it *means* to say that Jesus Christ is the fulfillment of the law, suppose ourselves to have completed the theological task, indispensable as the question of doctrinal and narrative meaning is. For by the Bible's own stipulation, the *truth* of what is declared here is the truth of a physically embodied reality that is actually achieved and accomplished in the temporal flow of history in the causal dynamism of space and time. The truth and reality of what is declared here, in other words, are not something that can be confined to the story of the textual narrative, even though this might indeed as a narrative be able to evince a certain response of deep meaningfulness on metaphorical, esthetic or literary levels. What occurs here is not merely something literary or metaphorical or phenomenologically saturated. Rather: 'he has reconciled you by Christ's physical body through death' (Col. 1.22).

The Bible itself therefore compels us – when we seek to understand and become accountable to what is declared as a living truth in real embodied life – to push these important and indispensable questions of doctrinal and narrative description further to their own grounding reality in the revelation of God in embodied history, and to seek a genuinely 'explanatory' account of *what really happens in the embodied world* in the event of Jesus Christ. Only after we have done this, only after we have sought to be attentive to what 'God himself did' in embodied history, to what he himself accomplishes here in Jesus's mortal life: only then will we be able to speak of the 'alien righteousness' that Christ *is*, no longer as an utterly remote 'other' righteousness, but rather, together with Bonhoeffer, as a 'better righteousness' which is alive and presently real at the center of life.

Notes

1 Franz Rosenzweig, *Star of Redemption* (Madison, Wisconsin: University of Wisconsin Press, 2005), p. 191 (hereafter *Star*).
2 *Star*, p. 191.
3 *CD* II.2 p. 548, emphasis added.
4 *Star*, p. 191.
5 *Star*, p. 191.
6 *Star*, p. 190, Deut. 6.5.
7 See e.g. Søren Kierkegaard, *The Sickness Unto Death* (Princeton: Princeton University Press, 1983), pp. 100, 120.
8 Kierkegaard, *Sickness*, pp. 96, 156.
9 'This is why', as Kierkegaard says, 'Christianity very consistently assumes that neither paganism nor the natural man knows what sin is; in fact it assumes that there has to be a revelation from God to show what sin is.' Indeed, as he continues, 'the qualitative distinction between paganism and Christianity is not, as a superficial consideration assumes, the doctrine of the Atonement. No, the beginning must start far deeper, with sin . . . as Christianity in fact does' (*Sickness*, p. 89).
10 *Star*, p. 193.
11 *Star*, p. 193.
12 *Star*, pp. 193–4.
13 *Star*, p. 194.
14 See e.g. Reinhold Niebuhr, 'The Relevance of an Impossible Ethical Ideal' in *From Christ to the World*, ed. Wayne G. Boulton (Grand Rapids: Eerdmans, 1994).
15 See e.g. John Howard Yoder, *The Politics of Jesus* (Grand Rapids: Eerdmans, 1994), pp. 103–7.
16 *Martin Luthers Werke: Kritische Gesamtausgabe* (Weimar: Hermann Böhlau, 1883–), Band 37, pp. 297–306.
17 See discussion above pp. 71–4.
18 The law is that which, in its generating of the awareness of an impossible culpability in the consciousness of sin, points us back to the original right- eousness from which we have become alienated. But the law itself – according to Romans and Hebrews especially, where this is worked through with a quite rigorous inner 'logic' – is unable to restore the relation to the communion with the original righteousness, precisely because it is that by which the awareness of the brokenness of communion with God comes. This is the divine power and efficacy and achievement of the law as 'holy, righteous and good'. But it is inevitable that the law, in its very righteousness as summed up in the great commandment, will become 'weakened by the sinful nature', which is to say that while the law points us back to the original righteousness, it is unable of itself actually to effect a full restoration. And the reason it is unable to do this

is because *what* it achieves within human nature – precisely *in* its pointing back to the original righteousness – is a culpability and obligation before this righteousness, an obligation which is impossible for the sinful nature to fulfil, for 'we suffer from unrighteousness' (Barth, *The Word of God and the Word of Man*, p. 11).

CHAPTER 8

CHRIST, REALITY AND HISTORY

I

1. The Bible declares that the incarnation of God in Jesus Christ is a real embodied incarnation that occurs in the history of this world in the real life of one man lived unto death. It is not merely something mythological or metaphorical that inspires humans to nobler and more sublime idealistic heights. It is rather an event which occurs within embodied history and which transforms decisively not only our history but also the relation of God to the world and the world to God. 'He has reconciled you by Christ's *physical body* through death to present you holy in his sight' (Col. 1.22). But the Bible declares just as forcefully that the resurrection of Jesus Christ, too, is a resurrection into *this* world and with real power into *our* history, and not into some alien realm or alien history. And this means that just as the real physical world of sensible-rational human life is the 'site' of the revealed reality of God in Jesus Christ in his mortal life, so it is also the site of the revealed reality of Christ's resurrection life, a life which through Pentecost is generatively and transformatively active with power today 'for all who are far off, for all whom the Lord our God will call' (Acts 2.39). Before we can address directly the question of the *present* reality of God, therefore (which we shall come to in the final chapter), we will need to turn our attention first to these 'foundational events' themselves and ask a different kind of question there, one that will need to be formulated in a certain way for apologetical purposes. The question is this.

What *actually happens in the world* when in the revelation of God in Jesus of Nazareth 'the Word became flesh', or when 'God becomes man'? Or what actually *happens in the world* when the reality of God enters into the reality of the world in the man Jesus Christ in spatio-temporal history? It is important to recognize that what is being asked here is something quite different than the question: what does it *mean* to say that God become man? This latter question is indeed also an important and indispensable one. Or as Karl Rahner says, the question of what 'God became man' *means* is 'a quite rudimentary question because it has to be answered in a sufficiently adequate way if we want to maintain that we *believe* in Jesus

Christ'.[1] What Rahner means by this is that it is impossible for us legitimately to claim to believe anything that in its very conceptuality is manifestly incoherent or unintelligible. Belief strictly entails the conceptual intelligibility of what is believed. What must be shown, in other words, is that when by faith we affirm that we believe that the man Jesus is God, or that Jesus Christ is the God-man, that this compound term 'God-man', although it may prima facie appear contradictory as it stands, is not really contradictory or conceptually unintelligible, in the way that, for example, the compound terms 'square circle' or 'spaceless body' are analytically incoherent or absurd, and therefore quite literally 'unbelievable'.

The way that the human incarnation of God in Jesus Christ is today perhaps most often rendered conceptually coherent or intelligibly meaningful is through Trinitarian theory. Barth does this, for example, in appealing to the 'unconditioned freedom' of God. God's unlimited freedom enables him to 'distinguish himself from himself; i.e. to be God in himself and in concealment, and yet at the same time to be God a second time and in a very different way, namely, in manifestation, i.e. in the form of something he himself is not'.[2] In this way Barth is able to give an internal doctrinal account of how the statement 'God became man' can be seen as conceptually coherent or conceptually meaningful – i.e. by defining God in such a way that his freedom allows him to be 'unlike' himself. But whatever its doctrinal merits as such, this account is concerned essentially with establishing the conceptual coherence of the statement or sentence 'God became man' itself, and it does not yet address itself to the question of the truth of what actually happens when the content of what the statement proclaims really occurs in history. Or likewise within Trinitarian theory, Wolfhart Pannenberg seeks to demonstrate the internal coherence and conceptual intelligibility of the statement 'God became man' through more eschatologically focused appeals to the 'reciprocal self-distinction' between the Father and the Son.[3] Or again, Elizabeth Johnson seeks to approach the question in important new ways through a dialectic of 'presence and absence' in which the Holy Spirit assumes a certain primacy.[4] Or yet again, the statement 'God became man' might be rendered conceptually intelligible and hence internally meaningful through various appeals to atonement theory, and so on.

Indeed, what we ourselves have done at the conclusion of the last chapter – i.e. in determining through the scriptures that what 'the fulfillment of the law' in Jesus Christ *means* is that he is the revelation of 'the righteousness which comes from God' revealed in 'the likeness of sinful flesh' – this as it stands is also in a way a descriptively theoretical or doctrinal response to the question of what it means that God became man. It is possible even to carry this somewhat further within doctrine itself into the directions that will concern us in the present chapter, as, for example, Karl Rahner has done. Rahner seeks to answer the question 'What does it mean to say that "God became man"?' by showing that as a *statement of faith*, 'God became man' can, on a certain theological interpretation, be found to be 'compatible' with an evolutionary view of the world.[5] But even that remains an essentially theoretical or internally doctrinal exercise because it confines itself to showing a *conceptual* compatibility or possible coherence between the faith-*statement* 'God became man' and evolutionary theory. It does not yet address itself to the question of the essential character of its truth as an actual occurrence in spatio-temporal history.

Now again, this kind of doctrinal and theoretical endeavor is not only right and proper but entirely indispensable for theology. It is where theology must begin as it attends to the scriptures and it is where most theological endeavor takes place. But we engage in an error when we consider the theological task to be essentially *completed* in them. For theology's task and responsibility, especially in engaging with this most central of all New Testament declarations – 'that Jesus Christ has come in the flesh' (1 Jn 4.2) – cannot be solely that of providing coherently descriptive accounts of its intelligible meaning as a '*statement* of faith', indispensable as this is. If theology is to be able to defend itself against the charge of expounding a mere mythology of God incarnate, it must also be able to provide an account of the truth of this statement of faith as a real dynamically causal occurrence in the world, a divinely causal initiative in the world in which the 'statement of faith' itself is grounded and apart from which faith collapses.

What we are searching for here, in other words, is an explanatory 'account' of a divinely causal initiative in space and time that grounds this statement of faith. We are searching for an explanatory account of a real embodied event in which God himself enters into human history and fundamentally transforms this history through the historical redemption of it. But in order to understand the depth of what is intended here, we must look more carefully at what we mean by this term 'history', especially with respect to the question of divine causality that becomes active in it.

2. As a science of cognitive enquiry, the intellectual discipline we call history is of course inevitably something interpretational and therefore something also concerned with meaning. But *as* the unavoidably interpretational discipline that it is, history also has a particular kind of interest. And let me quickly add that I do not mean 'interest' here in the polemical sense in which it has often come to be used under certain 'postmodern' (e.g. post-structuralist or deconstructive literary) influences. In these discussions, 'interest' is understood essentially as a kind of coercive 'power' that the thematizing or classifying mind unavoidably forces on its subject of focus in the very act of interpretation, in that every act of interpretation inescapably reflects the interests of the interpreter. According to such views, what is therefore required – because of the inescapability or 'hegemony' of interpretive interestedness – is a simultaneous and continuous act of deconstructing this interestedness so that no 'violence' is done to the subject of focus.

Without denying the literary and hermeneutical value and fruitfulness of such enterprises, however, the 'interest' I speak of here is meant in fact in the other direction. I mean the interest of an *observational attentiveness* to the real causal events of the past, an attentiveness or interest by which the science of history seeks to allow its source of concern to speak for itself.

In history, in other words, we return inevitably to the question of causality, or to an interest in real embodied cause–effect sequences in space and time. It is true of course that the science of history in most of its activity does not actually observe the unfolding of causal events in the present through sensible observation, in the way that the more strictly empirical sciences can. Nevertheless, even as it confines itself to historical accounts in texts, its interest remains that of coming to increasingly more accurate accounts, through those texts (combined perhaps with other evidence such as archeological evidence), of what actually happened in the cause–effect nexus in space and time. In short, history as a science is interested in distinguishing 'fact' from 'fiction'.

It is interested, for example, in whether Henry VIII really had six wives and how many of them he murdered; whether on August 28, 1963 Martin Luther King really walked onto a podium in Washington DC and delivered his 'I have a dream' speech; whether Abraham Lincoln was really assassinated on Good Friday, April 14, 1865, while attending a special performance of the comedy *Our American Cousin* at Ford's Theatre, and so on.

Let me be clear, however, that in saying that history as a science is interested in distinguishing 'fact' from 'fiction', I am not concerned with the philosophical question of what can be said about any theoretical principle by which 'fact' *in general* can be distinguished from 'fiction'. We need not, in other words, be concerned for present purposes with philosophically analytical discussions such as the Goodman–Hempel controversy, about the possibilities of determining which observed empirical regularities can be verified generally as genuinely law-like or inductively principled, and which observed regularities are merely 'accidentally general' and therefore not principled. Nelson Goodman, as is well known, seems to doubt whether a reliable inductive principledness which in general can distinguish fact from fiction is possible. But this does not mean that he himself is not willing to distinguish true fact from imaginary fiction *at all*. More specifically, even he will by no means deny that it is an historical fact and not merely an imaginary fiction that at some particular time and place he actually sat down and with his own hand put pen to paper as he wrote *Fact, Fiction and Forecast*, and that what he holds before him afterwards as he reads his own book is in part an effect caused by that factual effort. At any rate, it is with these factual events occurring in the causally sequential flow of embodied life in space and time, and not with the philosophical question of an inductive principledness of facticity, that history as a science is concerned.[6]

But now the science of history, which, in its concern to distinguish fact from fiction, is therefore concerned with real occurrences in the causal nexus of space and time, is not of course concerned with *all* causal events in space and time, but seeks to be attentive to a particular kind of causality. It is not interested, for instance, in past or present causal processes of the cosmic universe we inhabit: not in the causally dynamic orbits of the planets or the imploding of stars, even though we do indeed in the broadest sense of the term speak of our own solar system as having a 'history' of causal development.

Nor is it concerned with causal processes at work at the molecular or quantum level (where in the latter, causality seems to operate quite differently and paradoxically, but still with real physical or empirical effects), nor again with bygone dynamically causal fluctuations of the earth's climates, or in the causal shifts in its tectonic plates. These causal processes, including their causal pasts are the proper domain of astronomy, quantum physics, climatology, geology, etc.

The particular causal past that is most specifically of interest in the science of history is not the mechanistic causality of cosmic forces (where it seems to be deterministic) or of quantum forces (where it seems indeterministic), but rather more than anything, *the causality of free human agency*, which is to say the causality of *enacted decision*.

II

3. To explain what this means more exactly, especially for purposes of returning later to the question of divine causality, we can helpfully revisit the thought of Friedrich Schleiermacher. Schleiermacher's development will be focused toward different theological conclusions than ours but he begins from the same basic observations about causality under the evident influence not only of Aristotle and Kant but also Newton.

Schleiermacher, then, speaks of causes that are 'free' and causes that are 'not free'. Causes that are not free are those that proceed entirely from within the natural dynamic flow of what Schleiermacher calls the cosmic 'nature mechanism', that is, in the 'interaction of things which only react as such insofar as they have been acted upon'.[7] Earthquakes caused by the shifting of the earth's tectonic plates, meteors causing lunar craters, the growing warmth of the springtime sun causing mountain snow to melt, which in turn causes rivers to swell, are some obvious examples of this purely 'reactive' or 'deterministic' kind of causality. At any rate, in any such examples, where things cannot move themselves and are able to move only as they are moved, there is, as Schleiermacher says, 'a complete absence of freedom'.[8]

The question of 'free causes', then, begins to arise in the consideration of things which *are* able to move themselves in space.[9] And three vital things are to be observed here right at the outset. First, it will be immediately obvious that in the connection of free causality with the capacity for self-movement, we are concerned entirely with *living* things or with the domain of *life*, because only living things can move themselves. This means, secondly, that 'life' and 'the capacity for self-movement' are coterminous. And the third introductory point, which remains to be explained fully, is that insofar as living things are capable of self-movement in space, this movement as life-movement is always and intrinsically rooted in appetite or desire. Desire or appetition is the motivating dynamism of all embodied life. This is what Kant means when, echoing Aristotle, he says that '*Life* is the faculty of a being to act in accordance with the laws of the faculty of desire.'[10] Kierkegaard makes exactly the same observation in his own fundamental connection of life-existence to desire, or to what he thematically calls 'passion'. In his words, 'existing, if this is not to be understood as just any sort of existing [i.e. not inanimate existing] cannot be done without passion [desire, will]',[11] for 'passion itself is the impetus of motion'.[12]

But we need to look more closely at desire as the motivating source of all self-movement and therefore life, especially with respect to our more basic concern here with free causality and the domain of history. As we have seen in Chapter Five, all life-movement – insofar as it is movement generated by that life and not by external forces – is *motivated* movement; and insofar as it is motivated movement it is always movement rooted in some kind of appetite or desire. Now it may on the face of things seem strange to connect *all* life-movement to 'motivation' through desire. For it is of course true that even in human life (to say nothing of movement in plant life), we encounter what we would call purely involuntary and thus seemingly unmotivated movements, as when we jump reflexively at the sound of a loud noise, or when during sleep we gesticulate unknowingly, to say nothing of the unconscious and involuntary motion of the bodily organs. But a certain kind of appetitive life-'motivation' can be seen to be present here as well in a basic and rudimentary kind of way.

In the earlier chapter we saw this at work in a rudimentary way even in plant life where, as Aristotle and Aquinas called them, the life-motivating 'appetites' are purely 'nutritive'. Now there is of course no *self-conscious* 'motivation' in such a nutritive appetite. Nevertheless, the life-dynamism (or what Aristotle would call 'the soul') of an apple seed, for example, as it germinates and grows transformatively into a fruit-bearing tree, carries within itself a kind of causality that is not entirely dependent for its movement on being moved by external forces in the way that a slab of granite is, but is rather a movement generated by the internal life-dynamism itself. And the further point is that this transformative causality is exercised most fundamentally according to a constitutive or inbuilt nutritive *appetite*, an appetite which motivates the life-growth and the transformation from seed into fruit-bearing tree.

As we move into animal life, this motivated character of life-movement through appetite takes on new dimensions, especially in the emergence of movement in the avoidance of pain and in the attraction to pleasure. Black bears in British Columbia's rainforests, for example, will in the spring season eat the ripe sweet berries and leave the unripe sour ones, giving evidence already of the presence of what Aristotle and Aquinas call the 'sensitive' or 'sensible' appetite, which is not merely nutritive but suggests the entry of appetite based on certain kinds of pleasure. To be sure, there is not yet anything like a reasoning from means to ends here but rather something which seems to occur by a kind of instinct. But the main point at present is to say that in these animal forms of life there begin to be intimations in a rudimentary way of what might appear to be a kind of 'free causality', at least insofar as they have the capacity for ambulatory movement by means of their own life-dynamism. But this is not yet what is meant by free causality in the full or true sense of the term. For even in animals, as Schleiermacher says, the motivation to self-movement still springs essentially from physical or empirical sources which, as essentially physical and instinctual, are still traceable back to the causality of the nature-mechanism.[13]

In humans, however, we encounter something different. For through the faculty of the will (which is to say the 'intellectual appetite' as focused through motive or practical reason, which reasons from means to desired ends) humans understand themselves to be able to be causal agents in the world in a way that is not fully determined by the natural necessities of the nature-mechanism, and thus, within limits, to be able to be 'free' of it. Of course as physically embodied beings humans remain as susceptible to the causality of the nature-mechanism as any other physical bodies. But as both living and *rational* embodied beings, they understand themselves through the will or the motive intellect to be capable of contributing causally to the flow of their own temporal lives and surroundings in a way that is not reducible to the causality of the nature-mechanism.

But here we come to the real heart of free causality, especially with regard to its rootedness in intellectual desire or the will. For the indispensable basis of this as a genuinely *free* causality will be the introduction of *another law*, a law which is not reducible to the physical laws of the nature-mechanism. It is rather a law in adherence to which humans are able to be causal agents from *within* the deterministic laws of the nature mechanism, and to generate effects that the nature mechanism by its own laws could not have produced. What is this law? It is the *rational 'law of desire'*, as Kant calls, it following Aristotle, (i.e. the moral law).

The introduction of a new and autonomous '*law* of desire', in other words, is utterly indispensable for the possibility of *free* causality, including any concept of freedom derived from it. For the whole force of a genuinely *free* causality is precisely *not* the utter *absence* of every constraint or every law or every principledness. For that would not be freedom at all but merely blind randomness, arbitrariness and chaos. Free causality, and with it any genuine human freedom, in other words, requires law. The whole force of free causality is that as embodied beings, humans can through the *will* bring their own *rational* law of desire (i.e. another law of causal motion) to bear on the laws of the nature mechanism in a causal 'making real' of desired ends in embodied life through enacted rational decision. As Kant sums this up: '*Will* is a kind of causality of living beings insofar as they are rational, and *freedom* would be that property of such causality that it can be efficient independently of alien causes *determining* it, just as *natural necessity* is the property of the causality of all non-rational beings to be determined to activity by the influence of alien causes'.[14]

Applying this to our primary focus then, the point of this whole excursus has been to emphasize that it is *this* 'free causality' of human beings through the exercise of the will, and not the deterministic causality of the nature-mechanism, that is the true 'subject matter' of human history. Moreover, because the way that the will exercises itself through causal agency is always through decision, we can also say that the principal domain with which we are concerned in history is the domain of enacted decision. It is this free causal agency through enacted decision that history, as a science concerned with real events of 'factual' life-movement rather than fictional constructions, seeks to be the story *of*.

4. But before we can move on to address the central question of this chapter, all of this must be brought finally also to a further crucial threshold for theology. For on the witness of the Bible, theology must bring something else to bear on this question of human freedom and enacted decision in life-movement, something that philosophy cannot. The point is that while the Bible agrees that humans are indeed free causal agents in a way that allows for a genuine responsibility and culpability for what is caused, it also says that this 'law of desire' (the moral law) by which we are able, within limits, to be free of the causal necessity of the nature-mechanism, is in fact the law of '*covetous* desire', which is to say the law of sin and death in the knowledge of good and evil. This very 'law of desire' in the human will, in other words, by which humans are able to act causally in a way which is free from natural necessity, is also as the law of covetous desire and covetous freedom, the law of 'the will turned in upon itself', or as Luther puts it, the law of 'the heart turned in upon itself' (the *cor curvum in se*).

When we say therefore that God in Jesus Christ enters history, and that something real and divinely *causal* happens here in a way that transforms the relation of the world to God, the first thing that must be said is that we do *not* mean that something happens in the causality of the cosmic nature-mechanism per se. For in the original divine causality that creates the heavens and the earth out of nothing, the eternal Logos of God already fills and sustains all of this in every way from the beginning of all things: fills it, and continues to fill it *ex nihilo* in unspeakable glory and in the breathtaking beauty of a design which, in its own created causal processes and dynamic effects, day after day pours forth speech and displays knowledge (Ps. 19. 1–6). But the effects that human beings as *free* causal agents produce, especially as they have become a law of covetous desire unto themselves, are not the effects of the original creation which pours forth its own speech and knowledge. They are rather the effects of a divinely created, yet genuinely *free* causality, a freedom whose integrity God sustains by grace because of his love for creation, sustains it even when this freedom has come to be turned away from the desire of divine love and righteousness, and instead turned in upon its own law of desire and righteousness.

When we say, therefore, that God in Jesus Christ enters history and that something divinely causal happens here – just as something divinely causal is still happening *ex nihilo* in the unfolding physically causal processes of the created universe – we mean to begin with that God has entered causally even into that aspect of creation which the initial act of creation does not directly effect, but which God's allowance for free causality from within it effects. It is thus proved fully true that when Christ appears in history in the likeness of sinful flesh – that is, by inhabiting even the law of covetous desire and covetous freedom, or the law of sin and death, yet without sin: it is proved fully true that in the revelation of Jesus Christ in history we do indeed witness 'the fullness of him who fills everything in every way' (Eph. 1.23).

III

5. But we must now in light of this turn specifically to our central question in this chapter which remains unanswered. What happens in the world when the Word becomes flesh, or when God becomes man in history? What happens when the reality of God enters the reality of the world in Jesus Christ? What happens here really and causally in a way that transforms the history of the world itself? There is a specific, and different kind of question we will presently be asking in order to help to open this up. But as a foil against which to place that new question and develop it, let me begin from a few well-known statements by Dietrich Bonhoeffer, which seem to point in similar directions to our own, yet which because of the way they are framed remain opaque. Bonhoeffer's basic position, as already stated in Chapter One, is that because 'in Jesus Christ the reality of God has entered into the reality of this world' therefore theology may look nowhere else but to the reality of this world in its attentiveness to God.[15] Or likewise, 'the reality of God is disclosed only as it places me completely *into* the reality of the world'.[16]

These statements are grounded in others which envisage what remains an unclarified but still uncompromising 'unity' between 'the reality of God' and 'the reality of the world' announced in 'the reality of Jesus Christ'. It is a unity that has its basis in the reconciliation of the world to God in Jesus Christ, but which precisely as such is never to be understood in any kind of separation from the real world, or in some higher metaphysical abstraction from the world, but always only fully *in* the empirical contingencies of sensible-rational human life in space and time: 'There are not two realities, but *only one reality*, and that is God's reality revealed in Christ in the reality of the world'; and again, 'there are not two realms but only *the one realm of the Christ-reality* [*Christuswirklichkeit*], in which the reality of God and the reality of the world are united'.[17]

Now again, it is difficult, at least as these statements stand, to come to any clear or coherent theological rendering of what Bonhoeffer means by this 'unity' exactly. But it is at least quite clear, both from these passages themselves and other writings, what he does not or cannot mean by them. First, these cannot be *ontological* claims, for that would be to engage in a kind of pantheism that would never have entered into Bonhoeffer's theological field of vision, having been in so many ways the uncompromising Lutheran that he was. Secondly, while they do at first glance seem to contain certain *cosmological* overtones, they cannot be meant fundamentally or essentially in this way either. For such a cosmological interpretation would lead unavoidably to the kind of metaphysical understanding of God's relation to the world that Bonhoeffer resists throughout his writings. Just as little can they be seen as *faith-subjectivist* claims, which would be limited only to the believer's own new perception of reality in the decision of faith; nor by the same token can they be meant merely *metaphorically*, since they are explicitly claiming to be about 'ultimate *reality*'. And in fact, if one looks at these statements closely one will see that Bonhoeffer is quite careful to phrase them so that they cannot be interpreted in any inadmissible 'totalizing' sense, as discussed in Chapter Four. He is not suggesting, in other words, that on the *one* hand, we have 'the reality of God', and on the *other* hand, 'the reality of all that is not God' (the world, creation): as if these were simply two disparate segments of an alienated but still at bottom comprehensive *constitutive* 'whole' which, through the 'reconciliation' between 'the two' in Jesus Christ, could then simply be added together to form a cumulative unity or an objective totality.

If therefore what Bonhoeffer is seeking to express here is reflective of a valid and theologically proper insight, which I believe it is, and if we are to have any prospect of developing it further, then we must pursue it in a different direction than what he implies. I want to suggest that the question can be formulated better in a different way. The initial question cannot be: What is the unity of the reality of the world and the reality of God in the reality of Jesus Christ? It must rather be: What is the unity expressed in Jesus's statement that 'I and the Father are one' (Jn 10.19)? What is the unity with God, and therefore the reality of God in the world, that is expressed in Jesus's statement that 'anyone who has seen me has seen the Father' and 'I am in the Father and the Father is in me' (Jn 10.30; 14.9–10)? How are we to understand and explain the oneness of God with the man Jesus of Nazareth, and therefore the reality of God in the world *in* this man, 'in whom all the fullness of the Deity lives in bodily form' (Col. 2.9)? Let us address this first in a negative way in order to observe what it cannot be.

6. It will be fully clear to begin with, both from the immediately foregoing paragraphs and even more so from the discussions in Chapter Four, that this unity may not be explained through any speculatively ontological or meta-physical projections of the cognitively discursive understanding. That is, it will not be able to be understood theologically as if, on one side, we were able to set before ourselves 'ontologically' or metaphysically the 'being' of God as an objective 'existent' in the domain of the 'there is'; and on the other side 'ontically' the being of a man, so as from there through an exercise of our own cognitive intellect to fuse these together *speculatively* into an abstract ontologically idealized and totalized 'whole'. This is disallowed in the first place for the methodological reason that it would amount to a pure and unencumbered rationalism which has ceased to recognize its proper limits in that it has reified, without any possible rational justification (and thus irrationally) the abstract products of its own speculative activity (dogmatism). But it is much more importantly disallowed because it would not only violate the uncreated and therefore non-objectifiable reality of God – the 'I am' is *not* a 'there is' – but it would also rob Jesus Christ of his full humanity. For it would imply that the true reality of God in Christ is not in his embodied humanity but rather on some 'deeper' ontological level underlying this (always remembering that 'ontology' is a projective discipline of the speculative intel-

lect). We must on the scriptural stipulation be able to affirm that Jesus Christ, even and precisely in his oneness with God, is really a *man* – 'in *every way*' a human being as we are (Heb. 2.17) – indeed, a human being in 'the likeness of sinful man' as we are, and yet 'without sin' (Rom. 8.3, Heb. 4.15).

It is for this same reason that we may not diminish the real challenge of the 'two natures in one hypostasis' (or 'person') as set by Chalcedon, by reading these 'natures' abstractly and a-temporally as supra-sensible or subterranean 'essences' that are somehow taken to be 'more real' than the physically embodied reality itself; and which, by a purely speculative exercise of our own intellect we then postulate as being somehow intermingled on a *metaphysical* level of 'person'. The hypostasis, the person, *is* the physically embodied human being of Jesus Christ, and cannot be abstracted from this. What I am suggesting, in short, is that no amount of strategic appeals to supra-sensible essences or substances, which are always a product of the speculative imagination, will ever by themselves be able to account for or explain the unity expressed in 'I and the Father are one'.

Still more obviously as such, neither can the oneness of Jesus with the Father be conceived in any kinds of 'genetic' terms. In the conception of the child by the Holy Spirit in Mary, what the Holy Spirit generates is not a child whose 'DNA' is half human and half divine. For that – as ludicrous as it is to speak in such terms – would effectively be the creation of a demigod. What the Holy Spirit generates is a fully human man, with a fully human, created 'DNA' (the God whom Jesus calls Father does not have a 'DNA'), just as the first Adam is a fully human man and not a superman or demigod. It is in this real man that 'all the fullness of the Deity lives in bodily form' (Col. 2.9). It is this real man who is 'the image of the invisible God' (Col. 1.15).

How then are we to understand this fullness of God in the bodily form of one man? The first thing to be emphasized in answering this question is that we may not bypass, because God did not, the temporally constituted mortal embodied life which Jesus *actually lives* on earth. Or stated more strongly, we will not be able to answer the question of Jesus's oneness with the Father apart from attention to what Jesus Christ really accomplishes or achieves in the real embodied history of his mortal life lived unto death and into resurrection. It is not right, in other words, as we can be apt to do in doctrinal theory, to treat 'incarnation', 'cross' and 'resurrection' collectively as the three thematically central Christological loci without equally acknowledging that the real power and efficacy of these events hangs inalienably on what the man Jesus accomplishes in his mortal life. For it is the fullness of the righteousness and innocence that he accomplishes temporally in his lived life, which he then also carries with him into death, thus destroying death.

None of this is by any means to suggest that Jesus 'becomes' the God-man, or that he 'achieves' divinity through what he accomplishes in his life. It is not, in other words, to jeopardize Christ's divinity from birth, for he alone, in the words of John the Baptist, is the one to whom from his very conception 'God gives the Spirit without limit' (Jn 3.34). It is rather to take with full seriousness the clear scriptural stipulation that his genuine humanity, and all that goes with this, may not be compromised either. And what this means, as the epistle to the Hebrews makes clear, is that in his very divinity Jesus Christ participates in the natural limitations of the physical growth and temporal development of a single man, a man who is born in human infancy and who shares in the natural human maturing and learning process from boyhood to manhood. Or as the Hebrews passage states this explicitly, 'although he was a son', nevertheless in his real earthly life as a human being 'he learned obedience from what he suffered', and in *this* way 'once made perfect, he became the source of eternal salvation for all who obey him' (Heb. 5.8–9).

It is only in affirming with boldness and *theological* 'risk'[18] that God 'should make the pioneer of their salvation perfect through suffering', and that Jesus 'had to become like his brothers in every way': it is only in affirming this with boldness that we can also be assured that 'because he himself suffered when he was tempted, he is able to help those who are being tempted' (Heb. 2.10, 17, 18). It is not, in other words, as if alone by virtue of his conception by the Holy Spirit in Mary we could permit ourselves doctrinally to move directly from Bethlehem to Golgotha without equal attention to what on the scriptural testimony is achieved in his life. For again, it is through nothing less than what Donald MacKinnon calls 'the historically achieved innocence of Jesus',[19] an innocence and righteousness that he actually accomplishes in the temporal passage of his mortal life, that he is also able to carry this innocence with him into death, and so to conquer death.

7. When we attend to the scriptural witness in asking the question of what it is in Jesus's own life through which oneness with the Father is claimed, we will find that one answer presents itself with clarity and consistency. Jesus is the one man, the only man – the one to whom alone 'God gives the Spirit without limit' – who lives his entire life in the *perfect unity* and obedience of a *fully human will* with the *perfect will of God*. The oneness of Jesus with God, that is, the full divinity of the man Jesus, is not the unity of two speculatively generated supra-sensible essences coming together abstractly in an ideal realm of 'substance', as reassuring as such false dogmatic securities may be for the demands of a purely cognitive understanding of this oneness. It is rather the utter openness of this one real human being, and of this one real human will – an embodied being and will which inhabits fully the temptations of covetous desire (Heb. 2.18) in the consciousness of good and evil – to the divine will. And it is therefore a oneness that is able, from within the full habitation of human fallenness and temptation, to accomplish and fulfill the greatest commandment to love the Lord your God with all your heart and soul and strength.

To purely cognitive demands, which will always try to find a way for this to be 'resolved' on the level of concepts, this may seem an insufficiently 'satisfactory' and dangerous unity. But that concern would already be fundamentally to misperceive the full reality of the *lived* oneness here, the lived oneness of a humanly *embodied* will in history, as the domain of free causality, to the will of the Father. Indeed, it is the demand for a *conceptually* apprehensible unity of metaphysical 'substances' or 'essences' that is the real diminishment of the oneness and the real danger. For any such unity can never be anything more than a merely theoretically achieved 'unity' through the projections of the speculative intellect. The oneness of Jesus with the Father is not a theoretical or theorizable unity but rather a real divinely achieved oneness in embodied history, accomplished by the perfect unity and obedience of a fully human will with the perfect will of God.

Jesus himself does not say that he has 'come down from heaven' to make known the ontological 'essence' or 'substance' of God, or a phenomenological 'being given' of God, but rather 'to *do the will* of him who sent me' (Jn 6.38). Or again, he does not say that the 'nourishment' which sustains him in his oneness with the Father is drawn from a well of metaphysical 'substance', but rather that 'my food is to *do the will* of him who sent me and to *complete his work*' (Jn 4.34). And it is this '*very work*' that the Father has given me to finish, and *which I am doing*, [which] testifies that the Father has sent me' (Jn 5.36). The work which Jesus finishes, moreover, and which testifies to his relation of oneness with the Father, is in turn a work and relation that is always declared as a oneness of perfect obedience of the embodied will of Jesus to the *command* of the Father. 'I have obeyed my Father's commands and remain in his love'; 'I do as the Father has commanded me'; 'I received this command from my Father'; 'the Father who sent me has himself given me a commandment . . . and I know that his commandment is eternal life' (Jn 15.10; 14.31; 12.49–50). The oneness of Jesus with the Father, as the unity of a human will in perfect obedience to the will of God, is demonstrated in its greatest magnification in the prayer in the garden: 'Father, if you are willing, take this cup from me; yet not my will, but yours be done' (Lk. 22.42). It is in this way, in the perfect unity of real embodied human will with the will of the Father, and not on the level of metaphysical 'essences' or physically abstracted and thus purely speculative 'substances', that Jesus is 'the image of the invisible God' (Col. 1.15) and 'the exact imprint of his being' (Heb. 1.3).

We can carry this even further with regard to what the scriptures say about our own relation with God and knowledge of God. The scriptures do not say that in Jesus Christ God has made known to us the mystery of his ontological 'essence' or 'substance', but rather quite explicitly that 'he has made known to us the mystery of his *will*, according to his good pleasure that he set forth in Christ' (Eph. 1.9). Again, Jesus does not say that anyone who resolves to contemplate the ontological substance or essence of God will know whether Jesus's own teaching is from God, but rather that 'anyone who resolves to do the *will* of God will *know* whether the teaching is from God or whether I am speaking on my own' (Jn 7. 17). Similarly in Ananias' anointing of Paul, the commissioning declaration is not that Paul has been called to righteousness through the knowledge of the mystery of God's ontological essence of phenomenological 'givenness', but rather that 'the God of our ancestors has chosen you to know his *will* [and *thereby*] to *see the Righteous One* and to hear his own voice; for you will be his witness to all the world of what you have seen and heard' (Acts 22.14, 15). Or again in Romans, we are exhorted to be transformed into Christ's image, not so that we may be able to discern something ontological about God's essence or about the phenomenological 'meaning' of God's 'being given', but rather so as to 'be transformed by the renewing of your minds, so that you may discern what is the *will* of God – what is good and acceptable and perfect', as this is measured against the divine righteousness (Rom. 12.2).

The same requirement is just as evident in statements concerning the new creation and the coming Kingdom of God. The prayer that Christ taught us does not say 'Your kingdom come, your "essence" be given', but rather 'Your kingdom come, your *will* be done, on earth as it is in heaven' (Mt. 6.10). Or again, 'not everyone who says to me, "Lord, Lord", will enter the kingdom of heaven, but only one who *does the will* of my Father in heaven' (Mt. 7.21). Moreover, it is by the same measure that we ourselves are declared to be the 'brothers and sisters' of the incarnate Logos: 'for whoever does the *will* of my Father in heaven is my brother and sister and mother' (Mt. 12.50; see also Heb. 2.11–18).

When in light of all of this we return to the question at hand, of what 'happens' in the world when God becomes man, we can respond summatively in the following way. When God becomes man in Jesus Christ – the one man to whom alone the Spirit is given without limit – the righteousness of God is revealed. But it is not revealed primarily as an abstract conceptual 'essence' or the overflowing of an idea to cognitive consciousness. No, the righteousness of God is revealed as an *accomplished* righteousness, a 'better righteousness' through a 'historically achieved innocence' in a real life lived in the temporal flow of history, a life lived in the perfect obedience of a fully human will to the will and command of the Father. And it is in this fully temporal accomplishment that Jesus is really, in his body, also the fulfillment of the greatest commandment on which all other commandments hang.

Something *real* 'happens' here in what Jesus accomplishes in his historical mortal life lived in obedience unto death. Something real and *divinely causal* happens in the world through a physically embodied and this-worldly act of God himself, something that transforms the very nature of the relation of the world to God and therefore transforms the nature of creation itself from within embodied creation. But we must allow this history, as a history of free causality, to be the real embodied history that it is. In other words, let us not suppose ourselves to be able to plumb the depths of this historical reality better by abstracting it from the embodied history of free causality in which it actually occurs. Or let us not think it necessary to impose a subterranean or supra-sensible or phenomenologically superabundant 'dignity' onto what is *really* achieved here through the free causality of enacted *decision*, in order thereby to seek to ensure the proper depth of its meaningfulness.

There is quite enough depth in the bodily enacted decision Jesus takes to go up to Jerusalem where he will be crucified. Quite enough depth in this decision, which achieves its certainty, verification and truth not through being brought to analytical clarity through phenomenological meaning-analysis, but rather first through the real causal agency of bodily action and motion in obedience to the divine will by actually walking to Jerusalem. There is quite enough depth in what is really achieved in empirical history through this one causally enacted decision without requiring a deeper and more primary grounding of the freely causal event in a cognitive theory of meaning. This is by no means again to deny the importance and utter indispensability of interpretive meaning and conceptualization in theology, nor is it to deny that the true depth of its meaning cannot be apprehended except by conceptual reflection and interpretation. It is only to say that the conceptual depth of meaning in what happens derives from the reality of the free causal event itself – the real history of it – and not vice versa. The depth of interpreted meaning – and this is indeed a profound depth – springs from the decisional action in empirical life and not vice versa. The conceptual meaning is derivative of the motivated action in life.

8. But we must now in light of the foregoing turn our attention to the question of the *present* reality of God through what Christ accomplishes in his mortal life lived unto death and into resurrection, especially to the apologetical question of 'accounting' for this reality. Indeed, it will be the present reality of God which is generative at the center of life today that will 'account' more than anything for the truth of the 'foundational events' in Jesus Christ themselves. And the central statement around which this accounting or 'verification' will revolve is the following one.

The revealed righteousness of God, and therefore the reality of God in the world that Jesus Christ *is* through what he accomplishes in his *mortal life*, is the same righteousness and reality of God that he *continues to achieve* as a reality in the world today in his *resurrection life*. It is a 'better righteousness' and a resurrection-reality which through Pentecost is now made available to 'all who are afar off, for all whom the Lord our God will call' (Acts 2.39). Or one can state this summative point of departure also in the following way.

Just as then in his *mortal life* this 'better righteousness' was not revealed in any sort of conceptual or phenomenological 'essence' of it, but was rather a historically *enacted* and achieved righteousness and innocence: so also today in his *resurrection life* it is a righteousness and reality that demands to be enacted, achieved and made real in the world by faith. We will in the next chapter turn our attention directly to the question of an 'account' of the present reality of God in the better righteousness of his resurrection life. But in order to lead into that, we will need first to turn to some preparatory considerations on the question of faith. For the reality of God in the world that Jesus Christ *is* as 'the righteousness which comes from God' is 'a righteousness that is by faith from first to last' (Rom. 1.17).

IV

9. In the history of Christian thought there have been two quite different views on what the nature and activity of faith most essentially is, at its origin, as a human response to the gift of God in revelation: two different views that will have profound implications for the way the question of the relation of 'faith and reason' is understood. The one view of faith will be found to be an orientation to the transcendence of God in revelation along roughly 'Greek' lines, which is to say, as explained earlier, as a humanly impossible

referent or ideatum of thought. The other will accord much more closely with what we have discussed as a 'Jewish' view of the transcendence of revelation in the command and summons.

To state the point simplistically (but not incorrectly), the former of these sees faith as most essentially the divine gift of a special and new kind of 'illumination' given to the cognitive (phenomenological) or speculative intellect. And the insight into truth that faith is seen as providing, on this view, is thus essentially a cognitively 'referential' kind of insight, such that the question of 'faith and reason' – or more exactly the question of the 'truth of faith' and the 'truth of reason' – comes to be engaged fundamentally on these cognitively referential levels. We will come to some modern-day examples in a moment, but we can find this 'illuminational' view of faith articulated with especial clarity and explicitness, for example in Aquinas.[20] It is true that the following account of faith in Aquinas must be balanced out by what he says somewhat differently of faith at other places in the *Summa Theologica*,[21] and I do not wish to be unfair to him by painting an unduly one-sided picture. Nevertheless what follows does have a certain prominence in his account of faith overall, and it can serve at least as a useful starting point for the distinctions we are trying to set out.

Building from the Aristotelian framework, Aquinas sees faith as taking its place among the 'virtues'. And we should remind ourselves, as we have discussed in an earlier chapter, that the virtues in Aristotle and Aquinas are conceived more broadly than they are today, which is to say that they are there seen not only as practical sources of guidance for right action and moral judgment, but also in speculative terms as guiding sources of orientation for right thinking or epistemological judgment.

Now in Thomas, faith takes its place, along with hope and love, among the three very highest of all virtues, which he calls the three 'theological virtues'.[22] And Thomas sees the latter two of these – hope and love – as virtues relating fundamentally to the appetitive or motive nature. Love is the supreme theological virtue or 'perfection' in the *appetitive* or *desiring* and motive nature; and hope is likewise seen as a theological virtue of the desiring nature and motive intellect, although subordinated to love. Faith, however, alone among these three, is understood as the highest virtue for the *cognitive* or 'apprehending' intellect in its speculative exercise and not the motive intellect. And because the speculative intellect in Aristotle (whom Aquinas follows) is seen as the most pre-eminent of all human faculties, surpassing not only the senses but also the desiring and motive nature in purity and clarity, therefore it is also to this highest and purest of all faculties that, for Thomas, the divine illumination comes *first* through faith. Faith is thus given a certain pre-eminence among the three theological virtues in the 'order of generation' of these virtues (i.e. that the illumination of faith comes first and the other two follow from that); whereas love is given pre-eminence 'in the order of perfection', but is still dependent on the prior speculative illumination of faith.[23]

But now there is a particular reason why Aquinas, at least in this account, finds it necessary to view faith in this way, i.e. as essentially a divine 'illumination' of the speculative intellect; and this is that he still holds to a Hellenistic-ally influenced view of the reality of God as 'pure being'.[24] And it is true that *if* God's reality is considered as 'pure being' along Greek lines, then this must indeed and unavoidably be encountered, if at all, originally as an illumination of the speculative intellect. For it is only the cognitive intellect and not the motive intellect that is able to focus its attention on such an idea of pure being, inasmuch as the motive intellect is not concerned with the relations of ideas and referents in thought but with the relation of means to desired ends in life.

Now this 'Greek'-influenced view of faith – as most fundamentally a refer-ential illumination of the cognitive understanding into divine or transcendent truth – is strongly present in many of the most prominent apologetical discus-sions today on the subject of faith and reason. It is of course not always present in the same way – that is, often no longer in terms of insight into 'pure being' – even though it is indeed still present in this form, for example in several important Roman Catholic documents, whether tacitly or explicitly. It is openly present for instance in a recent address by Benedict XVI on faith and reason.[25] Benedict himself here calls explicitly for a 're-hellenization' (i.e. for Benedict a re-platonization) of Christian thought, a re-hellenization in which faith and reason come together within a 'universe of reason' where the being of the divine Logos – defined as 'both Word and reason' – takes his preeminent place 'precisely as reason'.[26]

But this view of faith – and with it also the truth of faith as essentially epistemically or referentially accessed truth – persists in Reformed and Prot-estant discussions as well, although in different forms, where the orientation is usually no longer Platonic but instead something either more Hegelian or Husserlian or philological or analytical. We encountered examples of this at the opening of Chapter Six where the efficacy of faith by grace was seen as resulting, for example, in the ability to see 'prophetically' into 'subterranean' domains of truth; or in an expansion of the horizons of discursive reason itself; or again, in a different direction, in an 'exemption' from the defining rigors of reason in order discursively to achieve theological purposes. But we can also see the commitment to the truth of faith as something essentially epistemically referential in some of the current non-theological (philosophical) apologetical discussions. Alvin Plantinga, for example, seeks to give a rational defense of the truth of faith by setting aside the theological problem of revela-tion entirely (as is proper in philosophy), or rather by collapsing the reve-lational reality of God which grounds faith into the essentially noetic status of 'Christian belief'. On this basis, faith can be 'warranted' self-guaranteeingly in terms of its 'proper basicality' for the Christian community, which is found to be as much within its own 'epistemic rights' for holding its beliefs as other communities are theirs.[27]

Now Plantinga's account is arguably indeed able – through what by any count are highly rigorous and ingenious epistemological strategies which are very difficult to refute outright (because they are self-guaranteeing) – to make 'Christian belief', as the belief of a religious community, noetically self-securing. But because it has found it necessary as a strictly philosophical enterprise to overlook its source in the reality of God which grounds faith, the merely epistemic securities it provides are not genuinely apologetical for *Christian* faith at all but rather apologetical for something else. What is effect-ively forgotten here is that *sola fidei* does not mean *faith* alone, but rather *by* faith alone. And *what* we know in Christian belief by faith is precisely that Christian faith is not epistemically self-sustaining or self-guaranteeing, but is rather fundamentally *dependent* on the reality of its ground. It is dependent on the reality of what faith is faith *in*, dependent on what the good news pro-claimed in the gospel is the news *of*. It is dependent, in short, on the *revelation* of God that precedes faith as its ground and authentication. Christian faith, in other words, can never be epistemically free-standing or self-guaranteeing for the simple but important reason that it is most fundamentally a human *response* through grace to the revealed reality of God. Christian faith is faith *in* Jesus Christ, who through the resurrection discloses himself as really alive today in power at the center of life and not merely as something 'basic' within the epistemic confines of 'Christian belief'. The resurrection reality of Jesus Christ does not collapse into the epistemic status of 'Christian belief' but rather makes Christian belief possible.

But while we must say, therefore, that everything in the discussion of 'faith and reason' depends on giving proper place to revelation in such consider-ations, it is equally clear that the discussion of faith and reason will depend just as much on how revelation itself is understood. In other words, if the confession of faith is the human *response* and assent to the gift of God in revelation, then the theological understanding of what revelation *is* will fun-damentally determine what kind of response faith must essentially be. And the point is that if revelation is indeed understood as 'primarily and pre-eminently' a discursive or cognitive 'communication', as it is in Barth and many others, then it will follow as a matter of course that faith too will come to be seen as most fundamentally the gift of a divine illumination giving dis-cursive or phenomenological insight, whether through an expansion of this use of reason or through an exemption from its natural rigors.

10. We have seen, however, that the revelation of God in Jesus Christ is pre-cisely not the revelation of an epistemic 'referent', whether that of a phenom-enological 'surplus' or a cognitively apprehended 'pure being' or essence, but rather the revelation of 'the righteousness which comes from God'. Moreover, this revealed righteousness in Jesus Christ is not the revelation of the supreme essence of the idea of 'the good' which he somehow radiates from his human frame just by looking at him. It is rather something that he accomplishes and achieves in the likeness of sinful man in his real mortal life, lived in perfect obedience to the command of the Father.

Now this latter view of revelation yields a quite different understanding of what faith *is* in its origin. It is a view of faith that is not only just as promin-ent in the theological tradition as is the 'illumination' view – for example, in Luther, Kierkegaard and Bonhoeffer, and also many others – but is the one that in fact is accepted and constantly practiced in the life and community of faith in the church. This view sees faith at its origin not as the granting of a special illumination referentially into divine truth resulting in an expansion of the cognitive vision, but rather as the response of *decision* confirmed in the action of *obedience*.

That the belief and 'knowledge of the truth' (2 Tim. 2.25) which comes by faith is indeed a belief and knowledge in this latter sense (through decision and action) can be shown not only in the first awakening of faith – that is in the movement from a state where faith in Christ is not present to one where it is – but also, as we shall see later, in the continuance of the life of faith. But for present purposes we can see this with especial clarity with regard to the former focus. For the belief and knowledge of the truth affirmed in the birth of faith, as we shall see, is not the product of having become cognitively convinced through logical or inductive plausibility argumentation and demonstration, in the way that we become convinced for instance of the truth of a mathematical postulate through logical demonstration. Again this is by no means to say that plausibility argumentation does not have an important secondary place in theology. It is only to say that the belief and knowledge of the truth that comes by faith is at its origin or birth the belief of a willed response to a call or summons, a response which is constituted originally by the decisional act of what the New Testament calls 'metanoia' or repentance. 'The kingdom of God is near. Repent (μετάνοιετε) *and believe* the good news' (Mk 1.15); 'God will grant them repentance (μετάνοιαν) leading them to a *knowledge of the truth*' (2 Tim. 2.25).

Now the term 'repentance', as metanoia, is not to be understood most essentially or primarily as the response of a kind of 'penance' or self-reproach, under a burdensome and condemnatory judgment of moral guilt. Indeed, as Romans says, it is through 'the riches of his kindness, tolerance and patience . . . that God's kindness leads you toward repentance' (Rom. 2.4). The belief of faith exercised in metanoia means rather a willed change of mind or a change of heart, a transformation of the mind through enacted decision. The belief of faith, in other words, is not, in its generation or origin, the same as the epistemic belief that results automatically and unavoidably whenever the intellect recognizes the plausibility, probability or necessity of some hypothesis or state of affairs on the basis of conceptual (deductive) or perceptual (inductive, abductive) demonstration through cognitive inference.

Or to put this somewhat differently, the belief of faith through a decisional change of mind is not equivalent to a change in cognitive opinion; or it does not mean purely or first a change in an apprehension and assessment of 'the facts'. The 'knowledge of the truth' that God grants in the summons to faith, and that is encountered through decision and action, is not, in other words, originally the knowledge of an 'illuminated' *referential* truth, in which God is now apprehended as a conceptual or perceptual or phenomenological 'referent' or ideatum whereas before he was not. It is not an apprehension of truth as something ontologically or phenomenologically 'excessive' or 'superabundant', not a cognitive 'more' that overflows this.

No, the knowledge of the truth through faith, as the decision and action of metanoia, is rather what Rosenzweig in a similar context calls a more 'ultimate knowing'.[28] And as an ultimate knowing it is not a knowing through an 'ultimate insight', not an ultimate speculative illumination into an ultimate signification or ultimate cognitive meaning. It is better to describe it – as Bonhoeffer does in speaking precisely of faith and metanoia – as the knowing that comes only through an 'ultimate honesty'.[29] We will discuss what this involves exactly in the next chapter. But for present purposes one might just summarize the difference in knowing here as a distinction between the knowing of a metaphysics and the knowing of a metanoia. The knowing of an ultimate insight through the illumination of the speculative intellect into a revealed 'ideatum' or cognitive 'donum' is the knowing of a metaphysics. Whereas the knowing of an ultimate honesty through enacted decision in response to a revealed call or summons or command is a knowing through metanoia.

But such a delineation as it stands still remains obscure and largely rhetorical. For while no one would be able to deny the importance of metanoia as 'ultimate honesty', it must be shown specifically what kind of theological and specifically apologetical function this can have, and again, we will turn to that in the final chapter. What will already be clear from the preceding discussions, however, is that such a response – of decision, metanoia and action – is intrinsically or most fundamentally a response of the motive and appetitive or desiring nature and not originally of the perceptual and conceptual (cognitive) nature. (Speculative thinking per se can be true or false, sound or unsound, but not honest or dishonest. Honesty and dishonesty are intrinsically tied to motivations.) And insofar as this response includes the activity of the understanding or reason, it is a response most fundamentally of the motive understanding and not the discursively cognitive or speculative understanding.

Any question of the relation of 'faith and reason', therefore, may not exclude the motive use of reason, but must in fact be focused first on this level. And as we allow ourselves to do this, we will find that the very question of faith and reason itself will come to expression in quite different ways than it will when considered first or only with regard to the demands of speculative or cognitive reason. None of this again is a diminishment of the importance of the cognitive, nor indeed is it to say that the cognitive use of reason is not active within all of this. It is only to say that in the decision of faith itself, cognitive attentiveness is subservient to motive attentiveness and is guided by it (as we have discussed in Chapter Five) rather than the motive being subservient to the cognitive.

Notes

1 Karl Rahner, *Foundations of Christian Faith* (New York: Crossroad, 1997), p. 213.
2 *CD* I.1 pp. 307, 316.
3 Wolfhart Pannenberg, *Systematic Theology*, Vol. 3 (Grand Rapids: Eerdmans, 1991), pp. 308ff.

4 Elizabeth Johnson, *She Who Is* (New York: Crossroad, 1997), pp. 124–8.

5 Rahner, *Foundations of Christian Faith*, pp. 212–28.

6 We can and do of course speak also of a 'history of ideas', which is a tracing of an interconnectedness – or the lack thereof – in the development of philosophical, literary or cultural thought from one thinker or generation or epoch to the next. It was Hegel again who sought to fuse these two and to make the causal history of the world essentially the history of mind. And it is astonishing the degree to which both the human sciences and theology still tacitly adhere to this in their basic methodologies, even after the stupefying grimness of the real, causally perpetrated and embodied violence – and not merely abstract interpretive 'violence' – of the twentieth century. The science of history itself, however, is concerned with such developments not so much in terms of their literary or philosophical content, but mainly in terms of their actual facticity within time periods, including the causes giving rise to them and the effects flowing from them.

7 Schleiermacher, *The Christian Faith*, p. 190.

8 *The Christian Faith*, p. 191.

9 It is true that there are those who question whether our seemingly self-evident perception of ourselves as human free causal agents is *really* free agency, and who maintain rather that this too is at bottom a product of the nature mechanism and therefore something illusionary. We cannot and need not go into this question here, except to say two things briefly. First, these kinds of views can never be absolutely refuted because they are a radical form of skepticism, and no radical skepticism is absolutely refutable. Thomas Nagel, writing from an atheistic perspective, after admitting that it is impossible to refute extreme skepticisms logically, adds in response that 'the best one can do [in the face of such extreme skepticism] is to raise its cost, by showing how deep and pervasive are the disturbances of the thought which it involves' (*The Possibility of Altruism* (Princeton: Princeton University Press, 1978), p. 143). Secondly, these kinds of views are not only utterly counter-intuitive but also essentially life-denying. Schleiermacher's own assessment of such counter-intuitive and utterly unlivable views, which deny the reality of free causality, is thus an assessment which still rings as true today as it did then. 'Fortunately, few have ever been capable of this self-annihilating renunciation, by which, after robbing the whole world of life, they sacrifice their own selves also to the completeness of their theory' (*The Christian Faith*, p. 191). At any rate, it seems clear where theology must stand on the question, given that the Bible affirms the free causal agency of humans in a way that allows for a genuine responsibility and culpability for what is caused.

10 *CPrR* 5:9, original emphasis.

11 Kierkegaard, *Concluding Unscientific Postscript to Philosophical Fragments*, Vol. I (Princeton: Princeton University Press, 1992), p. 311; hereafter *Postscript*.

12 *Postscript* Vol. 2, p. 73.

13 . . . although there are legitimate questions which arise at this point with regard to the higher mammals, but that need not concern us here.

14 *Groundwork of the Metaphysics of Morals*, in *Immanuel Kant, Practical Philosophy* (Cambridge: Cambridge University Press, 1996), 4:446, original emphasis.

15 Dietrich Bonhoeffer, *Ethics* (Minneapolis: Fortress, 2005), p. 59.

16 *Ethics*, p. 55.

17 *Ethics*, p. 58, original emphasis.

18 i.e. at the risk of forfeiting abstract conceptual or metaphysical securities, or theoretically comprehensive resolutions.

19 *Explorations in Theology*, p. 97.
20 See e.g. Aquinas, *Commentary on the de Trinitate of Boethius* in *Faith, Reason and Theology* (Toronto: Pontifical Institute of Medieval Studies, 1987), Q1, A1–A2; see especially pp. 19, 22 in this edition.
21 See e.g. *ST* Ia IIae Q56 A3.
22 See *ST* Ia IIae Q 62, especially A3 and A4.
23 See *ST* Ia IIae Q 62 A3 and A4.
24 *ST* Ia Q6 A1.
25 Benedict XVI, 'Faith, Reason and the University: Memories and Reflections', Address at the University of Regensburg, 12 September 2006.
26 'Faith, Reason and the University', §15, §5.
27 For a succinct overview of Plantinga's position on this, see 'The Reformed Objection to Natural Theology' in *Christian Scholar's Review* 11, no. 3 (1982) 187–98.
28 Franz Rosenzweig, 'Apologetic Thinking' in Paul Franks *et al.* (eds) *Philosophical and Theological Writings* (Indianapolis: Hackett, 2000), pp. 95–108, p. 108.
29 Dietrich Bonhoeffer, *Letters and Papers from Prison* (New York: Macmillan, 1979), p. 360.

CHAPTER 9

THE COMMAND OF GRACE

I

1. For Christian theology, everything depends on the present and living reality of God, as does everything in the Christian hope and everything in the Christian life. In this final chapter we return to the statement from which we began in order, on the basis of intervening discussions, to come to certain initial destinations with regard to the challenge it presents. That challenge itself, however – as a particular expression of the problem of 'revelation and reason' or 'transcendence and immanence' – has now been redefined in one important way. For as we have seen in Chapter Seven, we are now no longer searching for a reasoned understanding or 'account' of divine transcendence in revelation as the disclosure of an 'ideatum' which passes over into a reception at the frontiers of the discursive understanding. We are rather searching for a reasoned 'account' of divine transcendence as a revealed summons or motivating call to decision and obedience through faith in embodied life, a revelation whose 'passing-over' into a reception occurs at the threshold of the motive and desiring understanding. In this final chapter, then, we will be focusing our apologetical questioning at this latter threshold, a threshold at which the question of 'revelation and reason' will come to expression in a quite different way than it does at the cognitive or speculative threshold.

In order to proceed with this, however, it will be necessary to continue first with some further brief considerations on the question of faith and reason. And in light of the concluding discussions of the previous chapter this will have to be approached in a somewhat different way than it often is. We will not be approaching this relation by setting a generalized idea of 'faith' – loosely defined and presupposed as 'religious belief' or 'Christian belief' – before the cognitive gaze, to be analyzed under this gaze with a view to defending its reasonability or warrantability primarily according to the requirements of a cognitive rational analysis. For such a generalization would already not only be an abstraction of faith from the reality of its actual occurrence in life, it would also from the outset limit the possibilities of its reasonableness to cognitive or epistemic criteria of reason.

We will rather be looking first at the nature and activity of faith itself and asking about *its own* 'reasonableness' as a lived response to revelation. Because faith is a response of the whole human being, it includes an activity of the understanding or of reason. And the first task in considering the relation of 'faith and reason', therefore – if it is to be approached legitimately and fair-mindedly – must be that of observing or attending to the actual activity of the understanding that is involved in the response of faith itself. In order to explore this, we will be focusing more exactly on the nature and reasonableness of faith at one of its most difficult points: i.e. as an affirmation or response which carries with it *the assurance of a certitude* (Heb. 11.1). And we will be asking specifically about the precise status of its certitude as a 'reasonable' certitude, or how, if at all, it can be 'accounted for' as a certitude. If the certitude of faith is to be able to be apologetically 'defended' at all, then it cannot be *only* the subjective 'certitude' of an experiential conviction (while not wanting to take away from the importance of conviction), but must in some way be a reasonable certitude and assurance.

2. It is virtually axiomatically taken for granted today that when we speak of rational verification or warrant for anything affirmable with the assurance of a certainty, that such a verification or warrant, if it is to be genuinely rational, must be essentially a cognitive verification secured by a fundamentally cognitive certainty. There are of course varying grades of 'certitude' with which cognitive (perceptual and conceptual) enquiry will learn to be satisfied. The most secure certainty, as we have seen earlier, is that of 'necessity' based on the analytical definitions of terms and the operations of logic. The certainty here is called indefeasible or incontrovertible because it is deductive certainty, i.e. certainty which can be deduced logically and thus necessarily on the basis of accepted premises. But there are also other modes of reasoning by which we can legitimately claim at least a 'reasonable certainty', for example, through the probabilities demonstrable through inductive reasoning, or the plausibilities ascertainable through abductive reasoning (reasoning to the best explanation). All of these are modes of verification by which we support claims to cognitively reasonable certitude, which is to say *objective* reasonableness, in its varying degrees of assurance.

Now what we strive for in any of these verifications is the removal or the cessation of what C. S. Peirce calls 'the irritation of doubt'. And the way that cognitive or discursive reason, as a faculty of coherence, achieves this cessation of doubt is by coming to some state or other of conceptual 'resolution'. The irritation of doubt ceases automatically when problems are shown to be conceptually 'resolvable' in some way (hence conceptual 'resolution'). Now the initial inclination for theological apologetical thinking to strive for such states of conceptual resolution, and the cessation of doubt they automatically carry, and further to measure its apologetical success according to the degree to which it is able to achieve it, will be just as natural as it is for any other discipline of thinking. But as apologetical thinking strives for this kind of reasonableness, it also inevitably confronts another edge. For when it looks to its indispensable and defining source of concern – i.e. the revealed reality of God in life as witnessed to by the scriptures – it finds that it encounters a 'subject matter' that forbids any such resolution into cognitive securities, and indeed is not known by the natural capacities of either reason or sense alone but rather 'by faith'.

What becomes clear right from the start, therefore, is that the reasonability of the certitude affirmed in faith cannot at its root or ground be a *cognitively* verifiable certitude. For the verifiable certitude of a cognition *just is* the verifiability of its *objectivity* (in whatever grade, whether deductive, inductive, abductive or whatever); and the self-revealing God is not an object of any kind for cognition, whether perceptual or conceptual. Christian apologetics cannot, therefore – at least not when it concerns itself with its original ground and authenticating source – seek to account in this way for what is affirmed in faith with the assurance of a certitude.

In light of this, I want to suggest that we try to approach the problem in a different way. Let us take as our starting point the scriptural declarations that 'we live by faith, not by sight' (2 Cor. 5.7), and that in this life of faith 'we fix our eyes not on what is seen, but on what is unseen' (2 Cor. 4.18). Now we have seen in Chapter Five that a cognition of any sort – whether perceptual or purely conceptual – is, in Thomas's words, by nature a kind of 'apprehension' and thus intrinsically a kind of 'vision' or seeing. We see *per*ceptually through the bodily organ of the eye, and we see *con*ceptually through something being made rationally intelligible, or by gaining an intellectual 'insight' or illumination into something that was previously opaque or unclear, such as when we come to 'see' the answer to a mathematical problem after the basic logic of it has been made clear to us.

More than this, we saw that cognition as 'apprehension' in its very nature always has before it some object of reference, whether perceptive or conceptive. Or more fully, we saw that perceptual vision is intrinsically the perception *of* something that comes into view (otherwise it is not a perception); and conceptual vision or 'thinking vision' is always intrinsically thinking *about* a referent that a thought refers to, a referent which conception thus always has in view before it as its 'content' (otherwise it is not a conception).[1] It is intrinsic to the very nature of both perception and conception as the elements of cognition, in other words, that they always already have or possess or see their objects, to the extent that they would cease to be what they are as perception and conception without their objects in view.

When, therefore, 2 Corinthians says that 'we fix our eyes not on what is seen, but on what is unseen', this 'fixing' of the eyes on what is *unseen* cannot be first and foremost a cognitive (perceptual or conceptual) 'fixing'. For it is both physically impossible and logically contradictory for the eyes of the cognitive vision, whether perceptual or conceptual, to 'unsee' its object, since the seeing and possession of its object is intrinsic to what it is. Nor may we diminish or dilute the completeness of the cognitive 'unseenness' here by construing it as something which is unseen simply in virtue of its being perceptually 'too distant' or conceptually 'too difficult', thus implying that if our perceptual or conceptual capacities were only greater it might indeed become 'seen'. For again as Augustine says, even if these capacities were magnified innumerable times we would still catch no glimpse of the transcendence toward which faith orients itself.

3. But this now brings us to the really vital point of departure. For although it is indeed impossible and contradictory for the cognitive vision to fix its eyes on something unseen, it is not at all impossible to fix the eyes of the motive and desiring understanding on what is unseen. In fact, this faculty, as demonstrated previously, *never* has its object before it in any kind of visibility at all. It is of course true that a human being in its cognitive-appetitive unity will indeed, even in desiring and willing, hold objects in the cognitive view. But these perceived and conceived objects, as has been shown, are not themselves what is desired, but are rather simply the means to desired ends. We have illustrated this above where, in the simplest example of the nutritive desire of thirst, the real 'object' desired is not the cup of cold water itself which I see before me. The real object of desire is rather to be relieved of thirst. And *this* 'object' as a *desired* one, remains intrinsically not only unseen but un-see*able*. The real 'object' of desire is rather precisely what the human being lacks, and seeks to fulfill or 'make real' through an action.

Now the belief of faith, as a belief originating in a response of the motive and desiring understanding, which is to say in a response of the heart,[2] 'lacks' precisely such a cognitive vision of its object. 'We live by faith, not by sight' (2 Cor. 5.7). For it is the very nature of this faculty – that is, this willing and desiring understanding, or the heart – that it does not see or possess its objects at all but that it desires to make real what is neither already possessed nor within any visibility, but is rather hoped for. And this is indeed exactly how Ephesians amplifies what is meant by fixing our eyes on what is unseen: 'I pray also that *the eyes of your heart* may be enlightened in order that you may know the hope to which he has called you' (Eph. 1.18). Or again as Romans states this: 'hope that is seen [i.e. perceptually viewed or conceptually grasped] is no hope at all. Who hopes for what he already has?' (Rom. 8.24).

But here a further vital element emerges, an element that is fully consonant with everything we have been saying about the transcendence of revelation not meeting us originally as a transcendent 'referent' for the speculative understanding but rather originally the revelation of a summons, imperative or call. For when we ask about *what it is* exactly that does *not* 'come into view' and yet to which we are told to 'look' and 'fix our eyes' in hope, we will find that a clear answer is given directly in these passages themselves. We are to fix the eyes of the heart on 'the hope to which he has *called* you' (Eph. 1.18), and on 'the one hope of your *calling*' (Eph. 4.4).

We thus come back invariably and indispensably to the summons, the call, the command, which *as* a call and command is addressed directly to the motive and desiring understanding, an understanding that does not see what it hopes for but rather through the eyes of the heart desires that the hope of its calling be made real. Or we might state this point even more definitively in the following way. Just as we have seen that Jesus's own oneness with the Father – as the oneness of a fully human will in perfect unity of obedience with the will of God – is a unity that is inhabited and authenticated nowhere else than through attentiveness to the immediacy of the command of the Father in the motive nature:[3] so also, through what is achieved in the resurrection and Pentecost, the revelation of God addresses human beings in the character of a summons and command. 'If you obey my commands, you will remain in my love, just as I have obeyed my Father's commands and remain in his love' (Jn 15.10).

But now in Christ, and in the 'call of his grace' (Gal. 1.6) which is enabled through what he accomplishes in the historically enacted innocence of his mortal life into resurrection, we are now offered a new command. It is a command or summons in which, like the 'Thou Shalt Love', all the other commands of the law are summed up, or in which all the righteous require-ments of the law are fulfilled. Yet this command will be found to be no longer an 'impossible command' – and for that reason it is all the more a command of grace – in that it does not require us to achieve the 'better righteousness' by ourselves, but simply to follow in the way of the one who has achieved it. This new command is the definitive gospel summons of Jesus: 'follow me'.

In the ensuing paragraphs I want to focus on this injunction, 'follow me', as a paradigmatic point of concentration for pursuing the question of revelation and reason at the threshold or frontier of the motive understanding. For the call 'follow me' is a divine injunction and thus a revealed one, and for this reason it is not first and foremost a summons to an 'imitation'. This is not to say that imitation will not be important and necessary again as something derivative and secondary. It is only to say that what Christ accomplishes in his mortal life lived unto death and into resurrection is not just the achievement of a supreme example to be imitated. For that would confront us again only with another impossible ideal, because it is just as impossible to imitate the one who fulfils the greatest commandment as it is to obey the impossible commandment itself. The life of Jesus is not first and foremost an example to be imitated but rather, through his death and resurrection, the 'firstfruits' (1 Cor. 15.20, 23) and the 'pioneer' (Heb. 2.10; 12.2) in the achievement of a radically new *way* in which the human alienation from the righteous reality of God has been broken through and communion restored in history. As a divinely revealed injunction then, the call 'follow me' is not first and foremost a summons to imitation but rather at one and the same time *a summons to faith* and simultaneously *a summons to obedience*. That is, it is a summons to make real 'the righteousness which comes by faith' – i.e. to become in our *bodies* instruments of *his* resurrection-righteousness (Rom. 6.13) through enacted obedience, and therefore to become instruments of his resurrection-reality in the world.

II

4. Nowhere in recent Christian writing has the revelational authority of the call 'follow me' and the immediacy of obedience which follows been addressed more uncompromisingly than in Dietrich Bonhoeffer's *Nachfolge* (*The Cost of Discipleship*): 'The call proceeds, and without any other

mediation, the obedient action of the one who is called follows. The disciple's response is not a spoken confession of faith in Jesus but rather the obedient act. How is this immediate coaction of call and obedience possible? It is acutely offensive to the natural intellect which must strive to divide this unyielding fusion (*dieses harte Aufenander zu trennen*). Something must come between, something must be clarified. Some mediation must at all costs be found, something psychological, something historical.'[4] But, as Bonhoeffer goes on to say, no such interpretive mediation gives itself up for conceptual scrutiny in the immediate response of obedience to the call. Rather 'in this encounter the unconditioned, unmediated, unqualified authority of Jesus is witnessed. Nothing precedes this call and nothing follows it except the obedience of the one who is called . . . this call is his grace'.[5]

I want to use these assertions as a particularly exacting exemplification of the problem that confronts us in the relation of revelation and reason when revelation is heard as a call directly in the motive nature with the obligational authority of an imperative. And while I do not in the least wish to soften the force of what is being said here (even if in this formulation its force remains largely rhetorical), nevertheless for the apologetical task the following kinds of questions must inevitably be asked.

If the 'immediacy' of what occurs here is 'offensive' to the natural intellect ('immediate' means simply that the response of obedience has not been 'mediated' or facilitated through rational reflection), does this mean that the response of faith, in obedience to the call, lacks every and any kind of reasonability whatsoever? Must obedience to the divine call, in the immediacy of the 'absolutely pure present', remain even after the fact of it utterly inscrutable for any kind of rational attention whatsoever? Must it, by any human measure of reasonability, be seen in the end as essentially 'a move in the dark', as a blind faith in which reason is simply set aside? Or to state this in the other direction: by withdrawing the direct response of obedience from any rational 'mediation' whatsoever, how is Bonhoeffer here not engaging in essentially the same kind of fideistic positivism on the practical level of enacted obedience as he accuses Barth of falling prey to on the cognitive level of a divinely posited conceptual communication?

Bonhoeffer himself gives no direct answer to these kinds of questions, and one could perhaps be forgiven for supposing that he thus ends up in the same all-or-nothing 'like it or lump it'[6] terrain on the enacted level of 'praxis' as Barth does on the conceptual level of 'ratio'. Nevertheless it is possible, on the basis of our own foregoing discussions, to rescue Bonhoeffer from such a charge, especially in light of what Bonhoeffer himself later insists must be the full 'mental integrity'[7] of such a decision.

In the remaining paragraphs, then, I want to push these issues to a conclusion by returning first to a particular essay by Levinas where they appear in a very similar form. The destinations themselves as reached by Levinas, however, will not be acceptable for our purposes because they will retreat again into the securities of what is essentially an analytical truism of conceptual theory, in which the real difficulty of the problem is simply bypassed. But we will be able to utilize his insights helpfully nonetheless, both to sharpen the nature of the question before us, and from there to use them as a foil against which to put forward something different.

5. In his essay, 'The Temptation of Temptation',[8] Levinas is interpreting a Talmudic text based on the Book of Esther 9.27 in which he finds himself confronted with a very similar kind of problem to what we are facing in the relation of the revealed call of Christ and the obedience of faith. Or as Levinas will frame it more exactly, the problem will be in the relation of the act of obedience in response to the command, and the knowing of faith that it engenders. In the particular Talmudic text in question, the Israelites are commanded to commit themselves also to a 'doing *before* understanding', or to 'obeying *in order to* understand', or as Levinas also puts it, to 'knowing without examining', and to 'fulfilling before consciously accepting'.[9] Levinas's essay itself, as is the case with much of his work, does not admit of any easy deciphering into a 'linear' form of argument, but let me try to condense the main positions developed in an argumentatively connected way.

To begin with, the deeper and more basic underlying concern here, as it is also for us, is with the relation between divine revelation and the human reception of revelation, or between the message of truth and the reception of this message. And the defining problem that Levinas faces in the text is that the 'reception' of the message is said to come *through* obedience to it, such that *doing* what the command says *precedes* the cognitive *understanding* of its truth. Or in other words, it is the prior act of obedience to the command that is said to bring subsequently the knowledge of the truth offered in the command. For 'the recipient of the message cannot yet benefit from the discernment which this message brings to him',[10] and the 'reception' of the command comes only in the obeying of it.

Levinas's question, therefore, is this: Must such a commandment to 'doing before understanding' or to obeying before knowing be something utterly unreasonable? Indeed, there is an even deeper question underlying this, which Levinas himself does not state, but which runs to the heart of the problem we face in the immediacy of obedience to the summons in the Bonhoeffer passage: How can such a 'doing' be a genuine *obedience* at all – and not just the robotic reflex response of an automaton – if it is not in some way *understood* first, that is, if it is not the 'informed' and free decision that obedience as an act of the will would seem to imply?

At any rate, it appears initially that in responding to this question we are faced with only two alternatives, neither of which can be acceptable. Either (a) we allow the understanding of reason to have its proper place so that the genuine character of free obedience can be preserved. (But if we do this, then the requirement of the text to 'obey *in order to* understand' is negated.) Or (b) in order to preserve the integrity of the command as given in the text, we deny the rational understanding what seems to be its required place, and revert to an utterly blind step of 'faith', a rationally naïve trust, a 'move in the dark'. (But if we do this, then the integrity of true obedience as decision seems to be compromised, in that the doing appears to become something undertaken either coercively or by a kind of automation and not freely.)

Levinas now suggests, however, that these are perhaps not the only alternatives, and he goes on to offer a 'third way' which, as he hopes to show, will allow for a 'doing before understanding' that is not entirely unreasonable. Because this third way is interwoven with a sustained critique of the other two alternatives, however, we will need to give some brief attention to each of those critiques before considering his own option. More exactly then, in putting forward his third alternative, Levinas engages both (a) in a polemic against a certain 'notion of reason', and (b) in a polemic against a rationally blind fideism. Let us continue by looking first at the former of these.

The notion of reason that is attacked is what Levinas calls 'the philosophical notion of reason'. And this turns out to be essentially an intensification and broadening of what in Chapter Four we saw was his critique of the 'ontological' disposition of reason, that is, the totalizing disposition that seeks to 'comprehend' everything on its own terms. The intensification and broadening occurs in several ways but it is most generally evident in that the earlier statement (in *Totality and Infinity*) that 'Western philosophy has most often been an ontology'[11] is here expanded and magnified in its influence by being named now as 'the condition of Western man', and this in the first place as a description of 'his moral attitudes'.[12] At the methodological heart of this 'philosophical notion of reason' that Levinas is attacking is a view of reasonability in which 'consciousness and seeking are taken as their own preconditions'.[13]

But the specific terminological intensification that concerns us is that the 'philosophical notion of reason' which 'occupies a privileged place in Western civilization'[14] is in this essay referred to no longer as an 'ontology' but now rather as 'the temptation of temptation'. And the temptation of temptation, as the condition of Western man is then further identified most definitively and succinctly as simply '*the temptation of knowledge*'.

In order to explore what this means we will need to do some work that Levinas does not do but which is implied. To that end then, let us begin by looking at the condition of 'temptation' itself – i.e. in the single use of the term. Temptation (in the singular) is for Levinas a basic and unavoidable fact of human existence in that it means simply to be susceptible to sin, or in fact to be *in* sin through the knowledge of good and evil. Temptation (in the singular) is thus indeed already a kind of knowledge (i.e. it is moral knowledge in the consciousness of good and evil), but it is not yet the *temptation* of knowledge. For it is a knowledge of morality entirely from the 'inside', as it were, one that is expressed and known always with the inalienable attachment of 'scruples and remorse' in conscience.[15] One might say, therefore, that temptation (singular) is the knowledge of good and evil in the state of their 'perpetual conflict', to use Bonhoeffer's phrase.

The temptation of temptation, by contrast – as 'the temptation of knowledge' – is the temptation of the intellect to 'know' this state of temptation in which good and evil are in perpetual conflict, and thus conceptually to unify it or draw it together by seeking to 'comprehend' it on reason's own terms. In other words, it is the temptation to set at a distance before the cognitive gaze what must remain in perpetual conflict, in order to comprehend it 'in the whole or as a totality'. In this way evil is apprehended as no longer truly in *conflict* with good, but rather 'evil is added to good',[16] such that what was in temptation per se (singular) encountered from within the conscience-irritation of 'scruples and remorse', becomes now, in the temptation of temptation, the external enticement of a mere 'ambiguity'.

The temptation of temptation, as the temptation of knowledge, 'makes nothing irreparable'. To be tempted by temptation is 'to traverse the whole, to touch the depth of being, is to awaken the ambiguity coiled inside it'. In the temptation of knowledge 'the evil which completes the whole threatens to destroy everything, but the tempted ego is still outside. It can listen to the song of the sirens without compromising the return to its island. It can brush past evil, know it without succumbing to it, experience it without experiencing it, try it without living it, take risks in security'.[17] In short, the temptation of knowledge is the temptation of the cognitive intellect to 'know' the knowledge of good and evil at a distance, to comprehend it without inhabiting its scruples and remorse. Or more fully, in its 'merciless desire to bypass nothing', what is tempting in temptation is to be 'simultaneously outside everything' (that is, in the sense of setting everything before the cognitive gaze) 'and participating in everything'[18] (that is, in the sense of seeking to comprehend everything in its 'essence').

Now in one important way we cannot go along fully with the sweepingness of Levinas's condemnation of virtually all of 'Western thought' in this polemic. For as we have seen from previous discussions, it would be very difficult to make the case that most of Western thought has been exercised in the 'merciless desire to bypass nothing'. What does become clear, however, is that what Levinas is describing as the notion of reason in which 'consciousness and seeking are taken as their own preconditions' is exactly what we have also been describing as a cognitivist mono-vision, which seeks to make phenomenal consciousness and linguistic discourse the arbiter of everything real. And the Levinasian critique can therefore at least help initially to post yet another warning that the kind of reasonability we might be expecting for our problem – i.e. for the problem of the reasonability of 'doing before understanding' – may perhaps already be an improper expectation of reasonability, or may not be the only one available.

In any case, it will be quite obvious that to any such cognitively mono-visional kind of reasoning, which in everything privileges knowing over doing, the statement that one must obey *before* one understands, or obey in order to understand, will indeed be 'offensive' in Bonhoeffer's words. Or as Levinas puts it, for the 'consciousness obsessive' philosophic reasoning he has been attacking, such a statement 'shocks logic and can pass for blind faith'.[19]

But again, while acknowledging this, Levinas at the same time rejects any suggestion that the adherence to the doing before understanding that the text enjoins may be the response of a merely 'naïve spontaneity'. It cannot be a reversion to a 'naïveté of faith' or to a 'childish naïveté' of the intellect, for 'childhood [cannot] answer the Tempter in the long run'.[20] In a direct echo of what Bonhoeffer also speaks of as the immediacy of obedience to the call (i.e. that obedience to the call is not mediated by a prior interpretive weighing of it through reason), Levinas fully admits that 'the Torah is received outside any explanatory foray, outside any gradual development. The truth of the Torah is given without any precursor, without first announcing itself in its idea ... without announcing itself in its "essay", in its rough draft'. But despite the lack of an explanatory prolegomenon, he then reinforces the earlier insistence that the acceptance of its truth cannot be a naïve childlike response. For 'it is the *ripe fruit* which is given and thus taken and not that which can be offered to the childish hand, groping and exploring'.[21] In other words, if we are to undertake the task of 'go[ing] beyond the temptation of temptation', then this cannot possibly be 'the deed of an underdeveloped human nature'. It must rather be '*a perfectly adult effort*',[22] one which has available to it all the tools of rational maturity and sophistication.

6. We cannot here discuss in any great depth of detail Levinas's 'third way', and in any case, it echoes largely what has already been discussed in Chapter Four. It might only be admitted that the erudition and complexity of his response do indeed require a perfectly adult effort to follow. But let me try to summarize it in just a few short paragraphs here, and we can introduce this by saying that Levinas's alternative will be developed under the familiar Levinasian themes of subjectivity, freedom and responsibility. In a word, Levinas will seek to show the reasonability of 'doing before understanding' through an analytical redefinition of human *subjectivity*, in which the normal philosophical definition of subjectivity based in *freedom* is replaced by a new definition based in *responsibility*. So let us explore this briefly.

The 'subjectivity' of a morally rational being (a human being) has usually been defined in a way that makes human freedom central to such a definition. Indeed we have seen this ourselves in our own discussions of free causality above, where freedom was explicitly tied to the moral law (i.e. the rational 'law of desire' through which human subjects can act freely of mechanistic causes). Now Levinas acknowledges that the command issued by the text – i.e. of 'obeying in order to understand' and of 'knowing without examining'[23] – can seem not only a threat to our reasoned freedom (i.e. our ability to choose freely through rationally informed decision), but indeed even a contravention of such reasonable freedom. In fact, he willingly admits that what we encounter in the command of 'doing before understanding' is a kind of 'non-freedom', but he then quickly adds that 'far from being slavery or childhood [it] is a beyond-freedom'.[24] And so he undertakes to show, via an analysis of the 'deep structure of subjectivity', that 'the apparently upside-down order here is, on the contrary, fundamental'.[25]

The only way that Levinas will be able to achieve this, however – as the last quotation already indicates – is by retreating once again into the abstract assurances of conceptual analysis. More exactly, through a subtle juxtaposition of certain interrelated linguistic terms, coupled with an appeal to the undefended authority of abstract metaphysical ideals, Levinas will indeed be able to demonstrate not only the reasonability but indeed the guaranteed certainty of the position he is seeking to defend. But it will turn out once again to be the merely incontrovertible and self-guaranteeing certainty of a truism. Let me in the briefest of terms try to set out the basic logic of Levinas's argument.

First, Levinas takes as his point of departure a particular term in which the Talmudic text ends: *Temimut*, that is, 'integrity or uprightness'. And *Temimut* is then in turn taken as the definitional description of that subjectivity which has already committed itself to 'doing before understanding'. In other words, according to the text, the subjectivity which accepts the 'doing before understanding' is the subjectivity of 'uprightness' or *Temimut*. However, having quite rightly presupposed this on the basis of the textual authority, Levinas now secondly moves outside the text and invokes the speculatively metaphysical ideas of 'the true' and 'the good'. The metaphysical idea of 'the true' is held to be both (a) that which is mediated or received in any 'reception of Revelation';[26] (i.e. 'the true' is here made explicitly equivalent to 'Revelation'); and (b) 'the true' is also the destination toward which any subjectivity defined around uprightness will by logical definition have to be oriented. Thirdly, Levinas maintains that we can know from the very 'logical meaning'[27] of *Temimut* that the uprightness it signifies is not established and measured on the basis of the *freedom* of the ego but that it is defined rightly only in the basis of a *responsibility* to the other.

From these three definitional premises then, several things can be shown to follow analytically (i.e. with logical necessity). First, it follows that any *direct* relation with 'the true' (i.e. with 'Revelation')[28] can only come in responsibility before the face of the other, that is, only in a way that *precedes* my own rational freedom (since only the other mediates access to 'the true'). From this it follows secondly that my responsibility in the face of the other not only precedes my own freedom of choice but indeed also 'establishes the ego'.[29] That is, it establishes my own knowing-and-understanding subjectivity itself, because only responsibility before the other gives me access to 'the true' ('Revelation') and therefore also to the most basic truth about myself. Finally, because this other which establishes my subjectivity is now found to confront me as *a responsibility of doing* prior to my own *freedom of knowing-and-understanding*, therefore it follows with analytical necessity that the very structure of my subjectivity, as established by the other, has its integrity in *doing before knowing*.

It is difficult ever to take issue with the basic spirit of Levinas's work, or to argue with the importance of many of its destinations, and that is no different in this essay. Nevertheless there are three quite fundamental reasons why this account of the reasonableness of faith in 'doing before understanding' fails with respect to what is required for the immediacy of obedience to the divine call 'follow me'. The first has already been intimated. The essay can achieve its purposes only by retreating into a labyrinthine maze of self-referential conceptual analyticity which, however compelling its literary and syntactical beauty, remains thoroughly tautologous, inasmuch as the validity of the 'doing before understanding' is accomplished essentially through subtle strategic maneuvering among meanings of terms, and through the equation of the metaphysical idea of 'the true' with 'Revelation'.

But this confinement to analytical procedure in the logical analysis of sentences also has another side to it, which goes to the very heart of its failure for our purposes. The point is that what Levinas's phenomenological commitments require him entirely to bracket out, and what he thereby forgets, is exactly what must be most paramount in the immediacy of obedience with which we are concerned. What is forgotten is that doing is *not* doing at all until it is *physical motion*, which is to say the real motivated action of a living body in space. And *this* is where the reasonability of 'doing before knowing' as a living response of faith needs to be shown. One has little choice but to conclude, therefore, that because the 'reasonability' demonstrated is merely the theoretically guaranteed reasonability of an analytical truism, the result that Levinas achieves for the 'knowing of faith' in the 'doing before understanding' is no less removed from the dangers and vicissitudes of real life than is the 'temptation of temptation' he is attacking.

A second reason, stated briefly, for why this fails for our purposes is that it essentially inverts what is the true problem at issue by making the immediate 'epiphany' of the face of the other itself the mediator of revelation rather than the other way around. For Bonhoeffer, it is not responsibility in the face of the other that opens to the call of Christ; it is rather Christ and the immediacy of his call who makes possible a relation of genuine responsibility to the other.[30]

III

7. It is in the third reason, however, that we reach a point of comparison that will prove to be much more constructive and indeed decisive for our purposes. It has to do with a fundamental incompatibility between Levinas's stipulations for rational integrity and Bonhoeffer's stipulations for rational integrity. The point in short is that Bonhoeffer specifically ties the 'mental integrity'[31] of the decision of faith not to a *perfectly adult effort* but rather directly to the stipulation in Matthew 18.3: 'I tell you the truth, unless you change and *become like little children*, you will never enter the kingdom of heaven.' How is this to be understood? How can the childhood of the understanding in the obediential response, on the one hand, be reconciled with what Bonhoeffer claims must be the full 'mental integrity' of the response on the other? Or how exactly is the childhood of the intellect *not* the naïve credulity which Levinas takes it to be?

I want to suggest that what Bonhoeffer is seeing or intuiting here, in a quite undeveloped way, hinges exactly around the distinction we have been developing over the past several chapters: namely, that the cognitive (speculative) exercise of reason, and motive (desiring) exercise of reason, have their 'mental integrities' in quite different sources. We will explore what these are in a moment, but one thing will already be fully evident even at this juncture.

What is clear is that if we are to be able to give a truly 'reasonable' yet also appropriately 'childlike' explanatory account of the 'immediate' authority of revelation in the summons at all, then it will not be able to come through the subtleties and intricacies of a syntactically nuanced phenomenological and literary theory, such as the one Levinas has given us. The answer will have to be a much simpler one, an answer which, without forfeiting the reasonability and freedom required of obedience, even a 'less than perfectly adult' youth or child can follow. And there is indeed available to us a much simpler answer to this seeming dilemma. It is an answer in which most of the problems we have encountered thus far will effectively disappear, because they have arisen from attending to both revelation and faith in the wrong way or at the wrong place.

The point is that everything in the Levinasian picture still fixes its eyes through the cognitive vision, that is, through the conceptual and phenomenological use of reason, and supposes that 'immediacy' must be explained as a cognitive or phenomenological immediacy. And in this supposition it encounters an insurmountable problem. The problem is that every cognition *just is* already a mental interpretation (whether perceptual or conceptual); and interpretation in turn *just is* 'mediation'. (The 'interpretive' activity of cognitive reason *just is* its 'mediating' activity.) Levinas thus assumes that the problem he faces in explaining the reception of revelation is the following one. He assumes that he must show how an 'ideatum' or referent of cognition can arrive *non*-interpretively (i.e. im-mediately) into a consciousness which is *intrinsically* interpretive, that is, intrinsically 'mediating'. We have seen in Chapter Four that he tries to achieve this in one way through the introduction of the Cartesian 'idea of infinity' into the cognitive process, by which the intrinsically interpretive (mediating) character of cognition is, so to speak, cleansed or purged of its own interpretive 'hegemony'.

In the present essay, he does it first by simply positing what he calls an 'epiphany' of the other which arrives 'immediately' (non-interpretively) into interpreting consciousness in the face of the other. And in order then to explain the 'reasonability' of what seems to be a contradictory 'arrival',[32] he must resort to elaborate modes of analytical technique by which the 'reasonability' of the epiphanic or 'eschatological' arrival is defended through the construction of a complex truism by which 'the apparently upside-down order' is shown analytically to be 'on the contrary, fundamental'.[33]

But all of these often powerfully eloquent and quite beautifully formulated reasonings are predicated on a false problem, a problem that Rosenzweig exposes with especial force as false. For what Rosenzweig understands is that the revealed summons or command does not address itself *originally* to the cognitive (interpreting) intellect at all. It addresses itself rather originally to the motive understanding where *alone* it can be 'heard' as the 'absolutely pure present' which 'can imagine only the immediacy of obedience'.[34] (For Rosenzweig, like Bonhoeffer, it is not the immediate epiphany of the face that mediates the command 'Thou Shalt Love', but rather the immediacy of the command that mediates everything else.)[35]

8. This now brings us to the threshold of what I have been suggesting must be a much simpler answer for explaining the reasonableness of the immediacy of obedience in response to the revealed call. The immediacy of the command when heard correctly as an imperative is not that of a conceptual 'epiphany',

not that of an eschatological 'ideatum', not that of a 'concrete concept' suppositionally implanted by the act of God directly into cognitive (interpreting) consciousness. No, the immediacy encountered here announces itself rather as what we have seen in Chapter Five is the *only* immediacy that the motive intellect can possibly know. What is this immediacy? It is the immediacy of the command heard as *an end in itself*, that is, as an *obligation for its own sake*.

Bonhoeffer himself will also state this explicitly, but before coming to that we can clarify what is at issue here by reviewing briefly our findings in this regard in Chapter Five. We saw there that an 'ought' or an obligation to act confronts me either mediately, that is, to do something merely as a means some further end; or it confronts me immediately, that is, to do something as an end in itself. The pre-eminent example of this latter, as we have seen, is 'love of neighbor'. Or in a more philosophical terminology, the pre-eminent example is 'respect for persons', which is to say the obligation never to treat other persons solely as means to ends – i.e. solely as objects to be used – but to treat them always also with the dignity that befits them as fellow free subjects.

What was found to be unique about this obligation and others like it, is that we are aware of it as an obligation which is immediately evident in itself, or whose obligatoriness is not derivative of or dependent on any further good end to be achieved. That is, we are aware of it as an end whose binding authority and validity or rightness cannot be justified or warranted at all through a rational demonstration either (a) of some further utilitarian benefit that it results in, such as the maximization of happiness/pleasure; or (b) through a rational demonstration of some generally idealized 'good' that it seeks to emulate. We are aware of it rather as an obligation that has its reasonability within itself independently of any further reasonable end.

This is by no means to say, as we know all too well, that respect for the dignity of fellow human beings is always followed or even recognized. It is only to say that when it *is* recognized as an obligation, it is recognized intrinsically as one which is not 'reasoned to' – i.e. not as an obligation that is followed as a means to attaining some further good end – but one that carries its own obligational reasons indefeasibly and immediately within itself. Indeed, far from being the *products* of reason, these immediately recognized obligations were found, no less than conscience, to be among the basic moral endowments that actually constitute the very obligational consciousness or ought-consciousness on which our moral reasoning is based. They were found to be elementary to the very structure of the motive constitution in its moral exercise. The 'reasonableness' of such obligations, in other words, *is* their moral 'immediacy' as obligatory, and their moral immediacy as obligatory *is* their reasonableness.

Now this is exactly the authority in which the immediacy of the call 'follow me' is heard when heard as *revelation*, i.e. when heard in the motive understanding as the 'absolutely pure present' of an obligation for its own sake, an obligation which cannot first be 'understood' by being 'reasoned to' but which 'can imagine only the immediacy of obedience'[36] or disobedience. To repeat, the immediacy here means that the call of God in the 'follow me' is heard as demanding to be obeyed entirely for its own sake – for the sake of the one who calls – and not for any higher good or greater happiness or blessedness to which end the 'following' would be the means. Or as Bonhoeffer now agrees with this explicitly: 'The one who is called leaves everything, leaves all he has, but not thereby to do anything especially worthy, but *simply for the sake of the call*, because otherwise he cannot follow along behind Jesus.'[37] The 'follow me' in the call and command of Christ – just as the 'thou shalt love' of the greatest commandment which Christ alone fulfills – has no higher end to which it is the means. For the 'follow me', like the 'thou shalt love', is at its heart nothing less than the command, in David Ford's words, to 'love God for God's sake',[38] that is, as an end in itself, an obligation for its own sake.

We therefore have two grounds for saying that the immediacy of obedience in response to the call is not a blind fideism, not the 'doing before understanding' of a rational naïveté. The first is that to hear the 'follow me' as an end in itself, or as an obligation for its own sake, is already to hear it in the full *reasonability of its immediacy*. That is, to hear the 'follow me' as an obligation for its own sake just is to hear it as a command that carries its own reasonability within itself. Or more exactly, what is encountered in the summons heard as an end in itself, one might say, is precisely the reasonability of the impossibility of reason to 'reason to' it as an end in itself, that is, the impossibility of reason to 'mediate' between the command and the immediacy of the response through seeking to understand it before obeying it.

The second reason why it is not a rational naïveté is that even upon hearing the command in its immediacy as an end in itself, the choice can still be made for disobedience – which is just as immediate a response as is obedience. It is here, therefore, in the response of obedience, that the childhood of the intellect becomes decisive. For the childhood of the intellect is nothing less than what Bonhoeffer calls the 'ultimate honesty'[39] of motive mental integrity, which, upon hearing the voice of God in the call, is able to leave all, take up its cross and follow, solely for the sake of the call.

We can in light of this now state succinctly how the childhood of the intellect in faith is not a rational naïveté, and thus not the forfeiting of mental integrity. The childhood of the intellect in its speculative or cognitive exercise is indeed rational naïveté. But the childhood of the intellect in its *motive* exercise is by no means naïveté but rather – innocence. It is the innocence of an ultimate honesty of the heart, a motive and desiring honesty by which the call is experienced and responded to, as Rosenzweig has put it, in the obediential immediacy of an absolutely pure present. Or as Kierkegaard puts it similarly, 'the childlike is the immediately recognizable'.[40]

And we might just add here that there is a single most basic reason why Kierkegaard, like Bonhoeffer and Rosenzweig, can speak of the integrity of faith in this way without succumbing to rational naïveté,[41] while Levinas cannot. The point is that, like Levinas, Kierkegaard also addresses the question of the integrity of faith through 'subjectivity'. But subjectivity is engaged in Kierkegaard in markedly different terms than Levinasian subjectivity. In Levinas, remember, the motive or desiring nature – or what Kierkegaard will call the 'passional' nature – must, in both the sensible component and intellectual component (the will) of this nature, be entirely bracketed out of consideration for any of the questions before us, and this for two basic reasons. It must be bracketed first because in the Levinasian project of alterity the 'the other above all alienates the will'.[42] And it must be bracketed secondly because, as the *motive* nature, it is inalienably exercised in *embodied* reality (since even the will or the intellectual appetite exerts itself fundamentally as a free causality generating bodily motion or action). And as discussed at length in Chapter Four, embodied reality can have no place in the Levinasian scheme of things because it constitutes the final 'common frontier' by which 'the same' will always find a way of drawing the other back into its own possessive ('ontological') jurisdiction, and thus into 'the permanent possibility of war'.[43]

But this brings us to a departure between Levinas and Kierkegaard which could not be sharper. For what Levinas must reject as having no place whatsoever in the discussion of either subjectivity or faith, is for Kierkegaard the indispensable heart of everything subjective and the heart of every proper focus on faith: 'Passion [i.e. desire, will] *is* subjectivity and objectively [passion] does not exist at all.' Moreover, 'Christianity explicitly wants to intensify passion to its highest' and 'faith is indeed the highest passion of subjectivity'.[44] This already means something vital. It means that it is absolutely indispensable for understanding his work properly not to misinterpret the 'inwardness' of Kierkegaardian subjectivity (as can often be done) as primarily the *cognitively reflective* inwardness of the thinking-and-interpreting subject, which is to say the subjectivity which objectifies.

Kierkegaardian subjectivity, in other words, is not the subjectivity of the Kantian 'I think' or Kant's 'transcendental unity of apperception'; it is not the Levinasian thinking and objectively comprehending 'ego' which he designates as 'the same'.[45] Everything in the Kierkegaardian picture disallows this. For Kierkegaard sees all of this as already part of the intrinsically *objectifying* 'subjectivity' of cognition and speculation. And 'the subjectivity which objectifies' is thus for Kierkegaard not the genuine heart of subjectivity at all, but rather integrally already a defining constituent of what he calls the domain of 'objectivity'. His reasoning for this is straightforward. Because 'objectification' is itself the fundamental *function* of the thinking-and-interpreting subject, the domain of 'objectivity' for Kierkegaard therefore includes the subjectivity which 'does' the objectifying. It is against this that Kierkegaard's fundamentally different position must be understood: '*passion* [desire, will] is subjectivity', and 'Christianity explicitly wants to intensify [this] passion to its highest', the highest intensification of which is faith.

This is not of course to say that there are 'two' subjects: one thinking or objectifying, and another passional or desiring. It is only to point to a fundamental disagreement between Kierkegaard and Levinas as to what constitutes subjectivity at its deepest origin or ground. In Levinas, subjectivity is exercised integrally through the speculative intellect, as the ego receives its own *true* 'essence' from the other as this essence is mediated through the ego's own *speculative idea* of infinity. In Kierkegaard, by contrast, subjectivity is rooted in a bodily living existence that has its motivating and animating ground in desire or passion which always causally engenders *embodied motion*. Echoing our discussions of Aristotle, Kant and Schleiermacher above – where the domain of 'life' was defined as the domain of the capacity for self-movement which is always motivated by some kind of desire or appetite (whether merely nutritive in plants, or sensible or intellective) – Kierkegaard now also maintains that 'existing, if this is not to be understood as just any sort of existing [i.e. not inanimate existing] cannot be done without passion'.[46] For 'existence is like walking … existence is motion' and 'passion itself is the impetus of motion'.[47] And it is *this* subjectivity-defining and motion-generating passion that Christianity 'wants to intensify to its highest' in faith. We cannot go more deeply into Kierkegaard here. The reason for drawing on him has been simply to amplify in another way that the childhood of the intellect, in which 'the childlike is the immediately recognizable', need not be a rational naïveté.

9. Two important observations must now be added to this, however. Firstly, the fact that we are able by our own moral nature to orient ourselves to obligations that are not merely means to mediated ends but ends immediately to themselves, does not make this ability a 'capacity' or human merit for receiving the revelation addressed to us in the call as an obligation for its own sake. It is not an opening, in other words, for what Barth was critical of as 'natural theology'. Far from an enabling 'capacity', that the 'follow me' as the summons to faith addresses itself to the 'obediential potency' in our moral nature, is both the unmerited grace of the call, and the costliness of this call of grace. It is unmerited grace in that the revealed call or command addresses itself to the very heart of that 'principledness' which defines our alienation from God in our moral nature through the consciousness of good and evil (the sinful nature). And as commanding grace it is also costly grace because it is the command to be an instrument of the righteousness of God by taking up one's cross and following, that is, through sacrificial action in embodied life.

Secondly, the integrity of the motive intellect in the decision of faith does not mean that the integrity of the cognitive intellect is compromised or excluded. If we are to speak genuinely of mental integrity in the action of repentance through faith, then this must be able to accommodate and include cognitive integrity no less than it does motive. We have over the last few chapters been saying thematically that God's address in revelation does not declare itself originally at the threshold of the speculative intellect, as an illumination of this, but at the threshold of the motive and desiring intellect in the summons or command, because only the obligational understanding can hear the summons immediately as an obligation to be followed for its own sake (an end in itself). But this finding should not be misunderstood. For it does not mean that in the decision of faith the questioning activity of the cognitive intellect simply shuts down or capitulates, in the encounter with a kind of knowing which it has not interpretively mediated.

It is not the case that in this decision a cognitive troubledness or perplexity cannot arise or persist. This should not be misunderstood, however. For I do not mean that along with the assurance of faith through decision and action, there cannot also – and indeed often immediately does – come a cessation of the 'irritation of cognitive doubt'. I am only suggesting that it is not the case that in the motive decision of faith the discursive intellect must simply cease to engage in the perfectly adult effort of its own proper and legitimate questioning exercises. It does not mean that when the disciple immediately gets up and leaves all to follow Jesus, that this following cannot be accompanied by a kind of bewilderment over what has just occurred. Nor would the presence of such a bewilderment have to mean a hesitancy or unsteadfastness in decision. For the presence of cognitive perplexity or troubledness does not have to mean the presence of doubt.[48]

To the contrary, it is precisely because in the knowing of faith the cognitive intellect finds itself confronted with a knowing which it has not interpretively mediated, that when the follower reflects on what has just occurred, cognitive questioning must become active in even more critically sharpened ways, as it seeks to harmonize within the cognitive understanding what it already knows with motive integrity and decisional certainty in the 'yes' of faith. C. S. Lewis's well-known statement that upon coming to faith he was 'the most dejected and reluctant convert in all of Europe' illustrates this exactly. Indeed, it was out of the cognitive troublesomeness and bewilderment of what was encountered immediately in the 'yes' of faith, that Lewis went on to work out what came to be some of the most lucidly compelling apologetical writings of the twentieth century.

The integrity of the motive understanding in faith does not mean, therefore, that the cognitive intellect sacrifices its own integrity, or relinquishes its rightful function. It means only that it makes one central concession which it knows it must make in order to preserve its own integrity. It means only that in its recognition of having accepted a knowledge of truth that has not first passed through its own interpretive mediation but has rather been encountered immediately in the motive understanding, that it gives up its demand to 'comprehend' in concepts a truth that has not come by conceptual mediation. In a word, it gives up any supposition that God in his self-revelation, and the living truth of revelation, can be encountered or reflectively attended to *at all* as an idea or a concept.

IV

10. Among the main distinguishing features of the theological apologetics developed in this book is its advancement of a different way of understanding the transcendence of God, which in the revelation of Jesus Christ must be understood as a presently real transcendence at the center of human life. And the double-faceted destination reached in the immediately foregoing discussions – where on the one hand the motive use of reason at the threshold of faith assents to a 'knowledge of the truth' through the enacted decision of metanoia (2 Tim. 2.25), and where on the other the cognitive use of reason continues to wrestle with a knowledge that has not come by its own

mediation – this destination provides a key for expressing succinctly a proper orientation to the transcendence of God in revelation as presently real and living.

The most rigorous and rationally exemplary 'apophatic' theologies have long understood that it is impossible for the cognitive understanding to orient itself positively or indeed even negatively at all to the transcendent reality of God. For all the positive assessments of cognitive (perceptual and conceptual) apprehension are intrinsically objectifying, intrinsically spatializing, intrinsically temporalizing, intrinsically comparative, or in short, intrinsically 'mediating' and thus limiting within these kinds of quantifications. And even the negative assessments of the cognitive understanding in its speculative exercise (i.e. statements about what God is not) must themselves, as we have seen in Chapter Four, still inevitably be framed in such quantificational language, such that this language too remains inescapably comparative and therefore inadequate and improper.[49] 'To whom will you compare me or count me equal? To whom will you liken me that we may be compared?' (Isa. 46.5). Moreover, these intrinsic limitations of the cognitive or speculative understanding with respect to the transcendence of God in his eternal 'aseity' do not change in the consideration of divine transcendence for the 'economic' question of God's 'revelation' given for purposes of redemption. For in Christ, revelation is the *self*-revelation of God. And the God who cannot deny himself, and who admits of no naming, does not in his self-revelation give himself to be known as something he is not (i.e. as anything objectified or objectifiable).

This is why, while we must fully agree with Barth's central dictum on revelation, that 'God's being is in God's act', we must disagree with him about what this means. The revelatory 'act' of God is not, as Barth has it, a divine act of conceptual implantation occurring directly within *ratio*, whereby God's 'being' or reality is never truly dynamically present in life but is only nominally present through the theological ersatz of a 'concrete concept'.[50] To the contrary, while agreeing with the basic dictum itself, we have been saying rather that God's 'being' is the *real* presence of his *righteousness* in embodied life today. It is the 'being' and living reality of a 'better righteousness' that he himself really en-acts as we, in obedience to his call, 'offer the parts of [our] body to him as instruments of righteousness' (Rom. 6.13), so that in the resurrection-life of Christ through Pentecost *'we might become* the righteousness of God in him' (2 Cor. 5.21).

But at the methodological root of all of this is the inevasible scriptural demand, corroborated experientially in the witness of faith, that the initial act of God in the address of revelation is the address of a *call*. It is the address of a summons, a command, that is encountered genuinely as revelation only when heard in the immediacy of the motive or obligational understanding as a call to enacted decision. It is not at its origin the address of a 'concrete concept' implanted directly in discursive *ratio*;[51] not originally the address of a 'superabundance' of phenomenality, or an 'excess' of a phenomenal 'being given';[52] not originally an address that overflows our own speculatively ontological limitations as an 'ontological plus';[53] not originally the address of an 'epiphany' encountered immediately in phenomenal consciousness;[54] not originally an address understood in philological terms as a 'passage of gift' from Donor to donee expressed in various discursive configurations of 'asymmetrical reciprocity and non-identical repetition'.[55] All of these continue to try to fix the intrinsically mediating eyes of the cognitive vision on what is neither a perceptually nor conceptually mediatable address.

The address of revelation is rather the address of a call or summons heard *im*-mediately as an imperative in the motive nature as an obligation and a call for its own sake. It is the revelation of 'the one hope of your *calling*' (Eph. 4.4), of 'the hope to which he has *called* you' (Eph. 1.18). Revelation is the divine address by which we are '*called* to belong to Jesus Christ' (Rom. 1.6); '*called* by the grace of Christ' (Gal. 1.6); '*called* out of darkness' (1 Pet. 2.9); '*called* according to his purpose' (Rom. 8.28); '*called* to be holy' (1 Cor. 1.2). And because the human 'reception' of revelation as a call or command of grace is a genuine reception only as it is obedient action in embodied life in response to the call, therefore revelation reaches its full communicative reality only in the transformational living of embodied life itself.

The communicative 'passage of gift' in God's act of revelation, in other words, is not principally a phenomenologically discursive communication from subject to object in the noetic-noematic or conceptual structure; not principally a philologically analytical 'gift exchange' from Donor to donee in the conceptual hearing of a conceptual address. The 'act' of God in revelation is rather, through the call and summons – and here we return again to one of the main earlier emphases of the book – an address which is encountered *causally* as a *being acted upon* in life, an address which passes-over into a genuine 'communication' only in its 'reception' through bodily enacted obedience.

In order to amplify what is at stake here on this point of causality, we can return again to Bonhoeffer, who through Luther picks up on the medieval usage of the term *pati* (meaning 'to suffer' or 'to bear'). In relation to the revelation of God, Bonhoeffer says, 'human beings are in the position of those who suffer, or who are acted upon; Luther speaks of this as a *nova nativitas*' (a new birth or new creation).[56] The mode of existence of the *nova nativitas*, moreover, is in Luther 'defined as *pati*, as being acted upon . . . [as an] existence to which things happen' (*getroffener Existenz*).[57] God's act in revelation, then, is a divinely causal address which is encountered as a 'being acted upon' in embodied life. And the corresponding disposition of faith, in the reception of the dynamically causal act of God in life, is what Bonhoeffer calls '*die Stellung eines Leidenden*'[58] – that is, the disposition of one who in embodied life 'bears' or 'suffers' this being acted upon, a causal 'suffering' or 'bearing' which is expressed in its 'effect' as the obediential action of faith in life. 'The life I now *live in the flesh*, I live by faith . . .' (Gal. 2.20).

To reiterate, revelation is not a conceptual communication but a generative and causally transformative *life*-communication, or what Kierkegaard calls an 'existence communication'.[59] And this means that it is presently and fully real for human beings only as, in its reception, it is a *lived* transformation-reality in response to the revealed call, through obedience to which human beings '*are being transformed* into his likeness' (2 Cor. 3.18). Nor may the defining message of Romans be forgotten here, a message that always draws us back to the centrality and finality of the righteousness of God. For according to Romans, in this 'passage of gift' in revelation, the 'content' of what is given through 'God's abundant provision of grace' is once again nothing less than 'the gift of righteousness' (Rom. 5.17). And the gift of the righteousness of God, moreover, is received *as* gift not as it is cognitively and thus objectively 'apprehended' or recognized in its 'significance'; it is rather truly 'received' only as it is enacted in life, made real in life.

11. It must be stressed again, however, that the emphasis here on the motive and desiring nature as the threshold at which revelation passes-over into a communication is by no means to minimize or undermine the full integrity and necessary activity of the cognitive exercise of the intellect in the richness of either faith-understanding or theological understanding. Much less is it to say that cognitive questioning and enquiry must on its own lead to misguided and false destinations, or that there is a fundamental incompatibility between where cognitive enquiry leads in its questioning about God, on the one hand, and the summons or command which is met in motive obedience through free decision and action, on the other. When we say, therefore, that revelation meets us originally at the threshold of the motive understanding and not originally through the speculative, something must be added to complete this picture. The point is that we must be able to affirm that the God who meets us in the summons to the motive understanding at the center of life is indeed the cognitively unknowable God, the speculatively incomprehensible God, the discursively unspeakable God, the perceptually and conceptually invisible God.

But let us not go further and envision any abstract metaphysical 'term' at the end of this, whether positive or negative. For that would be to treat God as an ideational object of the speculative intellect, and God is not a cognitive object of any kind. No, if we are to be able to affirm that it is indeed the transcendent and cognitively (perceptually and conceptually) unknowable God who meets us at the center of life, then the two modes of intellection – motive and cognitive – must rather be held in harmony, and we can explain this harmony in the following way.

That God addresses us in revelation as a life-communication and a transformation-reality through the call, means that the 'reception' of revelation in faith is not primarily the reception of a cognitive illumination or epiphany through which something hitherto mysterious suddenly gains cognitive 'clarity'. To the contrary, as a divine call that grips and motivates immediately in the *motive* understanding or the heart, far from the clarification of something hitherto mysterious, revelation is rather now for the *cognitive* understanding, as Rahner puts it, nothing less than '*the dawn and approach of the mystery as such*'.[60] Or to return to John of Damascus's phrase, we might also say the following. It is in the motive response of decision to the divine summons, heard immediately as a call to obedient action, that God truly *is* '*known* in his unknowability'. For again, the God who is truly *known* through the motively obediential response of faith as a reality at the center of life, is indeed exactly and nothing 'other' than the *cognitively unknowable* God, the speculatively incomprehensible God, the discursively unspeakable God, the perceptually and conceptually invisible God.

What we are suggesting here then also gives a proper context to Rowan Williams's like-minded statement: 'Jesus is God's revelation in a decisive sense not because he makes a dimly apprehended God clear to us, but because he challenges and queries any "unusually clear" sense of God . . . not because he makes things plainer . . . but because he makes things darker.'[61] Or in the other direction, it gives proper context and content also to Bonhoeffer's statement that 'the beyond is not what is infinitely remote but what is nearest at hand'.[62] Or yet again, it gives a new context and content to Denys Turner's statement that God's transcendence may not be construed in 'metaphors of "gaps", even infinitely "big" ones'. For precisely in his transcendence of all creaturely distance, God is '*closer* to my creaturehood than it is possible for creatures to be to each other. For creatures are more distinct from each other than God can possibly be from any of them'.[63]

To summarize, just as we have two uses of reason – (a) cognitive reasoning in concepts and percepts with a view to questions of signification, and (b) motive reasoning in desires and motivations with a view morally to questions of obligation – so we have two modes of knowing or understanding. The cognitive understanding, within which theological thinking must operate, is intrinsically an inferentially mediated understanding or a discursively referential understanding in theory. But the motive knowing of faith at the center of life is not such an inferentially mediated knowing nor even a phenomenologically mediated 'epiphanic' knowing. It is rather a suffered knowing, a suffering knowing, which is to say a knowing that comes only through the sacrificial act of an embodied doing in immediate obedience to the call of God (Lk. 9.23), a doing through which alone the mystery that God *is* can first begin to be engaged cognitively with true earnestness and urgency, and not just in the esthetic enticement of a theoretical postulate or puzzle. Nevertheless, these two are in harmony. For what in the motive encounter with revelation through the enacted decision of faith is indispensably and originally a suffered knowing, is precisely the encounter by which the cognitive endeavor is enabled to begin to engage with revelation in full earnestness as 'the dawn and approach of the mystery as such'.

12. And in the meeting of these two, a theological apologetics or a fundamental theology now encounters a new challenge. For as it searches with earnestness and urgency into its own ground in the present reality of God at the center of life, it finds that the revealed life-communication of God is governed by a new *law of living*, which Romans calls 'the law of the *Spirit of life* in Christ Jesus' (Rom. 8.2), and which James calls 'the perfect law that gives freedom' (Jas 1.25). And this means that as theology searches intently into its ground in the present reality of God, it must now also begin to express itself as a concretely principled transformation ethics of the 'better righteousness' based on the law of the Spirit of life. What such a transformational ethics of the 'better righteousness' must look like in its 'principledness' is beyond what

the scope of this volume can consider, and that must await another study. But everything in the book has been pointing to it and indeed depends on it.

Several things can be projected briefly here in that regard, however, as we draw our present considerations to a close. First, such a transformational ethics of the 'better righteousness' would, as an ethics of a revealed life-communication, have to be an ethics focused fundamentally through the intrinsic *contingency* of life, and therefore it would indispensably have to come to expression in relation to a pneumatology (Jn 3.8). Secondly, it would unavoidably mean a return to a robust engagement with theological fundamentals through the moral nature in the knowledge of good and evil, which is to say unavoidably a return to the sinful nature. But this should neither surprise us nor deter us from pursuing such a venture. For what Christ accomplishes in his mortal life, on the cross, and in resurrection, is neither a termination of the sinful nature nor an escape from the knowledge of good and evil into which we have fallen. It is rather a redemption of it from within it through the living of the sinful nature unto death – yet without sin – thereby accomplishing the better righteousness through a historically achieved innocence.

We might say, therefore, that to engage robustly in a transformational ethics of the 'better righteousness' from within the knowledge of good and evil, would be a quintessential instance of embracing Luther's dictum, *Pecca fortiter, sed fortius fide et gaude in Christo* ('sin boldly, but believe and rejoice in Christ more boldly still').[64] The domain with which such an ethics would have to concern itself, in other words, as it searches out the concrete principledness of its ground in the revealed reality of God as a life-communication, is not the domain of an idealized 'eschatological vision' which guarantees the 'certitude of peace'.[65] To the contrary, it would lead theology to look first for the finality of the eschaton nowhere else than the place where divine grace actually achieves its purposes and efficacy with real eschatological finality in Christ. That is, it would have to look first nowhere else than to the domain of embodied life, which is not the domain of the guarantee of the 'certitude of peace' but rather nothing less than the domain of 'the permanent possibility of war'.[66] For the certitude to which God binds himself in Jesus's mortal life unto death is not the logically indefeasible certitude of analytical or metaphysical necessity, but rather the historically and temporally *irreversible* certitude of a lived contingency – understood as the free motive causality exercised in the real life of one man lived in perfect obedience to the will and command of God. 'Just as through the disobedience of the one man the many were made sinners, so also through the obedience of the one man the many will be made righteous' (Rom. 5.19).

Such a transformational ethics would therefore not fall into the danger of promoting a 'righteousness by works'; for its defining concern would rather be 'works by a better righteousness' (Eph. 2.8–10). And it would accordingly not be able to come to expression fundamentally around the normal and more narrowly focused questions of how, from a theological point of view, we are to be good or act well, nor could it take the form of a body-devaluing asceticism. Its concern would rather be with the kingdom of righteousness itself,[67] a kingdom which, according to the scriptures, even in this life we '*are* receiving' (Heb. 12.28), and with a righteous Christ-likeness into which even in this life we '*are being* transformed' (2 Cor. 3.18) as we look forward, in the words of 2 Peter, 'to a new heaven and a new earth, the home of righteousness' (2 Pet. 3.13). It would accordingly have to involve a whole political ecology of the *nova nativitas* or the new creation in the fullness of embodied life now, a whole political ecology of justice, goodness, freedom and compassion focused with single-minded attentiveness through what must be the foundational question of any theological ethics: What is the will of God?

Notes

1 See discussion above p. 83.
2 See the discussion on this above, pp. 87–8.
3 See the discussion on this above, pp. 147–50.
4 Bonhoeffer, *Nachfolge*, p. 45.
5 *Nachfolge*, pp. 45, 55.
6 Bonhoeffer, *Letters and Papers from Prison*, p. 286.
7 *Letters and Papers from Prison*, p. 360.
8 Emmanuel Levinas, 'The Temptation of Temptation', in *Nine Talmudic Readings* (Indianapolis: Indiana University Press, 1990), pp. 30–50.
9 'Temptation', pp. 43, 40, 41.
10 'Temptation', p. 36.
11 *TI* p. 43.
12 'Temptation', p. 32.
13 'Temptation', p. 49.
14 'Temptation', p. 34.
15 'Temptation', p. 43.
16 'Temptation', p. 33.
17 'Temptation', p. 33.
18 'Temptation', pp. 35, 34.
19 'Temptation', p. 42.
20 'Temptation', p. 35.
21 'Temptation', p. 46, emphasis added.
22 'Temptation', p. 42.
23 'Temptation', pp. 43, 40, 41.
24 'Temptation', p. 40.
25 'Temptation', p. 42.
26 'Temptation', p. 47.
27 'Temptation', p. 48.
28 'Temptation', p. 47.
29 'Temptation', p. 49.
30 As Bonhoeffer says, it is revelation – encountered in the direct and rationally unmediated authority of the call – which subsequently mediates every other relation: '*He is the mediator*, not only between God and humans, but between human and human, between humans and reality' (*Nachfolge*, p.88, original emphasis).
31 *Letters and Papers from Prison*, p. 360.
32 i.e. the seeming contradictoriness of the arrival of a non-interpreted or non-mediated referent into intrinsically interpreting or intrinsically mediating consciousness.

33 The point is that *any* desired result can be achieved and guaranteed with logical certainty in language via nuanced juxtapositions of terminological meanings, especially when coupled with the undefended equation of meta-physical ultimates – i.e. 'the true' = 'Revelation'.
34 Rosenzweig, *Star*, p. 191.
35 See discussion above pp. 118–20.
36 *Star*, p. 191.
37 *Nachfolge*, p. 46.
38 David Ford, *Christian Wisdom: Desiring God and Learning in Love* (Cambridge: Cambridge University Press, 2007), pp. 225ff.
39 *Letters and Papers from Prison*, p. 360.
40 Kierkegaard, *Postscript*, Vol. I, p. 596.
41 See C. Stephen Evans' important and excellently balanced study of this in *Faith Beyond Reason* (Grand Rapids: Eerdmans, 1998), Chapters 6 and 7: see especially pp. 106–12.
42 *TI* p. 240.
43 *TI* p. 21.
44 *Postscript*, Vol. I, pp. 131, 132.
45 See pp. 63–4 above.
46 *Postscript* Vol. I, p. 311.
47 *Postscript* Vol. I, pp. 413, 312; Vol. 2, p. 73.
48 Although it does not seem improper to say that the belief and assurance of faith can persist genuinely as something motivationally lived (2 Cor. 5.7) even when episodes of cognitive doubt and questioning might arise: 'I believe, help my unbelief!' (Mk 9.24).
49 For trenchant discussions on this, see Denys Turner, *The Darkness of God* (Cambridge: Cambridge University Press, 1995), pp. 36–9, 270–1; and *Faith, Reason and the Existence of God*, e.g. pp. 156–60.
50 Barth, *CD* I.1, pp. 290, 291; see discussion above, pp. 48–50.
51 Barth, *CD* I.1, pp. 290, 291.
52 Jean-Luc Marion, *Being Given* (Stanford: Stanford University Press, 2002), pp. 221–47, 236.
53 Jüngel, *God as the Mystery of the World*, p. 214.
54 Levinas, *Nine Talmudic Readings*, p. 47.
55 John Milbank, *Being Reconciled* (London: Routledge, 2003), p. xi.
56 Bonhoeffer, *Act and Being* (Dietrich Bonhoeffer Works in English [DBWE] 2) (Minneapolis: Fortress Press, 1996), p. 116.
57 *Act and Being* (DBWE 2), p. 116.
58 *Akt und Sein* (DBW 2), p. 113.
59 See e.g. *Postscript* Vol. 2, pp. 562–4, 570–2.
60 Karl Rahner, 'The Hermeneutics of Eschatological Assertions', *Theological Investigations*, Volume 4 (London: DLT, 1966), pp. 323–46.
61 Rowan Williams, *On Christian Theology* (Oxford: Blackwell, 2000), p. 138.
62 *Letters and Papers from Prison*, p. 376.
63 *Faith, Reason and the Existence of God*, p. 214, original emphasis.
64 Martin Luther, *Martin Luthers Werke: kritische Gesamtausgabe – Briefwechsel* Bd. 2 (Weimar: Hermann Böhlau, 1931), pp. 372, 84f.
65 Levinas, *TI* p. 22.
66 *TI* p. 21.
67 Isa. 9.7; 32.1; Mt. 5.10; 6.33; Rom. 14.17; Heb. 1.8.

INDEX